In the
Vanguard of
Cultural Transfer

Cultural Transmitters and Authors in
Peripheral Literary Fields

Studies on Cultural Transfer and Transmission

Volume 2

Series ISSN

1879-7350

Series editor

Petra Broomans

Faculty of Arts

University of Groningen

P.O. Box 716

NL-9700 AS Groningen

p.broomans@rug.nl

www.petrabroomans.net

Series publisher

Barkhuis

Zuurstukken 37

NL-9761 KP Eelde

info@barkhuis.nl

www.barkhuis.nl

All volumes in the series can be purchased
via your academic bookseller
or directly from the publisher

In the Vanguard of Cultural Transfer

Cultural Transmitters and Authors in Peripheral Literary Fields

Edited by **Petra Broomans and Marta Ronne**

Barkhuis
Groningen
2010

Cover design and typesetting: ColtsfootMedia, Nynke Tiekstra, Noordwolde
Book design: Barkhuis & Nynke Tiekstra

ISBN 9789077922811

This publication was supported by a grant from
the Netherlands Organisation for Scientific Research (NWO)

Table of Contents

Preface

The project 'Peripheral Autonomy? Longitudinal analyses of cultural transfer in the literary fields of small language communities', financed by the Netherlands Organization for Scientific Research (NWO), started in 2006 and was one of the spin offs of the project 'Scandinavian literature in Europe: the influence of language politics, gender and aesthetics', itself part of the research programme 'Autonomy and the "new" Independence in the Arts', which was undertaken by the Groningen Research School for the Study of the Humanities (GRSSH). Three universities are involved in the project: Ghent, Groningen and Uppsala. The first workshop 'Reflection on theoretical and methodological points of departure', was held in Ghent in December 2006. Selected papers from the workshop were published on the project's website, which was developed to function as a scholarly environment favourable to intellectual exchange concerning the 'Peripheral Autonomy' programme. The website contains several forums and a database where previous and upcoming papers are presented, edited and discussed. Only registered users can fully participate.

In December 2007 the second workshop 'The Development of Literary Fields and the Influence of Foreign Literature from the Late Nineteenth Century until 1950', was held in Groningen. Scholars belonging to various disciplines from Belgium, the Netherlands and Scandinavian countries participated in the workshop, which focused on cultural transfer from the late nineteenth century until 1950. Attention was paid to the institutional conditions of cultural transfer, the social role of cultural transmitters and the functions of transferred literature. Gender aspects of cultural transfer were also studied, as well as the connection between changing national identities and varying definitions of national literatures. The essays in this volume, the second in the series Studies on Cultural Transfer and Transmission (CTaT), are based on contributions to the workshop.

We would like to thank the co-organiser of the workshop, Daan Vandenhaute (University of Ghent), and we are also grateful to Marijke Wubbolts for helping organise the workshop and Ester Jiresch for assisting us with the index.

Petra Broomans and Marta Ronne

In the Vanguard of Cultural Transfer

« Petra Broomans and Marta Ronne »

When studying the reception history of foreign literature, we discover that it is not only literary historians or literary critics who have mapped the influence of foreign literature, but also cultural transmitters. Sometimes they are the first to make an inventory of what has been translated and by whom. In the Dutch-speaking region, Margaretha Meyboom (1856-1927) provides us with a good example of this.

The article by Meyboom in *De Boekzaal* from 1911, 'Skandinavische literatuur in Nederland' (Scandinavian literature in the Netherlands), is one of the first studies of the reception of foreign literature in the Dutch-speaking region.[1] In her article, Meyboom provides an overview of the history of the reception of Scandinavian literature in the Netherlands from 1847 until 1909, noting a tendency on the part of many publishing houses to produce novels concerning peasants and family chronicles, rather than modern poetry and modernistic novels. Consequently, according to Meyboom, the public no longer had a balanced view of Scandinavian literature. Whereas around 1900 the image of Scandinavian literature as progressive and 'new' was clear, over the next ten years it became increasingly diffuse.

Meyboom formulated some basic questions that are still relevant to research in the field of cultural transfer and transmission: What was translated? Who were the translators and what was the actual extent of the work translated? Meyboom was of the opinion that the media, newspapers and magazines, could exert great influence, but that an inventory based on such sources would probably be impossible. Research of this kind in the field of reception and media studies is difficult for individual scholars to carry out such tasks alone.[2] In this regard, Meyboom expressed a critical reflection well ahead of her time, given that she was not working as a scholar at a university. Meyboom divides the period under investigation

....

1 Margaretha Meyboom, 'Skandinavische literatuur in Nederland', *De Boekzaal* 5 (Zwolle, 1911), pp. 45-49.

2 Meyboom, 'Skandinavische literatuur in Nederland', p. 47.

into three shorter periods, 1851-1882, 1883-1902 and 1903-1909, basing her survey on book retailers' sales lists without pretending that her survey is complete. Despite this it is one of the sources that biographers make use of when collecting material.

Which Swedish authors can be found in Meyboom's overview?[3] For the first period, Meyboom mentions the Swedish authors Esaias Tegnér (1782-1846) and Emilie Flygare Carlén (1807-1892). It is remarkable that she does not include Fredrika Bremer (1801-1865), who was known in the Netherlands and was translated into Dutch and sold in the bookstores. In the bibliography of translations of Swedish books into Dutch that we currently work with, Bremer has 26 hits, with the first translation being from 1841 and the last from 1871.[4]

In the second period, from 1883, more Swedish writers were translated, mostly writers from the Modern Breakthrough (1870-1890), a period of realism and naturalism in Scandinavia. Meyboom refers to Swedish authors such as Anne Charlotte Leffler (1849-1892), Victoria Benedictsson (1850-1888) (who used the male pseudonym Ernst Ahlgren), Selma Lagerlöf (1858-1940), August Strindberg (1849-1912) and Gustaf af Geijerstam (1858-1909). In general, Meyboom evaluates the translated books from the North positively, suggesting that the works chosen were mostly of literary merit, that the writers introduced to the Netherlands already had good reputations and that their works were treated with esteem. 'Rightly so, as they belonged amongst the best writers in their countries'.[5]

The last period Meyboom discusses begins with an increase in the number of translations: in 1903, 29 translations were published, and in 1904, 30, but in 1905 a reaction is noticeable, with only 18. In 1906 a peak is reached, with 32 translations, and in 1907, 28 translations were published.

....

3   See also Ester Jiresch, 'Margaretha Meyboom (1856-1927) – "Cultural Transmitter", Feminist or Socialist?', in: Petra Broomans, ed., *From Darwin to Weil. Women as Transmitters of Ideas* (Groningen, 2009), pp. 110-111.

4   Petra Broomans, Jos Groen and Ingeborg Kroon, 'Zweedse Literatuur in Nederland en Vlaanderen en supplement Fins – Zweeds in vertaling', in the series Studies on Cultural Transfer and Transmission (CtaT) (forthcoming).

5   'En terecht. Ze behoorden ook in hun vaderland tot de allerbesten.', Meyboom, 'Skandinavische literatuur in Nederland', p. 47.

In the following years the number of translations again decreased, with only thirteen in 1908 and 14 in 1909. Meyboom comments that there are many unknown names amongst the new authors, and pseudonyms as well. Because of the good reputation of some authors, translators and publishers had become too greedy: 'Books were chosen with less good sense, and translated with less care'.[6] She does not mention specific names here but they can be found in the separate surveys accompanying her text. According to Meyboom, Selma Lagerlöf would survive this flood of lesser quality literature, with her books maintaining their strong position in the Dutch literary field and being reprinted. Another critical comment by Meyboom concerns why so few of the works of authors such as the neo-Romantic writer Verner von Heidenstam (1859-1940) had been translated. She states that the Dutch public could easily gain the impression that lesser authors were more highly regarded than Heidenstam.

In her article, Meyboom also makes a clear distinction between good ('high') literature and trivial ('low') literature, advocating a translation policy that promotes good authors such as Heidenstam. Did the appeal to the Dutch publishers have any results during Meyboom's lifetime? What does an initial analysis of the material in the Swedish bibliography reveal concerning the period from 1911 – the year Meyboom published her article – to 1927, the year of her death?

An initial examination of the bibliography for the period 1911-1927 reveals that 38 authors were translated, with only one or two books by many of them. However, there are some authors who are represented by a substantial number of works:

Selma Lagerlöf: 19
Runa: 15
August Strindberg: 14
Emanuel Swedenborg: 14
Samuel Duse: 11
Anna Wahlenberg: 6

Certain genres can be pointed out on the basis of this list. Strindberg and Lagerlöf can be regarded as the authors of highbrow literature, Runa

....

6 'Er werd met minder oordeel gekozen, met minder zorg vertaald.', Meyboom, 'Skandinavische literatuur in Nederland', p. 48.

(Elisabeth Maria Beskow, 1870-1928) wrote popular fiction, Duse (1873-1933) crime fiction, Swedenborg (1688-1772) religious literature and Wahlenberg (1858-1949) children's literature. The authors from the Modern Breakthrough, so popular at the end of the nineteenth century, have almost disappeared, being represented by only one or two translations (sometimes a reprint). In this period, Heidenstam was only translated once, in 1919, this being his book on Saint Birgitta of Sweden (1303-1373), which was translated by Dien Logeman-Van der Willigen (1864-1925). A previous translation of a novel by Heidenstam was made by Philippine Wijsman (1837-1907) in 1900, and after 1927, one historical novel was published in 1928. Moreover, in 1964 Heidenstam's book on Birgitta of Sweden was published in a new version by an anonymous translator.[7]

Meyboom remarks in her article that many women made an effort to popularise Scandinavian literature and she places herself in the tradition of women cultural transmitters.[8] One of her colleagues was Dien Logeman-Van der Willigen, with whom she edited the journals *Scandia. Maandblad voor Scandinavische Taal en Letteren* (1904) and *Scandinavië-Nederland. Tijdschrift voor Nederlandsche en Scandinavische Taal, Letteren en Kultuur* (1905-1906).[9] The latter is a fine example of cultural transmission, containing information about both Scandinavian and Dutch literature and

....

7 From the lemma in the Swedish bibliography. Heidenstam, Verner von – Endymion / Endymion (1889) – vert.: [naar het Zweedsch] Ph. Wijsman – Van Dishoeck 1900 Amsterdam Heidenstam, Verner von – De pelgrimstocht van de Heilige Brigitta / Heliga Birgittas pilgrimsfärd (1901) – vert.: [geaut. uit het Zweedsch] D. Logeman-Van der Willigen – Honig 1918 Utrecht. Heidenstam, Verner von – Karolinerna. De geschiedenis van Karel XII / Karolinerna (1897-1898) – vert.: [uit het Zweedsch] August Vanhoutte – Die Poorte 1928 Oude-God-Antwerpen. Heidenstam, Verner von – De pelgrimstocht van de Heilige Brigitta / Den heliga Birgittas pilgrimsfärd (1901)- in: Roman, gedichten, verhalen Heidenstam, Verner von, Erik Axel Karlfeldt, Johannes V. Jensen– vert.: N.N. – inl.: Staffan Björck – De Toorts 1964 Haarlem.

8 Petra Broomans. '"The splendid literature of the North". Women translators and intermediaries of Scandinavian women writers around 1900', in: S. van Dijk, P. Broomans, J. van der Meulen, P. van Oostrum, eds., *'I have heard about you', Foreign Women's Writing Crossing the Dutch Border: from Sappho to Selma Lagerlöf*, Verloren, Hilversum, 2004:b, pp. 307-323.

9 Petra Broomans, '*Scandia* i Nederländerna. Om Margaretha Meijboom och hennes nordiska tidskrifter', *TijdSchrift voor Skandinavistiek* Vol. 22 (Amsterdam, 2001:1), pp. 155-167.

culture. In addition, Logeman-Van der Willigen is mentioned 20 times as a translator in the period 1911-1927. She translated for the H. Honig publishing house in Utrecht, amongst others, with Honig publishing the most titles in the period 1911-1927 (20 translations). Other translators in this period were A. Lukkien, with eighteen translations, and Margaretha Meyboom herself, with seventeen translations. The reason that Meyboom published so many titles was due to the fact that she translated Selma Lagerlöf, who was published by Becht of Amsterdam.

Logeman-Van der Willigen's translation oeuvre is much more heterogeneous than that of others, as shown convincingly by Ester Jiresch in her article on Logeman-Van der Willigen and Marie Belpaire (1853-1948) in this volume. A. Lukkien translated thirteen books by Runa, which were published by D.A. Daamen, The Hague, so her/his translation oeuvre could be called homogeneous. However, we still do not know who A. Lukkien was. More research into archives, including those of the publishing houses, is needed, for bibliographical sources do not give the full name or date of birth. Perhaps it was the A. Lukkien who was an author of religious texts? Some of the works by Runa were published by Kok Kampen, a publishing house that is known for religious and moral literature.[10]

Logeman-Van der Willigen, A. Lukkien and Meyboom are the 'top' translators in this period. Fourth in this ranking is Henriëtte M.J. Bok, who translated six titles. In relation to the publishing houses, some of them focus on one specific author, for example W. de Haan (Utrecht) published twelve translations, ten of which were by Duse, while Meulenhoff (Amsterdam) published ten works, all translations of Strindberg. Some of the translated authors were reviewed, others not, and some writers who were discussed in articles and essays were never published in Dutch translation. The examination of the material in the Swedish bibliography resulted in 88 hits for reviews of Strindberg, mainly due to his stage productions. Ellen Key (1849-1926) had ten hits, Lagerlöf seven, Swedenborg four and Birgitta of Sweden four. The author Per Hallström (1866-1960) was not translated, but had four reviews, while Meyboom's favourite, Heidenstam, was discussed in three reviews.

....

10 PiCarta, the portal to the Dutch Union Catalogue and other databases, and sources such as DBNL (http://www.dbnl.org/) do not provide any information about the translator A. Lukkien, who could be Albert Lukkien (1862-1941) or his wife Annigje Knol, see http://home.planet.nl/~conter/noord/schrijf4.htm (accessed November 15, 2010).

Translated, but without reviews in the period 1911-1927, were the works of 28 authors, including Duse, the crime fiction writer. There were only eight authors who were both translated and reviewed: the above-mentioned Strindberg, Key, Lagerlöf, Birgitta of Sweden, Swedenborg, Heidenstam (his novel on Birgitta), as well as the world-famous explorer and travel writer Sven Hedin (1865-1952), with five translations and three reviews, and the journalist, feminist and author Elin Wägner (1882-1949), with one translation and one review.

Using the Swedish bibliography as a point of departure to answer the question of whether or not Meyboom's quest for good Scandinavian, in particular Swedish, literature was fulfilled, it is obvious that there was no 'breakthrough' for Heidenstam. The material in the Swedish bibliography shows that both 'high' literature (Strindberg and Lagerlöf for example) and 'low' literature (for example, Duse and Runa) was translated. Other genres that can be defined are children's literature (Wallenberg) and religious literature (Swedenborg and Birgitta, including the book on Birgitta by Heidenstam). Two feminist authors also reached Dutch readers – Key and Wägner.

The number of women cultural transmitters was high. Logeman-Van der Willigen and Meyboom herself were still translating. The 'old generation' maintained what Bourdieu calls their 'cultural capital', but a 'new generation' of translators, such as A. Lukkien and Greta Baars-Jelgersma (1911), were about to take over, as shown in the contribution by Janke Klok about Baars-Jelgersma in this volume.

An initial analysis of the material concerning 1911-1927 provides a good example of how a bibliography can be the first step and a basis for research into the reception of foreign literature. However, a bibliography does not present the *content* of reception documents.[11] To investigate whether or not the 'diffuse' image described by Meyboom continued in the period 1911-1927, the content of the reception documents must also be considered, making it possible to define tendencies in the changing images of foreign literature.

The flood of foreign books between peripheral language areas, as well as the cultural transmitters who were active, can be made visible by bibliographies, lists and surveys, while the genres that were popular in a certain period can also be revealed. How a foreign author is received

....

11 See Stella Linn, 'Meten is weten? Kanttekeningen bij de compilatie van een bibliografie als basis voor receptieonderzoek naar de Nederlandse literatuur in vertaling', in: Petra Broomans et al., eds., *Object: Nederlandse literatuur in het buitenland. Methode: onbekend* (Groningen, 2006), pp. 36-55.

and how the image of a foreign literature is shaped can be researched in many different ways: imagology (including Dyserinck and Leerssen), institutional research (including Bourdieu, Sapiro and Heilbron, Even-Zohar, Meylaerts), network analysis (SNA or Latour) or from a historical perspective (reception studies, cultural transfer and transmission history).[12] In this volume various theories and methods are applied and tested. A selection of papers presented at the first workshop of the project 'Peripheral Autonomy? Longitudinal analyses of cultural transfer in the literary fields of small language communities' were published on the project's website. The contributors to this volume took this input as their point of departure. Additionally, the article by Petra Broomans on the reception of Strindberg, which provides a definition of the concept 'cultural transmitter' and a proposal for several phases in the process in cultural transfer, was also published on the website.[13]

The proposed phases in cultural transfer are:

1 Introduction. A cultural transmitter discusses or reviews the literary work of an author based on the author's original literary works and/or these works in translation.
2 In the second phase the selected author is 'in quarantine'. A cultural transmitter attempts to find an interested publisher or another way to publish the work in translation or perhaps even in the original.
3 In the third phase the author's work is translated. The translation is the point of no return and can be regarded as an important event in the process.
4 In the next phase, an in-between phase, the author and his/her translated work is 'in quarantine' once again. The translation might be bought and read.
5 In the final phase the author undergoes a second phase of reception in the form of reviews, articles, lectures, books, etc., and due to this follow-up we can speak of a successful cultural transfer.

....

12 The question of how to do research within the field of cultural transfer has been addressed in Petra Broomans et al., eds., *Object: Nederlandse literatuur in het buitenland. Methode: onbekend* (Groningen, 2006).
13 Papers by the following authors were published: Joep Leerssen, Gisèle Sapiro and Johan Heilbron, and Reine Meylaerts. See http://www.peripheralautonomy.org/node/38 (accessed November 15, 2010). Petra Broomans, 'Reception and Ideology. "Wild Volcanism" and Other Varieties on Strindberg', in: T. Naaijkens, ed., *Event or Incident. Special Issue, Genèses de Textes/Textgenese(n)* (Bern, 2010), pp. 107-120.

If a translation does not follow the first phase, the process of cultural transfer will not continue. In addition, if the fourth phase does not receive follow-up in the form of reviews, articles, lectures, books, etc., the process of cultural transfer will not be completed. If an author has been 'received' in the target language by means of translations that have been read and reviewed, the process of cultural transfer can be considered to be 'successful'. This volume makes clear that the cultural transmitter is still a very important factor in cultural transfer and transmission. She/he is active or present in all phases.

Four contributions to this volume explore the role of single cultural transmitters, most of them women, and of the international networks they created as translators or literary critics. Even if they have often tended to disappear from literary history, or were pictured as moving on the outskirts of their home literary fields, many female cultural transmitters in small language communities are now being rediscovered for their impressive ability to gather both social and cultural capital, and to move between translations on the one hand and literary critique on the other. As Margaret H. McFadden has pointed out, Scandinavian women possessed an extraordinary ability to create networks,[14] as did female cultural transmitters such as Meyboom from Belgium and the Netherlands.

Meyboom had a large network in the Dutch-speaking region and Scandinavia.[15] The Norwegian authors Arne Garborg (1851-1924) and his wife Hulda Garborg (1862-1934) contributed to Meyboom's journals, amongst other topics writing about the language situation in Norway. Around 1900, language politics had a degree of influence on the reception of Scandinavian literature. This was especially the case in Flanders, where Flemish writers and cultural transmitters found a similar language situation in the form of a struggle for the emancipation of Dutch in Belgium.

In the first contribution '*Spread the Word*. Arne and Hulda Garborg as Cultural Transmitters of Nynorsk', Roald van Elswijk discusses the position

....

14 Margaret H. McFadden, *Golden Cables of Sympathy. The Transatlantic Sources of Nineteenth-Century-Feminists* (Lexington, 1999), p. 4 and pp. 171-188.

15 See Broomans, '*Scandia* i Nederländerna' and Petra Broomans, 'Hur skapas en litteraturhistorisk bild? Den nordiska litteraturens "fräschhet" i Nederländerna och Flandern', in: *Videnskab og national opdragelse. Studier i nordisk litteraturhistorieskrivning* (Vol. 2), Per Dahl and Torill Steinfeld, eds., *Forskningsprogrammet Norden og Europa*, Nord 2001:30, pp. 487-541.

of Arne and Hulda Garborg with respect to the Norwegian language debate and their promotion of the Nynorsk language. Van Elswijk investigates how the Garborgs 'spread the word' about Nynorsk in the Dutch-speaking region and what role they played in cultural transfer between the two peripheral fields of Nynorsk and Dutch literature. Van Elswijk also deals with the nationalist-folkloristic debate in Scandinavia, taking as his point of departure Reine Meylaerts' paper on the study of cultural transfer in the literary fields of small language communities and how this can contribute to 'the vital broadening of the study of ("national" and other) literary identities and to new literary historiographies of peripheral literatures'.[16] In his thorough analysis, Van Elswijk shows that through their efforts Arne and Hulda Garborg realised stronger intercultural contacts between the two peripheral literary fields and, furthermore, a more profound knowledge of Nynorsk language and literature in Europe.

As mentioned above, Meyboom, Dien Logeman-Van der Willigen and her husband Henri Logeman (1862-1936) were the co-editors of the journals *Scandia* and *Scandinavië-Nederland*. Logeman-Van der Willigen lived in Ghent with her husband Logeman, who became the first professor in Scandinavian languages at the University of Ghent. Ester Jiresch discusses the work of Dien Logeman-Van der Willigen and compares this with that of Marie Belpaire in her article 'Marie-Elisabeth Belpaire and Dina Logeman-Van der Willigen: Two Cultural Transmitters in Flanders – in the Same Literary Field?'. Jiresch uses the definitions of the phenomenon 'cultural transmitter' developed by Grave and Broomans, and examines the applicability of these definitions to the work of Logeman-Van der Willigen and Belpaire, describing the networks of the two cultural transmitters and their respective roles in transmitting Scandinavian literature. Belpaire only translated neo-Romantic literature with a religious motive, such as the hagiographies of the Catholic Johannes Jørgensen (1866-1956). Jiresch argues convincingly that Belpaire might have thus obstructed the transmission of modernist contemporary Scandinavian literature and that her network was relatively small. Logeman-Van der Willigen, by contrast, had a large network and translated various Scandinavian authors, without a clear favourite. Though Logeman-Van der Willigen was to some extent guided by strong religious beliefs, this did not result in her developing a similar profile to that of Belpaire. Jiresch comes to the conclusion that

....

16 Reine Meylaerts, p. 1.

the two colleagues and friends were both cultural transmitters but chose different kinds of literature. While Belpaire focused on Flemish cultural life, Logeman-Van der Willigen became part of an inter-Scandinavian literary field.

In the next two contributions, the focus is again on individual cultural transmitters, firstly Greta Baars-Jelgersma, who belongs to the 'new' generation of cultural transmitters after, amongst others, Meyboom and Logeman-Van der Willigen. Janke Klok discovered Greta Baars-Jelgersma so to speak and interviewed the translator in 2007 and 2010. In 'Greta Baars-Jelgersma, Cora Sandel and the Dutch Literary Field, 1925-1950. Aspects of Cross-national Literary Transfer', Klok follows Baars-Jelgersma as she becomes a translator, exploring her translation oeuvre and discussing the reception of the Norwegian author Cora Sandel (1880-1974) in the Netherlands in the period 1925-1950. Sandel is one of the many authors Baars-Jelgersma translated. The investigation of both the reception of Sandel and the translation oeuvre of Baars-Jelgersma is made in order to define Baars-Jelgersma's position within the Dutch literary field and to point out the timing of the changing image of Scandinavian literature in the period 1925-1950. Klok uses various theoretical perspectives, including those of Meylaerts and Even-Zohar, in order to show that in the 1940s and 1950s, the Dutch literary field, as a literary system, had become closed, in contrast to the situation of the 1920s and 1930s. In effect, Scandinavian literature had been 'depowered' in a context in which the national literature of the receiving country came to be regarded as innovative, an observation that endorses the findings of Kees van Rees and Gilles J. Dorleijn, who state that the Netherlands was generally a closed nation in the nineteenth and twentieth centuries. Klok also uses the five phases of the process of cultural transfer, as described by Petra Broomans. In the case of Cora Sandel all five phases were completed and the process of the cultural transfer of Cora Sandel's works a 'success'. Klok further proposes a sixth phase – is a successful transfer followed up in the form of the canonisation of the author?

Although Baars-Jelgersma did not have a great deal of cultural capital in the Dutch-speaking region, the Swedish critic Margit Abenius (1899-1970), on the other hand, came from a well-educated, middle-class family, which together with a thorough academic education helped her to become one of the most influential Swedish critics in the 1940s. In '"There is Always an Invisible Reader ..." The Swedish Critic Margit Abenius and the Making of a Female Cultural Transmitter', Marta Ronne analyses several aspects of Abenius' career as a critic and her work of translating and introducing highbrow foreign writers to Sweden, such as Franz Kafka, Simone Weil and Cora Sandel. Abenius is considered a middle-class intellectual and an acknowledged arbiter of taste in the Swedish literary field of the mid-twentieth century. Ronne's argument is based on some general ideas concerning the mechanisms of cultural transmission and its agents, as presented by Broomans, Meylaerts, and Heilbron and Sapiro. Meylaerts, as well as Heilbron and Sapiro, stress the importance of a single literary agent and of her interaction with literary institutions, when analysing mechanisms of literary transmission. According to Heilbron and Sapiro's twofold concept of translation as a means of accumulating cultural capital, Ronne also discusses Abenius' possible influence as a critic. She shows that Abenius' translation and introduction of Simone Weil follows the five stages of transmission proposed by Broomans. However, Ronne not only studies Abenius' strategies as a transmitter of foreign literature to Sweden, but also her ability to oscillate between highbrow and more popular literature, and between different groups of readers and listeners. From a gender perspective, the disappearance of Abenius and other female Swedish critics from manuals of literary critique during the last four decades is also discussed.

Transmitting literature may lead to literary motives being introduced to a new language area. In order to fully understand the mechanisms of their introduction, linguistic and cultural aspects as well as social and political ones have to be taken into account. In the next contribution, 'Walking the Streets of Helsinki. The Flâneur in Early Finnish Prose Literature', Lieven Ameel discusses how a literary *topos* can be transferred from a dominating language area (in this case France) to a peripheral literature. In his study of how the notion of the flâneur was adapted to both Finnish and Finland-Swedish literature at the turn of the twentieth century, Ameel compares the novels on Helsinki by Eino Leino (1878-1926), Juhani Aho (1861-1921) and Arvid Järnefelt (1861-1932) with those of Finland-Swedish writers from the so-called *dagdrivare* (idler) generation. Based on Meylaerts' thoughts on multilingualism in literature within small language communities, his study aims to show how a literary theme from an international literary movement can be adapted in different ways by peripheral national literary traditions. According to a tradition established by the works of Charles Baudelaire (1821-1867) and Edgar Allan Poe (1809-1849), the flâneur, the lonely, male, middle-class city walker, has been the very symbol of modernity and of the urban space in transition. Ameel suggests that linguistic and literary elements, as well as political and social ones, explain why the Finland-Swedish writers from the 'idler' generation were the first authors in Finland to provide insightful descriptions of Helsinki and to develop the flâneur motif on local ground. The paper also briefly discusses the gender aspect of the motif.

The influence of Swedish, the former dominant language in Finland, and the development of national literature in Finnish are investigated by Anders Nilsson in his 'One Nation – Two Literatures? From Finnish to Swedish: Some Themes in the Translation of Finnish Literature into Swedish, 1900-1950'. Using Gisèle Sapiro's ideas on the conditions of translation as entailing the transfer of symbolic goods as his theoretical framework, Nilsson discusses the translators and the literary institutions that promoted translations of Finnish authors into Swedish between 1900 and 1950. He points to the influence of the writer Elias Lönnrot (1802-1884), as well as the Hegelian philosopher Johan Vilhelm Snellman (1806-1881), in the promotion of the idea of Finnish as the one and only national language. He also investigates the possible political and social reasons for Finland developing a 'national literature' in two languages, Indo-Germanic Swedish and a Finno-Ugric Finnish, in the late nineteenth century. As Nilsson aims to show, from the turn of the twentieth century and until 1950 there was an ongoing, albeit fluctuating, level of interest in translations of Finnish authors into Swedish. He identifies a number of key translators, such as the modernist poet and critic Hagar Olsson (1893-1978), whose main reasons for continuing the promotion of Finnish literature in Swedish is found to be personal interest, networking in the literary field and a need for income.

These motives are also manifest in the work of the other cultural transmitters discussed in this volume, while another common interest is the introduction and promotion of what they regarded as good literature. Such figures discovered new authors and genres, and they shaped, reconstructed or deconstructed images. Whether or not the foreign literature was received on fertile soil and became part of a new literary field, they were pioneers and in the vanguard of cultural transfer.

Spread the Word

Arne and Hulda Garborg as Cultural Transmitters of Nynorsk

« Roald van Elswijk »

This article aims to establish the social and cultural views of a prominent author couple from nineteenth-century Norway, Arne (1851-1924) and Hulda Garborg (1862-1934). I will concentrate on their points of view concerning the Norwegian language debate, more specifically on their ideas about Nynorsk, the minor of the two official written forms of Norwegian. I will also assess their roles within the nationalist movement and their ways of 'promoting' the Nynorsk language outside Norway. As a case study, I will provide an outline of the way Arne and Hulda Garborg spread the word about Nynorsk through their contacts within literary fields in the Netherlands and Flanders. Thereby, I hope to provide insight into the role of these two cultural transmitters in the intercultural relationships between the two peripheral literary fields of Nynorsk and Dutch literature. For a broader perspective, I will make some comparisons with the nationalist-folkloristic debate in the other Scandinavian countries, especially the works of scholar and folklorist Artur Hazelius (1833-1901) in Sweden. In terms of theory, I will focus on the thoughts of Reine Meylaerts in her article from 2006,[1] specifically her ideas on the imagological study of peripheral literatures and the dynamics within these fields.

The Norwegian language question

From its start in the first half of the nineteenth century, the Norwegian language debate was embedded in the broader Scandinavian and European discourse on ethnonationalism and folklore. Therefore, it may prove worthwhile to analyse the rise of Nynorsk in the wider context of nationalism and the representation of Norwegian identity. An interesting

....

1 Reine Meylaerts, 'The study of cultural transfer in the literary fields of small language communities: Some preliminary thoughts' (Ghent, 2010). Accessible at http://www.peripheralautonomy.org/node/35.

work concerning the theoretical background of the debate was published by
the historian Kåre Lunden (1930), and this is one of the first studies to place
the nationality issue in a broader, non-Norwegian context.[2] In general, two
historical traditions can be distinguished when discussing the Norwegian
nationality debate. Firstly, some scholars regard the rediscovery of a
Norwegian national identity explicitly as the result of the dissolution of the
political union between Denmark and Norway in 1814. That is to say, only
the creation of a semi-independent state led to feelings of being 'Norwegian'.
One might even take this a step further: Norwegian nationality only became
imminent with the Treaty of Kiel in 1814, thus due to events *outside* Norway.
Today, this is the theory supported by most scholars. Secondly, however,
there is the point of view predominantly taken by earlier scholars, such as
Ernst Sars (1835-1917) and Halvdan Koht (1873-1965), according to whom, a
strong nationalist sense existed prior to 1814 amongst the social and cultural
elite, while the working classes lacked a common sense of culture, political
interests and literary taste.[3] However, the participation of the peasantry in
the latter, more active stage of the rise of Nynorsk proved indispensable in
its evolution. The elevated level of 'målreising', or language rise, coincides
with what Czech scholar Miroslav Hroch (1932) calls 'Phase C', where a
broader social movement comes into being after folkloristic activism has
laid the foundations for a national identity (Phase A) and a larger group of
followers have claimed a territory, in this case more metaphorically, of their
own (Phase B).[4] In the late-nineteenth-century nationalist debate and the
(re)construction of a national Norwegian identity, Arne Garborg and his wife
Hulda were to play key roles, albeit in different ways.

Arne Garborg and the concept of nationality
Arne Garborg is generally regarded as one of the most important authors,
thinkers, critics and essayists of late-nineteenth and early twentieth-
century Norway. He was an avid writer who produced some 2,000 texts on
linguistic, political and religious issues. Garborg was born in the southern

....

2   Kåre Lunden, *Norsk grålysing. Norsk nasjonalisme 1770-1814 på allmenn bakgrunn*
     (Oslo, 1992).
3   *Op. cit.*, p. 37.
4   Miroslav Hroch, *Social Preconditions of National Revival in Europe* (New York,
     [2]2000), p. 180.

region of Jæren and never renounced his rural Norwegian background. Nevertheless, he wholeheartedly embraced the European spirit and was what one of his biographers has referred to as 'a Jæring as well as a European'.[5] Garborg's European outlook and the ideological concept of a good European may well have been influenced by the philosophical thinking of Friedrich Nietzsche (1844-1900), especially by his work *Jenseits von Gut und Böse* (*Beyond Good and Evil*, 1886). It is a known fact that Arne Garborg had read many of Nietzsche's works as well as the political essays of Georg Brandes (1842-1927), the theorist behind the Modern Breakthrough.[6]

From an early age, Garborg had been interested in the Norwegian language debate. An interesting choice of words can be found in a letter to philologist Kristofer Janson (1841-1917), in which young Garborg comments on '(...) your high and holy cause: the resurrection of the Norwegian language'.[7] By calling it a resurrection, Garborg's view on the matter is clear: Norwegian was in need of revival due to the Danish domination it had endured for more than 420 years. Garborg felt that only the rise of Nynorsk would ensure a truly independent Norway.

One of Garborg's key programmatic works, the 1877 collection of polemical essays *Den ny-norske Sprog- og Nationalitetsbevægelse. Et Forsøg paa en omfattende Redegjørelse, formet som polemiske Sendebreve til Modstræverne* (The new Norwegian language and nationality movement. An attempt at an elaborate elucidation, in the form of polemical epistles to opponents) can be seen as the most elaborate and influential attempt in contemporary Norway to define the concepts of nation and nationality on a linguistic basis.[8] Here, he presents his theory of a 'kløvying' (split) in Norwegian society, his well-known 'two-nation theory', by which he meant that the geographical and political nation of Norway in fact consisted of two linguistically separate cultures. According to Garborg, one of the central questions had to be how and to what extent these two 'nations' were to influence each other, other than by means of linguistic differentiation.

....

5   Tor Obrestad, *Arne Garborg. Ein biografi* (Oslo, 1991), p. 168.
6   *Op. cit.*, pp. 175-179.
7   '(...) Deres høie og hellige sak: det norske maals gjenopreisning', after Morten Haug Frøyen and Sveinung Time, *Arne Garborgs kulturnasjonalisme. To studiar* (Oslo, 1993), p. 111.
8   The word 'ny-norsk' in the title, whose literal meaning is 'new Norwegian', may well have given its name to the Nynorsk language. There seems to be little clarity about where this name derives from.

Garborg formulates his views on nation and nationality most poignantly in his fifth essay, entitled 'Den norske Nation' (The Norwegian nation), where he states that the existence of a Norwegian nationality will simply manifest itself:

> How does one prove that a Norwegian nationality exists? How does one prove that this nationality needs a Norwegian language? etc. – useless discussions. Gentlemen! If a 'Norwegian nationality' does exist – then it will simply demonstrate itself by objectifying itself in an independent form. If it fails to do so, then it does not exist – as a nationality.[9] (original quotation marks)

To Garborg, this 'independent nationality' seems to be one of the most direct implications of a new language for Norway: for the concept of a Norwegian nationality to be viable, its independence and thus that of the Norwegian language has to be evident. In the book's introduction, Garborg had already argued that 'The process of raising a language and nationality is (...) a *historical phenomenon*, made possible by certain *historical preconditions*. That is to say: *it is an objectivity*' (original emphasis).[10] The Norwegian linguist Lars Vikør elaborates on this, in his words, 'Darwinian interpretation of linguistics', in an article from 1990.[11]

Less of a theorist, Arne Garborg's wife Hulda had a more practical view where the nationalist debate was concerned. Her reintroduction of traditional Norwegian dance and cooking, and also the establishment of an all-Norwegian theatre, proved important in the conceptualisation of an independent Norwegian culture.

....

9   'Hvoraf beviser man, at der er en norsk Nationalitet? Hvoraf beviser man, at denne Nationalitet trænger et norsk Sprog? osv. – Ørkesløse Diskussioner. Dersom der er en "norsk Nationalitet", Mhrr.! – saa vil dette [simpelthen] aabenbare sig deri, at den objektiverer sig i en selvstændig Form. Gjør den ikke dette, saa existerer den ikke – som Nationalitet nemlig', Arne Garborg, *Den ny-norske Sprog- og Nationalitetsbevægelse* (Kristiania, 1877), p. 15. All translations in this article are my own, unless stated otherwise.

10 'Sprog- og Nationalitetsreisningen er (...) et *historisk Fænomen*, indtraadt i Livet i Kraft af bestemte *historiske Forudsætninger*. Det vil sige: *den er en Objektivitet*', *op. cit.*, p. 14.

11 Lars Vikør, 'Linjer i nyare språkhistorie', *Eigenproduksjon* 37 (1990), pp. 1-116.

Hulda Garborg and Norwegian traditional culture

1. The forgotten valkyrie

According to her biographer Tor Obrestad, Karen Hulda Garborg née Bergersen was one of the great spirits of her time. He calls her '(...) an important link in modern Norwegian history from awakening nationalism via the Modern Breakthrough until the global thinking of today'.[12] Ivan Kristoffersen, who wrote the article on Hulda in *Norsk biografisk leksikon*, Norway's main biographical lexicon, characterises her as 'a versatile author and cultural figure'[13] as well as 'an inspirational spirit and a pioneer'.[14] In conclusion, he defines her as an intellectual woman who in many aspects was ahead of her time.[15] From an early age, Hulda took an active part in the social debate, gave speeches across the country and wrote essays and articles on topics such as traditional cooking, the gender debate, art, the language question and costumery.[16] However, Hulda Garborg felt an unhappy and unrequited love for her native Norway, which never fully acknowledged her accomplishments within the social, political and cultural debate.

Karen Hulda Bergersen grew up in eastern Norway and went to primary school in Hamar. From 1875 she lived in Kristiania (Oslo). At a young age, she started reading works by modern authors and surrounded herself with left-wing idealists who believed in a strong, independent Norwegian nation. Steadily Hulda became drawn into the pending language debate. In Kristiania she met famous Norwegians of the time, including well-known authors such as Bjørnstjerne Bjørnson (1832-1910) and Hans Jæger (1854-1910), as well as the aforementioned philologist Kristofer Janson. The poet Nils Collett Vogt (1864-1937) was very impressed by Hulda's spirit and enthusiasm and called her 'somewhat of a valkyrie to the idealists amongst

....

12 '(...) eit bindeledd i den moderne norske historia frå den vaknande nasjonalismen, over det moderne gjennombrotet, og fram til dagens globale tenking', Tore Obrestad, *Hulda* (Oslo, 1992), p. 7.

13 '(...) ein allsidig forfattar og kulturperson', Ivan Kristoffersen, 'Hulda Garborg', in: *Norsk biografisk leksikon* (Oslo, 2000), vol. 3, p. 258.

14 *Ibidem.*

15 *Ibidem.*

16 For more information on Hulda Garborg and traditional costumery, see Tjitske Sijtsma-Oma, 'Fra kistebunn til opphavsrett. Drakt og nasjonalidentitet. Nåtidens motiver for nasjonaldraktbruk i Norge og Fryslân – en komparativ analyse' (unpublished MA thesis, Groningen, 2010).

the youth here'.[17] In 1887, Hulda Bergersen married Arne Garborg and they moved to Kolbotn, east of Oslo. As she was from the east of Norway and he from Jæren in the south, they were very different in spirit. However, Arne and Hulda felt united in their views on national, political, religious and social questions. They complemented each other in several ways and both used material from their lives in their literary works.[18]

2. Enlightening the people

The awakening of Norwegian nationalism and the subsequent rise of Nynorsk were greatly influenced by German national-romanticist thinking, specifically by Johann Gottfried Herder's (1744-1803) concepts of *Volksseele* and *Volksgeist*. His ideas closely connected the nation with nature, that is to say, the expression of culture and thereby that of a nation, according to Herder, were influenced and inspired by nature's design.[19] Herder also placed much emphasis on the notion that the peasantry, considered as the 'common people', were the heart of a nation. This 'positivist' thinking concerning nature and the populace was a key element in the rise of nationalism, and it also considered practical housework, agricultural labour and healthy meals as important aspects of tradition. It was this folkloristic, more practical side of Norwegian culture that interested Hulda Garborg, of which she became an advocate. She wanted to share much of the knowledge she had gathered during her travels to mainland Europe. This resulted in an 'enlightening project' which was very broad and included tips for running a good household and for healthy cooking, traditional clothing, arts and literature. Hulda Garborg believed that Norwegian customs and traditions should be the cornerstones of a strong Norwegian culture, as reflected in the ideas of the time.

In neighbouring Sweden, the folklorist and scholar Artur Hazelius had begun a similar project of enlightenment. To Hazelius, national culture was

....

17 'Visst noe av en valkyrie for de ideelt bevegede blandt ungdommen her', quoted in Obrestad, *op. cit.*, p. 37.

18 A recent article argues that Arne perhaps used too many private details from his own and Hulda's life in his works. Cf. Arnhild Skre, 'Huldas liv i litteraturen', *Syn og Segn* 3 (2010), pp. 14-23.

19 Sverker Sörlin, 'Artur Hazelius och det nationella arvet under 1800-talet', in: Cecilia Hammarlund-Larsson, Bo G. Nilsson and Eva Silvén, eds., *Samhällsideal och framtidsbilder. Perspektiv på Nordiska Museets dokumentation och forskning* (Stockholm, 2004), pp. 11-63.

something real, almost tangible. He felt it his duty to reveal the national soul of the Swedish people, which was revealed in folklore, costumery, storytelling and other traditions.[20] However, in the 1870s and 1880s he could not find an audience for his ideas. Contrary to Norway, the Swedes felt less of a direct need to address questions of nationality, as a Swedish nation-state had been in existence from the Middle Ages. It was not until the 1890s, when national-romanticist ideas also became popular in Sweden, that Hazelius' ideas were received with interest. Artur Hazelius had taken a keen interest in traditional costumes and other artefacts, and his large personal collection formed the basis of an ethnographical museum, Skandinavisk-Etnografiska samlingen (the Scandinavian ethnographical collection), which opened in Stockholm in 1872. One of its major objectives was 'to raise and nourish the love of the homeland' and to preserve the memory of all the Swedes who had played a role in maintaining the national heritage.[21] Eight years later, it was re-named the Nordiska Museet (Nordic Museum) and it remains Sweden's largest cultural-historical museum today. Like Hulda Garborg, Artur Hazelius felt that ethnographical folklore was an important part of a nation's heritage; however, his beliefs had less of a European outlook.

In 1902, Hulda travelled to the Faroe Islands and learned the local folk dance, which she thought shared a basis with ancient Norwegian dance. On her return, she started publishing books and essays on Scandinavian folk songs and organised cultural *soirées* during which she performed traditional dances. In 1911, Hulda established Det Norske Spellaget (The Norwegian Theatre Company), a dance company which would later become Det Norske Teatret (The Norwegian Theatre). Hulda Garborg may have initiated this renewal of the Norwegian dance tradition but it does not appear that she attempted to re-establish it systematically. She was too busy with other projects, including the theatre, her greatest love. Although it was Arne Garborg who first raised the question of a people's theatre in the vernacular, it was actually his wife Hulda who laid the foundations for future Nynorsk drama.

As to Hulda Garborg's thoughts on the nationality debate, there is less textual evidence to consider, compared to the huge number of essays, pamphlets and articles written by her husband. However, Hulda's diaries

....

20 *Op. cit.*, p. 44.
21 *Op. cit.*, p. 11.

Arne and Hulda Garborg in their home at Låbråten, ca. 1910. Photographer: A.B. Vilse

do provide us with some points for discussion. On several occasions she wrote about the more programmatic side of the nationalist movement. Concerning the Nynorsk orthography by the 'founding father' of Nynorsk, Ivar Aasen (1813-1896), she comments:

> Aasen's dictionary was a great achievement, but considering it was the first [of its kind] it could not [comprise] the entire Norwegian language. The advocates of Nynorsk who stare blindly at Aasen and (...) who do not want to believe that development and richness exist beyond Aasen, therefore cause great harm.[22]

Although Hulda Garborg certainly had her own ideas on nationalism, she seems to have been more practical in her beliefs than others. By travelling a lot and teaching the Norwegian people about the things she cared for, she proved a pragmatic link within the Nynorsk network. Through her contacts with cultural transmitters across the European continent, for example with the Dutch Margaretha Meyboom (1856-1927), she became an important advocate of Nynorsk culture.

....

22 'Aasens ordbok var et storværk men som den første kunde den jo ikke bli hele det norske sprog. (...) Stor skade gjør derfor de målfolk, som stirrer seg blinde på Aasen og (...) ikke vil tro på, at der er udvikling og rigdom udenfor Aasen', Karen G. Koht and Rolf Thesen, eds., *Hulda Garborg. Dagbok 1903-1914* (Oslo, 1962), p. 29.

Cultural transfer between the Nynorsk network and the Low Countries

1. Travelling Europe

The textual evidence seems to suggest that both Arne and Hulda Garborg regularly corresponded with authors, critics and intellectuals all over Europe. Both of them saw their travels as an important way of getting to know other cultures and literatures. However, the pair had very different ways of looking at the world when travelling. Arne Garborg saw the world as a stage for his inner drama and experienced everything on the basis of his own emotions, while Hulda was the journalist and observer and put the world itself on centre stage.

Both Arne and Hulda Garborg seem to have been interested in the Netherlands and Belgium, both countries they visited at least once. Arne Garborg took a particular interest in the Belgian language debate, which he mentions in *Den ny-norske Sprog- og Nationalitetsbevægelse*, quoting a French magazine: 'la [Flamand] est un jargon corrumpu du Hollandais, qu'on ne parle que quand on n'en sait pas d'autre'.[23] According to Garborg, the word 'Hollandais' in this citation could easily be substituted by 'Danish' and 'Flamand' by 'Norwegian', since many thought (and think) that Norwegian was just a dialect of Danish. Garborg also mentions Belgium in the context of his short essay 'Norsk eller dansk-norsk? Svar til Bjørnson' (Norwegian or Danish-Norwegian? An answer to Bjørnson) from 1887.[24]

In July 1889, Arne Garborg travelled to Germany via Amsterdam. It is not known if he stayed in the Netherlands or whether he was just passing through. In Germany, he became a leading cult figure for Scandinavian naturalist literature. His first German translation was published in 1887 and all of his early novels would follow. Garborg lived in Munich and Berlin from July 1889 until April 1891. He also spent some time there in 1905. During these years, he was more popular – and the German public considered him to be more important – than Hamsun, Strindberg or Tolstoy.[25] One German critic even wrote: 'Ich nehme gar kein[en] Anstand, Garborg geradezu für den grössten Techniker im Roman überhaupt zu

....

23 Garborg, *Den ny-norske Sprog*, p. 163.
24 An abridged version can be found in Arne Garborg, *Vor Sprogudvikling. En Redegjørelse. Med et Tillæg* (Kristiania, 1897), pp. 340-347.
25 Cf. Johannes A. Dale, *Garborg-studiar* (Oslo, 1969), p. 116.

erklären'.[26] Arne Garborg's travels gave him the intellectual stimulation he needed, which was reproduced in the characters of his books. In 1906, Hulda Garborg spent a month in the vicinity of Amsterdam, where she met up with the Dutch translator and scholar Margaretha Meyboom. Their correspondence over the years can be characterised as genial, perhaps even friendly. In the following sections, I will examine this correspondence in more detail and discuss the cultural transfer of Nynorsk literature to the Netherlands and Flanders.

2. Correspondence between Hulda Garborg and Margaretha Meyboom

In the University Library in Oslo, there are twenty-seven letters and postcards from Margaretha Meyboom to Hulda Garborg. Meyboom was an important figure in the process of cultural transfer between Northern Europe and the Low Countries around the *fin de siècle*.[27] These twenty-seven documents span the period of 1909-1925. Most are dated, although others are undated and/or damaged.[28] Unfortunately, no letters from Hulda Garborg to Margaretha Meyboom are known to have survived.

The correspondence between Meyboom and Garborg provides an insight into the nature of the contact between these two female cultural transmitters, and into the connections between the Nynorsk network and the Netherlands and Flanders. Firstly, there is the way that Meyboom refers to Hulda Garborg and her husband Arne. In most letters, Meyboom addresses Hulda as 'Kjære fru Garborg', 'Dear Mrs Garborg'. The pronoun she uses is always 'De' (you, formal), a pronoun which is rarely used in modern Norwegian. However, in one letter Meyboom addresses Garborg as 'Du' (you, informal), which may prove that they knew each other well enough to dispense with strict formalities.[29] In the same letter, Meyboom includes a poem by the German poet Christian Morgenstern entitled *An eine Freundin*, a poem she says had helped her overcome some difficult periods

....

26 Quoted in Obrestad, *Arne Garborg*, p. 171.

27 Cf. Petra Broomans, '*Scandia* i Nederländerna. Om Margaretha Meyboom och hennes nordiska tidskrifter', *Tijdschrift voor Skandinavistiek* 22 (2001), pp. 155-166.

28 I would like to thank Ester Jiresch (University of Groningen) for providing me with copies of these letters.

29 Fragment of a letter from Margaretha Meyboom to Hulda Garborg, undated and damaged. At the beginning of the twentieth century, Norwegian personal pronouns were still written with a capital ('Du'), as in modern German.

in life.[30] This suggests that the contact between Meyboom and Garborg was not purely professional. The letters also provide evidence that Meyboom visited Arne and Hulda Garborg in Norway at least once,[31] while Hulda also visited Meyboom in 1909. Unfortunately, there is no mention of the 1909 visit in Hulda's diary, although it does mention her travelling to Germany at the end of April 1909. This may suggest that she travelled to the Netherlands via Germany.[32] Reading these letters, one gets the feeling that there was some sort of friendship between Arne and Hulda Garborg and Margaretha Meyboom. The latter certainly shows a more personal and vulnerable side in mentioning her financial difficulties and the stress she feels when overcome with work.[33] She also wrote a heartfelt letter to Hulda in August 1924 after learning of Arne's death on January 14 earlier that year.[34]

One would think that in these twenty-seven letters and cards, Scandinavian authors and literature in general would be an often-mentioned subject. This is not the case. Although Hulda Garborg sent Meyboom, amongst other works, her play about Iroquois Indians, *Den store freden* (The Big Peace) and the play *I Huldreskogen* (In the Enchanted Forest), there is less talk of literature than one might expect. However, Meyboom does mention that she would like to write an article on Nynorsk, despite Arne Garborg having already published an extensive essay on Nynorsk literature in *Scandia* in 1906.[35]

3. Traces of Nynorsk in Dutch and Flemish literature

Although Margaretha Meyboom was one of the prime cultural transmitters of Scandinavian culture in the Netherlands, she was not the first scholar to direct her attention to the North. As early as 1860, a Dutch literary history of Scandinavian literature was published, *Noordsche letteren (talen, letterkunden, overzettingen) als vervolg op de reisbrieven uit Dietschland en Denemark* (Scandinavian literatures [languages, literatures, translations] as a continuation of the travel letters from Germany and

....

30 *Ibidem.*
31 Postcard from Meyboom to Garborg. Westerbro, Rijswijk, December 22, 1915.
32 Koht and Thesen, eds., *Hulda Garborg. Dagbok 1903-1914*, pp. 134-135.
33 Cf. for example the letter from Meyboom to Garborg. Nieuw Westerbro, Voorburg, April 10, 1925.
34 Letter from Meyboom to Garborg. Broederschapshuis, Bilthoven, August 18, 1924.
35 Letter from Meyboom to Garborg. Westerbro, Rijswijk, February 9, 1910.

Denmark).[36] However, this book by Constant Jacob Hansen (1833-1910), does not contain any references to Nynorsk. However, in the context of this article it is interesting to note the nationalistic tone that Hansen uses in the preface to this work. It gives us an interesting insight into the representation of the Nordic peoples in the Dutch-speaking area and, more prominently, of his strong personal opposition to the increasing influence of French in Belgium.[37]

One of the first if not the very first mention of Arne and Hulda Garborg's works in a Dutch magazine is the article by G.A.E. Oort entitled 'Arne Garborg' in *De Gids* in 1896.[38] The article most probably also introduced the term 'New Norwegian' to the Dutch-speaking area. In her contribution to *De Gids* – which was founded in 1837 and is the oldest existing literary magazine in the Dutch-speaking area – Oort introduces the author from Jæren and depicts him as 'melancholic and timid'.[39] Oort also finds Garborg to be an 'important' author and 'an honest and relentless fighter, to whom *life* means working and thinking' (original emphasis).[40] The article also features translations – some lengthy – of fragments from novels by Arne Garborg. I take these fragments to be the first literary translations from Nynorsk into Dutch. The first complete translation would be the short story *Han Lars i lia*, from 1904.[41] Six years after the article by Oort, Richard C. Boer, professor of Dutch and Early Germanic in Amsterdam, published an extensive article[42] on Garborg in *De Gids*, where he compared the Old Norse poem *Völuspá* (The vision of the prophetess) to certain parts of Arne Garborg's lyrical cycle *I Helheim* (In hell, 1901). Here, Boer also describes the historical background of Nynorsk and mentions that it is worthwhile learning the language because 'first-class writers' write in it:

....

36 Constant Jacob Hansen, *Noordsche letteren (talen, letterkunden, overzettingen) als vervolg op de reisbrieven uit Dietschland en Denemark* (Ghent, 1860.

37 For more information on Hansen and his views on nationalism, see Petra Broomans, 'Ibsen als God en duivel. Scandinavische literatuur in Vlaanderen rond 1900', in: Raf de Bont, Geraldine Reymenants and Hans Vandevoorde, eds., *Niet onder één vlag. Van Nu en Straks en de paradoxen van het fin de siècle* (Ghent, 2005), pp. 245-264.

38 G.A.E. Oort, 'Arne Garborg', *De Gids* III (1896), pp. 255-283.

39 '[D]roefgeestig[en] en vreesachtigen', *ibidem*.

40 '[En] voor dezen eerlijken onvermoeiden strijder beteekent *leven* werken en denken', *ibidem*, p. 282.

41 Arne Garborg, 'Onze Lars', *Scandia* 6/7 (1904), pp. 96-98.

42 Richard C. Boer, 'Twee Noorweegsche gedichten van de eeuwigheid', *De Gids* III (1903), pp. 23-64.

Only the national movement of the nineteenth century put the
Norwegian dialects, which lead a despised existence, little by little into
their rightful place. (...) The prominent thought here is that Norway
will never be a unity and that the common man will never raise himself
from ignorance if the language used in literature is not one understood
by each inhabitant of the country. (...) If you would like to know what
first-class writers have to say, from now on you will have to take the
trouble of learning the Norwegian farmers' language.[43]

Over the years, *De Gids* featured other articles on authors from Norway,
such as Knut Hamsun and Henrik Ibsen. A later, but more specific
source of knowledge for the cultural, linguistic and literary conditions
in Northern Europe, was the bilingual magazine *Scandia. Maandblad
voor Scandinavische Taal en Letteren* (Scandia. Monthly Magazine for
Scandinavian Language and Literatures, 1904). It featured articles and
essays on different aspects of the culture, literature and the languages
of the Scandinavian countries and the editor-in-chief was Margaretha
Meyboom. As a follow-up to *Scandia*, in 1905 Meyboom founded yet
another magazine concerned with the Nordic countries, *Scandinavië-
Nederland. Tijdschrift voor Nederlandsche en Scandinavische Taal,
Letteren en Kultuur* (Scandinavia-Netherlands. Journal for Dutch and
Scandinavian Language, Literatures and Culture, 1905-1906). In *Scandia*,
Arne and Hulda Garborg are mentioned as being among the journal's
'reporters'. Other frequent contributors included Herman Bang, Georg
Brandes, Jonas Lie, Johan Ludvig Runeberg and Juani Aho. These authors
also submitted original work.

In the March 1904 edition of *Scandia*, both a novel by Arne and one
by Hulda are reviewed. Linguistically interesting is that this review also
mentions that Arne Garborg writes in 'Boeren Noors' (farmers' Norwegian)
while his wife writes in 'Danish-Norwegian, but uses a lot of Norwegian

....

43 'Pas de nationale beweging der negentiende eeuw hielp langzamerhand de
Noorweegsche dialecten, die een veracht (sic) bestaan voerden, tot hun recht. (...) De
gedachte, die hier op den voorgrond staat, is deze, dat Noorwegen nooit een eenheid
zal wezen, en dat de gemeene man nooit uit zijn onwetendheid zich zal verheffen,
zoolang niet de taal der litteratuur er eene is, die door iedere inwoner van het land
verstaan wordt. (...) Wie voortaan wil weten, wat de dichters van den eersten rang
hebben te zeggen, moet zich de moeite getroosten, de Noorweegsche boerentaal te
leeren', *op. cit.*, pp. 38-40.

dialect'.[44] Hulda takes central stage in *Scandia*'s next edition, with a six-page essay on the Faroes entitled 'De Færöer eilanden' (The Faroe Islands),[45] which she refers to in her diary.[46] From a linguistic point of view, it is interesting that Faroese is described as 'a type of Norwegian'.[47] At the same time, however, Hulda also calls Faroese 'the country's own language'.[48]

One of the most interesting essays in the context of the transmission of Nynorsk culture, is Arne Garborg's essay in *Scandia*'s only double edition, 'Nieuw Noorsch' (New Norwegian).[49] It concentrates on Danish supremacy in Norway from 1387-1814 and the first attempts by Ivar Aasen to reconstruct an authentic Norwegian language based on the heritage of Old Norse and Norwegian dialects. These attempts to 'Norwegianise' the Danish language, which led to the Bokmål language, Garborg calls 'a blending of languages, or linguistic confusion'.[50] Notable is his use throughout of the term 'Nieuw Noorsch', whereas the Norwegian parliament did not change the *målform*'s name from 'Landsmål' to 'Nynorsk' until 1929. Garborg also uses the term 'Landsmål' in his essay, which is alternately translated as 'landstaal' (language of the country) or considered as a name proper. The same issue of *Scandia* features a translation of Arne's short story *Han Lars i lia*, now entitled *Onze Lars* (Our Lars), the first complete translation from Nynorsk into Dutch. It features the *post scriptum* 'Naar 't "Nieuw-Noors"' van Arne Garborg' (After the 'New Norwegian' by Arne Garborg).

In 1922, Richard C. Boer published the book *Noorwegens letterkunde in de negentiende eeuw* (Norway's literature in the nineteenth century).[51] Its second chapter, 'De taalbeweging en de oudste schrijvers in Landsmål' (The language movement and the earliest writers in Landsmål), deals specifically with the rise of Nynorsk and its most important advocates. As Boer sees it, the core of the language debate was not the fact that an independent Norwegian language did not exist, but rather that the language was not yet

....

44 Henri Logeman, *Scandia* 6/7, p. 44.
45 Hulda Garborg,'De Færöer Eilanden', *Scandia* 4 (1904), pp. 49-54.
46 Koht and Thesen, *Hulda Garborg*, p. 27.
47 *Ibidem*.
48 '[D]e eigen taal van het land', *ibidem*.
49 Arne Garborg, 'Nieuw Noorsch', *Scandia* 6/7 (1904), pp. 86-90.
50 '(...) een taalvermenging, of taalverwarring', *ibidem*, p. 88.
51 Richard C. Boer, *Noorwegens letterkunde in de negentiende eeuw* (Haarlem, 1922).

unified and only lived in various Norwegian dialects.[52] Boer also comments on the artificial character that some say characterises Nynorsk:

> This [the rise of Nynorsk] being successful, is surely one of the most extraordinary things the cultural life of the nineteenth century has seen. Whatever one might say of artificial languages – this artificial language has become a living one. However, I need to add that only up to a point is it an artificial language and not in all respects a living one. The language builds on living dialects and therefore does not have the rigidity so typical of schematic creations deriving from a dehydrated calculation, but the language is actually not spoken anywhere. It is a written representation of the unity of Norwegian dialects, slightly divergent in the different regions.[53]

Note the unifying character of Nynorsk and the fact that it is mostly a written, not a spoken language, which Boer refers to in this book. It is interesting that in this book, and also in other material I have analysed, the Norwegian language question and Nynorsk are readily mentioned subjects. The fact that the term 'New Norwegian' was introduced in the Dutch-speaking area quite early, may point to an interest within the Netherlands and Flanders in the ethnonationalist debate in Norway, and in the interests for which the Nynorsk network stood.

4. Early translations from Nynorsk into Dutch

An important source of information for early literary translations from Norwegian, is the Dutch bibliography *250 jaar Noorse literatuur in Nederland 1743-1993. Bibliografie van vertalingen en recensies* by Jos

---

52 *Op. cit.*, p. 95.
53 'Dat dit gelukt is, is wel een der merkwaardigste dingen, die het cultuurleven der negentiende eeuw heeft zien gebeuren. Wat men ook van kunstmatige talen mag zeggen – deze kunstmatige taal is eene levende geworden. Er dient echter bijgevoegd te worden, dat zij slechts tot op zekere hoogte kunstmatig, en dat zij niet in alle opzichten levend is. Zij is uit levende dialecten opgebouwd en heeft daarom niet de starheid, die aan de schematische schepselen van een dorre berekening eigen is, maar gesproken wordt zij eigenlijk nergens. Zij is een in verschillende streken eenigszins uiteenloopende schriftelijke representant van de eenheid der Noorweegsche dialecten', *op. cit.*, p. 95.

Groen (250 years of Norwegian literature in the Netherlands 1743-1993. A bibliography of translations and reviews, 1994). For this book, Groen, an antiquarian and bookshop owner, consulted numerous bibliographies, name registers, catalogues, indexes and other sources. The result is by no means comprehensive, nor is it free of mistakes or omissions. However, the book is quite well organised and is a good source for a reference bibliography of early Norwegian literature in Dutch.

Based on references in both *Scandia, Scandinavië-Nederland* and the above-mentioned bibliography by Groen, I have compiled a list of literary translations from Nynorsk into Dutch up to 1935. I have listed fragments of literary translations of all genres, as well as articles and essays which specifically deal with the rise of Nynorsk and/or Nynorsk literature. Since Hulda Garborg only started writing in Nynorsk in the latter half of her life, none of her early works are mentioned in this overview.

List of translations Nynorsk-Dutch and articles on Nynorsk, 1895-1935

1896	Garborg, A., 'Vrede' (*Fred*, 1892). Fragment. Translator: G.A.E. Oort. *De Gids*, 60th vol., III, pp. 255-256.
1896	---, 'Boerenstudenten' (*Bondestudentar*, 1883). Fragment. Translator: G.A.E. Oort. *De Gids*, 60th vol., III, pp. 258-261.
1896	---, 'Bij moeder thuis' (*Hjaa ho Mor*, 1881). Fragment. Translator: G.A.E. Oort. *De Gids*, 60th vol., III, pp. 263-265.
1896	---, 'Een vrijdenker' (*Ein Fritenkjar*, 1881). Fragment. Translator: G.A.E. Oort. *De Gids*, 60th vol., III, pp. 266-269.
1903	---, 'Boerenstudenten' (*Bondestudentar*, 1883). Fragment. Translator: Henri Logeman. *Den Gulden Winckel*, 1903, pp. 200-203.
1903	---, 'In de woning van Hel' (*I Helheim*, 1901). Fragment. Translator: Richard C. Boer. *De Gids*, 21st vol., III, pp. 33-37; 41-45; 47-49; 57-62.
1904	---, 'Nieuw Noorsch' (Essay on the rise of Nynorsk and the language question). Translator unknown [Margaretha Meyboom?]. *Scandia* 6/7, pp. 86-90.
1904	---, 'Onze Lars' ('Han Lars i lia'). Short story. Translator unknown [Margaretha Meyboom?]. *Scandia* 6/7, pp. 96-98.
1905	---, 'Boerenstudenten' (*Bondestudentar*, 1883). Novel, edited. Translator: Henri Logeman. Baarn: Hollandia.
1905	---, 'De verloren vader' (*Den burtkomne faderen*, 1899). Novel. Translator: Margaretha Meyboom. Amsterdam: Becht.
1913	---, 'Bij moeder thuis' (*Hjaa ho mor*, 1890). Novel. Translator: Michaël Zeeman. 's-Gravenhage: Loman & Funke.

1913	---, 'Slaapmiddeltjes' ('Sleeping powder', original title unknown). Short story. Translator unknown. Leeuwarden: Leeuwarder Courant.
1917	Garborg, A. and H., 'Buiten in de bergen. Brieven van Kolbotn' (*Kolbotn-brev, 1887-1888*). Diaries. Translator: Henri Logeman. Leiden: Sijthoff.
1918	Garborg, H., 'Vrede' (*Fred*, 1892). Novel. Translator: Henri Logeman. Utrecht: Honig.
1935	Vries, J. de, 'Taal- en spellingstrijd in Noorwegen' (Essay on the rise of Nynorsk and the Norwegian language question), *De Nieuwe Taalgids*, 15th vol., pp. 203-217. Groningen, etc: J. B. Wolters.

An interesting element of these early translations from Nynorsk is the fact that the words 'uit het Nieuw Noorsch' (from the New Norwegian) or even 'uit het Nieuw Noorsch Landsmål' are often mentioned explicitly on the title page.

Now as before, relatively few literary works are translated from Nynorsk into Dutch, compared to books in Bokmål. The novel *Bondestudentar* (1883) by Arne was the first book in Nynorsk to be translated into several major languages, such as English and German. As the Swedish scholar Claes Ahlund argues in his 1990 work, *Den skandinaviska universitetsromanen 1877-1890* (The Scandinavian university novel 1877-1890), not only is *Bondestudentar* of high artistic value, there has probably been more written on this particular book than on all other books discussed in his dissertation put together.[54] After 1920, more Nynorsk literature was translated into Dutch, such as several novels by the well-known author Olav Duun (1876-1939), as well as three books by Tarjei Vesaas (1897-1970), also translated into Frisian.[55]

The text corpus and these early translations seem to suggest that the Dutch audience took a certain interest in the Norwegian language debate, and also in Nynorsk. Scholars such as Richard C. Boer and Jan de Vries published lengthy articles on the rise of the language, and translators such

....

54 Claes Ahlund, *Den skandinaviska universitetsromanen 1877-1890* (Uppsala, 1990), p. 160.

55 Frisian is a minority language spoken in the bilingual province of Fryslân. Interestingly enough, Frisian literary magazines in the 1950s and 1960s paid much attention to Nynorsk and the Norwegian language debate. Cf. Roald van Elswijk, 'Noarwegen en de wrâld. Over de Noorse taalstrijd', in: Pîter Boersma and Goffe T. Jensma, eds., *Philologia Frisica. XVIIIe Frysk Filologekongres* (Ljouwert [Leeuwarden], 2010), [s.p.] [in print].

as Henri Logeman and Margaretha Meyboom were instrumental in finding this young, peripheral literature an audience. Hulda and Arne Garborg played an active part in the cultural transmission of Nynorsk culture in Europe, for example in the Netherlands and Flanders. Not only did they keep in contact with relevant cultural transmitters and literary networks, they also supplied original work which was published in magazines such as *Scandia*. In the Netherlands specifically, Arne and Hulda befriended Margaretha Meyboom, who was one of the most active translators of Scandinavian literature at the time. The efforts of Dutch and Flemish cultural transmitters and those of Arne and Hulda Garborg in Norway, paved the way for more elaborate intercultural contacts between two peripheral literary fields, Nynorsk in Norway and Dutch in the Netherlands and Flanders, and for a wider knowledge of the Nynorsk language and its literature in Europe.

Conclusion

In her 2006 article, Reine Meylaerts argued that the study of cultural transfer in peripheral literatures may provide an insight into the intricate role of intercultural contacts in the dialectics of the construction of a peripheral literary field.[56] My article retraced the role played by Arne and Hulda Garborg in the Norwegian nationalist movement and their endeavours as cultural transmitters to spread the word about Nynorsk across Europe, especially in the Dutch-speaking area. I used material from their diaries and private correspondence as well as from their literary and scholarly output. This enabled me to take a closer look at the late-nineteenth and early twentieth-century intercultural relationship between two peripheral literary fields, Nynorsk and Dutch, and the cultural and social context in which Arne and Hulda Garborg worked.

As the Norwegian language question is embedded in a broader discourse on nationality and national-romanticism, Arne and Hulda's points of view on the concept of nationality proved interesting. In his programmatic work, *Den ny-norske Sprog- og Nationalitetsbevægelse* from 1877, Arne Garborg offers several theories in the field of nationality studies. According to him, a nation is a historical, objective phenomenon which only manifests itself when a people realise that they form a national

....

56 Meylaerts, 'The study of cultural transfer', 1.

unity: only then will they rise and institutionalise their language. A nation can thus only exist by virtue of its own, cultural language. Garborg offers several ideas as to the realisation of an independent, strong Norway with its own language, Nynorsk – albeit in a European context.

Due to Arne Garborg taking such a special position in Norwegian history, the works of his wife Hulda Garborg née Bergersen are sometimes overlooked. There is sufficient reason to change this perspective. Hulda Garborg was a 'self-made', modern woman, who was extremely active in the field of folk dance, traditional cooking and folk music. She initiated the first theatre in Nynorsk, Det Norske Teatret, which is still a successful theatre company. Although she may have operated on another level and in a different way than her husband, her works and accomplishments are proof in themselves of her important position within the Nynorsk network. Both Arne and Hulda Garborg were oriented towards Europe, without neglecting their rural Norwegian background. They travelled extensively throughout Norway and Europe, and beyond. The literary evidence from their correspondence, diaries and other literature shows that they were in frequent contact with foreign writers, publishers and critics – in short with the cultural intelligentsia of a rapidly changing Europe.

The role Arne and Hulda Garborg played in the cultural transmission of Nynorsk seems to have been an active one. Not only did they maintain contact with Dutch translators such as Margaretha Meyboom, they also wrote essays and articles about Nynorsk for the Dutch and Flemish media. It was probably Arne's 1904 essay in *Scandia* that introduced the term 'New Norwegian' to the Dutch-speaking area, and the transfer of Nynorsk literature towards the Netherlands and Flanders would follow suit by means of extensive articles on the Norwegian language debate and a number of early translations.

The Dutch professor Richard Boer has referred to the rise of Nynorsk as 'surely one of the most extraordinary things the cultural life of the nineteenth century has seen'. The Norwegian language question is still very alive today, and emotions tend to become heated. Although the number of Norwegians who use Nynorsk as their *hovudmål* is decreasing, the impact that Nynorsk has had on Bokmål and on Norwegian society as a whole, is substantial. To many Norwegians, Nynorsk represents an important part of their life and their cultural background: language, identity and nationality are closely intertwined. Any forced change would mean a loss of identity. In Arne Garborg's own words: 'Language is the body of nationality, and a soul cannot change its body'.

Marie-Elisabeth Belpaire
and Dina Logeman-Van der Willigen

Two Cultural Transmitters in Flanders – in the Same Literary Field?

« Ester Jiresch »

Central to this paper are two women, Marie-Elisabeth Belpaire (1853-1948) and Dina Logeman-Van der Willigen (1864-1925), who were contemporary translators of Scandinavian literature into Dutch.[1] They lived in close geographical proximity, were good acquaintances and on different occasions even worked together. The nature of their relationship, their exchange of thoughts about literature, work and life in general, can be retraced in forty-three letters.[2] Concerning their work, I am going to use the terms 'cultural transmission' and 'cultural transmitters' to describe their occupation. Jaap Grave, who was one of the first Dutch scholars to use the term 'transmitter' rather than 'translator' in his work on Dutch literature in Germany between 1890-1914, indicates the variety of tasks of those involved:

> They [the transmitters] searched actively for literature abroad, contacting the authors in many cases, and it was not uncommon that they bought the rights of a book and therefore became closely financially involved in the success or failure of their own translations.[3]

....

1 This article forms part of a PhD research project that is currently being conducted at the Institute for Scandinavian Studies at the University of Groningen. The project investigates the work and networks of female cultural transmitters of Scandinavian literature around 1900 in the Dutch/Flemish region and in the Austrian/German region.

2 The remains of the exchange of letters from Logeman-Van der Willigen's side are stored in the Archive and Museum of Flemish Cultural Life in Antwerp (AMVC).

3 'Zij [de bemiddelaars] zochten actief naar literatuur in het buitenland, namen in veel gevallen contact op met de auteur en het kwam niet zelden voor dat zij de rechten van het boek kochten en op deze manier financieel nauw betrokken waren bij het slagen of mislukken van de door hen gemaakte vertaling'. All translations are by the author of this article. Cf. Jaap Grave, *Zulk vertalen is een werk van liefde. Bemiddelaars van Nederlandstalige literatuur in Duitsland 1890-1914* (Nijmegen, 2001), p. 13.

Another, more recent and considerably more elaborate definition of 'cultural transmitter' was developed by Petra Broomans in the context of a discussion of cultural exchange between Scandinavia and German-speaking countries:

> A cultural transmitter basically works within a particular language and cultural area. She/he often takes on various roles in the field of cultural transmission: translator, reviewer, critic, journalist, literary historian, scholar, teacher, librarian, bookseller, collector, literary agent, scout, publisher, editor of a journal, writer, travel writer, or counsellor. Transmitting another national literature and its cultural context to one's own national literature and cultural context is the central issue in the work of a cultural transmitter. Transmission often reflects a bilateral situation. Even the transmission of one's own literature takes place. The motivation can be aesthetically, ideologically, politically and/or economically based.[4]

Building on these definitions I would like to show their applicability to the work of both of my protagonists. I will concentrate on the various aspects of their complex roles, as well as their interest in a specific geographical area and the motives behind their commitment. The investigation of the two women's roles in the literary field will be accomplished in two parts: firstly their life and work will be examined and secondly their professional networks will be scrutinised. Concerning the latter, I would like to refer to a prior article in which I discussed the development of a suitable network model for cultural transmitters, combining literary discourse analysis and social science theories.[5] The final section of this paper will compare the women's roles in transmitting Scandinavian literature in the Flemish

....

4   Petra Broomans, 'Introduction: Women as Transmitters of Ideas', in: Petra Broomans, ed., *From Darwin to Weil. Women as Transmitters of Ideas* (Groningen, 2009), p. 2. In another recent article, Petra Broomans presents an in-depth look at the various stages of cultural transfer. See Petra Broomans, 'Reception and Ideology. "Wild Volcanism" and Other Varieties on Strindberg', in: Tom Naaijkens, ed., *Event or Incident. Special Issue, Genèses de Textes/Textgenese(n)* (forthcoming Bern, 2010), pp. 107-120.
5   Ester Jiresch, 'The problem of demarcation in the investigation of literary networks. Margaretha Meyboom as a cultural "border crosser"', in: Clas Zilliacus et al., eds., *Gränser i nordisk litteratur. Borders in Nordic Literature. IASS XXVI 2006* (Åbo, 2008), pp. 727-735.

literary field and will propose categories for a possible comparison of their networks. As mentioned, this article forms part of an ongoing PhD research project, and the determination of the most suitable categories for comparing the network models in question has not yet been finalised. It should thus be understood as a work in progress. I will begin with an analysis of the life, work and network of Marie-Elisabeth Belpaire, followed by Dina Logeman-Van der Willigen, before turning to a comparison and some concluding remarks.

Marie-Elisabeth Belpaire

1. Biography

Marie-Elisabeth Hyacinthe Belpaire was born on January 31, 1853 in Antwerp, where she lived until the end of her life on June 9, 1948.[6] She was the youngest daughter of Alphonse Belpaire (1817-1854) and Betsy Teichmann (1821-1900), the latter from a very wealthy and distinguished family. Growing up in her grandfather's house – Theodore Teichmann (1788-1867) was governor of the province Antwerp at the time – Marie came into contact with important figures in the cultural and intellectual world of Antwerp at an early age.[7] The importance of education for girls was highly valued in her home, with Marie mainly being taught by private teachers, her older sister and her aunts. After having developed an extensive knowledge of several foreign languages, she was able to read much literature in the original. Initially she became fond of French, English and German Romanticists, although personal contact with contemporary Flemish writers such as Johan Alfred de Laet (1815-1891) and Hendrik Conscience (1812-1883) soon turned her interest to Flemish literature.[8] It might also have led her to choose Dutch as the language of her own literary work.

....

6   Jan Persyn, 'Belpaire, Maria Elisa. Letterkundige en Kunstbeschermster', in: Koninklijke Vlaamse Academiën van België, eds., *Nationaal Biografisch Woordenboek* (Brussels, 1966), p. 51.

7   Jan Persyn, *De wording van het tijdschrift Dietsche Warande en Belfort en zijn ontwikkeling onder de Redactie van Em. Vliebergh en Jul. Persyn* (Ghent, 1963), p. 57; Ria Christens, 'Het is moeilijk haar eigen wezen achter te halen. De vele gedaante van Marie Elisabeth Belpaire', in: Aline Dereere and Helga van Beeck, eds., *Marie Elisabeth Belpaire 1853-1948: Facetten van een levenswerk* (Antwerp, 2002), pp. 10-11.

8   Christens, 'Het is moeilijk', p. 13; Persyn, 'Belpaire, Maria Elisa', p. 52.

Being surrounded by strong women in her family laid the foundation for Marie Belpaire's feminist point of view. Higher education for girls and women was a great concern to her and this led to her founding several institutions, such as the Katholieke Middelbare beroepsschool voor Juffrouwen[9]– Catholic professional school for young women and the Extension universitaire pour les femmes – university education for women.[10] Moreover, Belpaire also followed another family tradition, engaging in charity work throughout most of her life.[11] In this regard she mainly supported young artists – usually writers and musicians – as she believed art should be available to everyone and that it 'should elevate the people'.[12] The role of her Catholic faith was probably of greatest significance to Belpaire and always remained central in all of her life's pursuits.[13]

Through her acquaintance with the Flemish writers Hilda Ram (pseudonym of Mathilde Ramboux 1858-1901) and Louisa Duykers (1869-1952) – who became her closest confidants – Belpaire came into contact with the Flemish Movement and the Christian social women's movement in Flanders.[14] Although very interested in various local women's clubs, Belpaire decided not to join the national Belgian women's league because it was too strongly related to the clergy for her taste. Instead she established her own women's association (inspired by the German Catholic women's movement), which was supposed to function as an umbrella organisation and to motivate the founding of further local women's organisations. Disappointingly for her, this organisation was never approved by Church authorities because they found it too emancipatory.[15]

Even though Belpaire descended from a French-speaking family, she felt great sympathy for her fellow Flemish citizens and became strongly

....

9   Lutgarde Govaerts, 'Marie Elisabeth Belpaire en haar onderwijsinitiatieven', in: Dereere and Van Beeck, eds., *Marie Elisabeth Belpaire*, pp. 38-41; Ria Christens et al., 'Marie Elisabeth Belpaire (1853-1948). Een hoger "doel" voor de vrouwen', in: Dorinda. Dekeyser et al., *Vrouwenfaam op straat: Vrouwen maken naam* (Leuven/ Apeldoorn, 1999), p. 63.
10 Irene Smets, 'De Katholieke Hogeschool voor Vrouwen', in: Dereere and Van Beeck, eds., *Marie Elisabeth Belpaire*, pp. 72-74.
11 Christens, 'Het is moeilijk', p. 14.
12 Persyn, *De wording*, p. 57.
13 Christens, 'Het is moeilijk', pp. 15-16.
14 Govaerts, 'Marie Elisabeth Belpaire en haar onderwijsinitiatieven', p. 45.
15 Christens, 'Een hoger "doel"', p. 65; Christens, 'Het is moeilijk', pp. 21-22.

involved in the Flemish Movement, associating herself with a subgroup of the movement, the so-called 'cultural Flemingants', who advanced the cause of the Dutch-speaking citizens, that were treated as, arguing that they should be supported for the collective good of Belgium and the Catholic Church and promoting equality and official bilingualism. [16] In this and in many of Belpaire's enterprises which were interconnected and intended to support the arts and underprivileged people, her work was carried out in the Roman Catholic spirit.

2. Literary activities

In her endeavour to support the Flemish Movement, Belpaire founded a small society called Eigen Leven with the Catholic priest August Cuppens (1862-1924). This society's intentions were to strengthen the Catholic element of the Flemish Movement and thus to counteract the liberal element which they considered too predominant. In particular, they planned Flemish Catholic initiatives and projects. [17] Their greatest achievement was without doubt the merger of the existing Flemish journals *Het Belfort* and *Dietsche Warande* into the *Dietsche Warande en Belfort (DWB)*. The original editorial staff consisted of Belpaire, Cuppens, Ram, Duykers, Lodewijk Scharpé (1869-1935) and others, with the young lawyer Emiel Vliebergh (1872-1925) as its chief editor. Founded in 1900, this journal still exists today and thus numbers amongst the oldest literary journals in the Dutch-speaking region. Even though Belpaire never officially held the position of editor-in-chief, her influence was strongly felt over 40 years. Also, as the funds to maintain this enterprise came mainly from Belpaire's own fortune, at least until the First World War, she more or less considered it 'her magazine'. [18] The *DWB* generally promoted neo-Gothic and Romantic ideals and strongly opposed the modernists' development of realistic and naturalistic currents. [19]

With respect to Scandinavian literature, Belpaire contributed thirteen articles to the *DWB*, ten of them concerned with her favourite author,

....

16 Govaerts, 'Marie Elisabeth Belpaire en haar onderwijsinitiatieven', p. 49.
17 *Ibidem*; Geraldine Reymenants, 'Marie Elisabeth Belpaire: Bezielster van het Tijdschrift DWB', in: Dereere and Van Beeck, eds., *Marie Elisabeth Belpaire*, pp. 163-165; Persyn, *De wording*, pp. 43-44, 52; Persyn, 'Belpaire, Maria Elisa', p. 52.
18 Reymenants, 'Bezielster', p. 191.
19 Persyn, *De wording*, pp. 161-163.

the Dane Johannes Jørgensen (1866-1956). At the beginning of his career Jørgensen was a follower of Georg Brandes (1842-1927), the leading man of the Modern Breakthrough in Scandinavia. These modern writers propagated realistic literature, which examined actual problems within society, such as gender and social inequality, the hypocrisy of the Church and marriage and the liberty of the individual.[20] Jørgensen soon distanced himself from these 'modernists' and converted to Catholicism, from then on writing mainly about his travels and the legends of the saints. Belpaire, who vigorously disapproved of the modernist movement, grew very fond of the Catholic convert and writer Jørgensen. She considered him to represent the ideal of the searching soul, having realised the inconsistency of non-belief and consequently turning to the salvation of the Catholic belief.[21] Comparing Jørgensen's autobiography to Hans Christian Andersen's (1805-1875) she stated her opinion quite clearly:

> It is true that Andersen's art dwells on the general spirituality of the poetic emotion. His 'Levenssprookje' solely sketches the fading conditions of the common lad, like a butterfly fluttering from the darkness of misery to the light of fame, whereas Joergensen, in his 'Legende', aims to enlighten us about how he broke out of the dungeon of confusion and disbelief and moved into the bright sun of Catholic truth.[22]

With respect to her translations, it was again Jørgensen who was the focus of Belpaire's attention. In Catholic circles she was certainly a well-respected and recognised critic. The education she had received thanks to her wealthy family may have laid the proper ground for her critical work; nevertheless, she did choose quite a biased approach in her work, which, as we will see

....

20 Nils Ingerwersen, 'The Modern Breakthrough', in: Sven Hakon Rossel, *A History of Danish Literature* (Nebraska, 1992), pp. 262 ff.

21 Persyn, *De wording*, p. 228.

22 'Blijft toch waar dat Andersens kunst bij het algemeen godsdienstige van 't poëtiek gevoel verwijlt. Dat zijn "Levenssprookje" enkel de tijdelijk toestanden teekent van den volksjongen stijgend, een vlinder gelijk uit de duisternis der ellende tot den luister van de faam, terwijl Joergensen in zijne "Legende" voor doel heeft ons voor te lichten hoe hij zich losworstelde uit den kerker van dwaling en onvolledig geloof tot de volle zon der katholieke waarheid'. Cf. Marie Elisabeth Belpaire, 'Johannes Joergensen volgens eigen getuigenis', *Dietsche Warande en Belfort* (1919/1), p. 106.

below, resulted in severe criticism
from other philosophical and
political camps. The liberal author
and journalist August Vermeylen
(1872-1945), for example, accused
her of being narrow-minded and
overly religious in her orientation
several times.[23]

Belpaire had a very high
standard for works she deemed
worthy of translation. As a result
she was completely committed to
each of the pieces she translated.
These were four books by
Jørgensen,[24] one by Bjørnstjerne
Bjørnson (1832-1910) – *Synnøve*
Solbakken, an idyllic peasant
novella – and several fairy tales by

Marie-Elisabeth Belpaire, date unknown,
From Collection AMVC-Letterenhuis, Antwerp.

Hans Christian Andersen, Christen Asbjørnsen (1812-1885) and Jørgen Moe
(1813-1882), which she published together with her colleagues and friends
Ram and Duykers in a collection of international fairy tales.[25]

3. Belpaire's role in transmitting Scandinavian literature and culture

The picture of Scandinavian literature that Belpaire transmitted, as one
can read in articles she published mainly in *DWB*, was extremely partial.
She focused exclusively on neo-Romantic literature, in which belief and
God were central. In addition to the work of the Catholic Jørgensen, who
was almost her only Scandinavian concern, one novella by Bjørnson also
captured her interest, although all the more intensely. In 1902 Belpaire
wrote a book[26] on literature of the nineteenth century, focusing on five

....

23 Kaatje Aerts, 'Marie Elisabeth Belpaire en de kunst' in: Dereere and Van Beeck, eds.,
    Marie Elisabeth Belpaire, p. 211.
24 Johannes Jørgensen, *Levensleugen en levenswaarheid* (Ghent, 1900); *idem, De*
    uiterste dag (Ghent, 1902); *idem, Klokke Roeland* (Bussum, 1916); *idem, Over Goethe*
    (Bussum, 1919).
25 Marie Elisabeth Belpaire, ed., *Wonderland: Vertellingen*, Vol. 1-6 (Ghent, 1894-1896).
26 Marie Elisabeth Belpaire, *Het landleven in de letterkunde XIXe eeuw* (Antwerp/
    Ghent, 1902).

countries: Germany, England, France, Flanders and Norway. The chapter on Norway singularly provides an appraisal of *Synnøve Solbakken*,[27] as if it was the ideal representation of contemporary Scandinavian literature. Jan Persyn called her whole treatise 'nothing other than a great hymn to the romantic characters of Western European literature, a glorification of *heimatliteratur*'.[28] In the work, Belpaire describes the Northern peoples as 'young and childish, wild and without life experience',[29] putting herself in an objective, superior position. However, she also called Scandinavian literature 'fresh' and 'pristine' and considered that others could learn and benefit from it.

The following statement by Belpaire makes very clear what she felt to be positive about Bjørnson's novella and Scandinavian literature in general:

> Only a few stories are so dedicated: the purity of morals, the freshness of invention, the plainness of speech, everything is in accord with the nature of our people and our literature. As a language, Norwegian stands in much closer affinity to our Flemish than does German, and this is due to its nobility and frugal gracefulness.[30]

Stressing the kinship of the Dutch-speaking and Northern peoples was quite popular at the time,[31] and Belpaire not only referred to the affinity between the languages but also claimed a relatedness in terms of folk spirit and morality. Belpaire is a very good example of how a cultural transmitter connects their own ideologies with the transmitted work. As Petra Broomans

....

27 Petra Broomans, 'Ibsen als god en duivel: Scandinavische literatuur in Vlaanderen tijdens het fin de siècle', in: Raf de Bont et al., eds., *Niet onder een vlag: Van Nu en Straks en de paradoxen van het fin de siècle* (Ghent, 2005), p. 262.
28 Persyn, *De wording*, p. 161.
29 Belpaire, *Het landleven*, p. 202.
30 'Weinig verhalen zijn er zoo voor geschikt: de reinheid der zeden, de frischeid der ingeving, de eenvoud der taal, alles is in overeenkomst met den aard van ons volk en van onze letterkunde. Ook staat het Noorsch, als taal, in veel nauwer verwantschap met ons Vlaamsch dan met Hoogduitsch, en wel voornamelijk om zijne eenvoudige zwierigheid'. Cf. Marie Elisabeth Belpaire, 'Het landleven in de letterkunde: VIII – Noorwegen', *Dietsche Warande en Belfort* (1902/3), p. 13; Broomans, 'Ibsen als god en duivel, pp. 262-263.
31 Broomans, 'Ibsen als god en duivel', pp. 250-251.

clearly points out in her article 'Reception and Ideology', this phenomenon was quite widespread in the Dutch-speaking region around 1900 and at the beginning of the twentieth century. One persisting ideology maintained by Belpaire, as we saw above, was her strong Christian belief, around which she focused her critical work. In Broomans' article we see a likeness with fellow countryman Piet Schepens (1901-1967), who in his reception of August Strindberg (1949-1912) focused on the latter's search for faith. Another ideology that can be traced in Belpaire's reception work was clearly language politics. During this time, this geographically based ideology was of special interest in Flanders, where many people considered the Norwegian language situation, the development of New Norwegian, as a source of motivation and inspiration for their own struggle for emancipation.[32]

As we saw above, Belpaire only transmitted a very restricted and narrow picture of Scandinavian literature and culture. One could argue that she might have obstructed the transmission of a large part of contemporary Scandinavian culture by almost completely ignoring the outstanding 'modernists' of the North such as Henrik Ibsen (1828-1906) and Jens Peter Jacobsen (1847-1885). Despite the fact that Ibsen's name did appear a few times in the *DWB*, Belpaire no doubt ensured a certain restriction of 'modern' ideas in *her* magazine. Moreover, while she did find that some – in her eyes – typical 'Scandinavian' traits were of literary value, her actual 'hidden' agenda, namely promoting Christian beliefs, can always be sensed.

4. Scandinavian network

The transmitting of Scandinavian literature took a secondary position in Belpaire's life, as pointed out. Thus, it should not be surprising that her 'Scandinavian' network – the present focus of my analysis – also turns out to be rather small, although it should also be pointed out that this network only constitutes one cluster, thus a subgroup of Belpaire's entire professional network, an analysis of which is yet to be made. Geraldine Reymenants has already investigated another of Belpaire's sub-networks, examining the connections between female writers represented in Catholic magazines in Flanders.[33]

....

32 Broomans, 'Reception and Ideology', p.113.
33 Geraldine Reymenants, 'Vrouweninvloed in het literaire veld: De medewerking van vrouwen aan katholieke Vlaamse tijdschriften, weekbladen en kranten 1900-1940' (unpublished dissertation, Ghent, 2005).

In search of a Scandinavian network, I determined the time frame as the period between 1898 (meeting Jørgensen) and 1932 (Belpaire's last article in *DWB*), with Belpaire slowly reducing her work towards the end of the 1920s. Concerning the members of this network, all those who were in any way involved in Belpaire's work concerning Scandinavian literature are included. The primary and secondary materials that have been used in this research are letters to/from Belpaire, her articles and translations concerning Scandinavian literature, Jan Persyn's history of the *DWB* and Reymenant's thesis.

Diagram 1 shows a model of Belpaire's Scandinavian network. The colours of the dots indicate the nationalities of the network members: white=Dutch, light grey=Belgian, grey =Danish, dots=Norwegian, and black indicates the central member or *ego*.

Diagram 1[34]

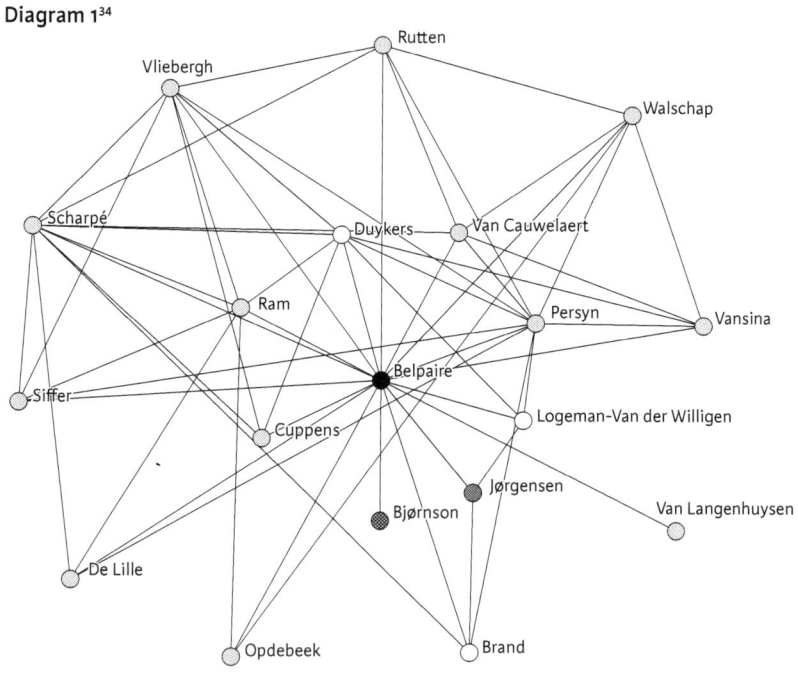

....

34 The diagrams in this article were created by the author with the help of the software
    UCINET: Stephen P. Borgatti, Martin G. Everett and Linton C. Freeman, *Ucinet for
    Windows (Version 6): Software for Social Network Analysis* (Harvard, MA, 2002):
    Analytic Technologies.

The period in question spans 34 years.[35] Bjørnson's status is marked as virtual[36] as there is no evidence that he and Belpaire actually had personal contact. However, his work made such an impression on her that it contributed considerably to the formation of her view on Scandinavian literature. This cluster (sub-network) includes editors and co-workers from *DWB*, as well as publishers and Scandinavian authors. The inner circle consists of those people Belpaire had significantly[37] more contact with in comparison to those in the outer circle.

As I mentioned above, this cluster cannot be seen as an independent network, as it largely overlaps with a group that might be called the core *DWB* network, in which Belpaire definitely also held a central position.

....

35 The period of time is quite broad, which might create the impression that the network in question was a stable entity which persisted in the same configuration throughout the years. However, the networks presented should be seen as highly simplified abstractions of given data. Networks consisting of individuals constantly fluctuate. Certainly there were contacts that persisted over several years or at the same time. To provide more insight into the actual relationships, there will be an in-depth analysis of individual contacts through a textual discourse analysis following the network analysis. Unfortunately this cannot be presented here due to space limitations. For further information, see Ester Jiresch, 'The role of networks in the work of female cultural transmitters of Scandinavian literature and culture in Europe around 1900: A comparative study of the Dutch/Flemish area and the Austrian/German-speaking regions' (dissertation to be submitted 2010, Groningen). The diagram is first and foremost intended to provide an overview of the persons with whom the central figure worked and their mutual contacts.

36 Margaret H. McFadden's investigation of nineteenth-century women's networks describes women who felt part of a specific female tradition in an international context. They often had female role models and found support and inspiration from their writings and lives without actually knowing them personally – McFadden calls such connections 'virtual' networks, Margaret H. McFadden, *Golden cables of sympathy: The transatlantic sources of nineteenth-century feminism* (Lexington, 1999), pp. 67-68.

37 The evaluation of contact 'strength/intensity' posed a severe problem. Naturally no contact will ever be the same as another, as relationships between people are always unique. However, it seemed reasonable to distinguish at least two categories of 'closer' and 'more distant' contact so that possible influences were visible in the diagram. In the case of Belpaire, I considered people who were in contact with her over decades and/ or for a shorter period on a daily basis to fit into the inner circle – 'close contact' – and the rest to remain in the outer circle as 'distant contacts'. It cannot be stated strongly enough that the network figures presented are highly simplified abstractions of reality.

Network analyst Jeremy Boissevain uses the term 'entrepreneur' for a person who builds up and manages a network in order to pursue profit, which does not necessarily have to be financial profit. He also distinguishes two kinds of resources to which such an entrepreneur needs access: direct or *first order resources*, that is, personal capital or knowledge; and indirect strategic contacts with persons (*second order resources*) who control direct resources. 'Patrons' dispose of first order resources and 'brokers' of second order resources. Boissevain defines a broker further as:

> (...) a social broker places people in touch with each other, either directly or indirectly for profit. He bridges gaps in communication between persons, groups, structures and even cultures.[38]

Thus, Belpaire actually fills both positions: that of a patron and a broker. On closer examination of the network, three subgroups emerge:

- Editorial staff and co-workers of the *DWB*
- 'Real' Scandinavian and Scandinavia-related contacts (Logeman-Van der Willigen, Jørgensen and 'virtual' Bjørnson)
- Publishers of Belpaire's translations

Diagram 1 reveals a very dense interconnection between the editorial staff and co-workers of the *DWB*, which indicates an active network inside the journal itself. Members of the Scandinavian network with a lower number of contacts are the publishers of Belpaire's translations, the 'real' Scandinavian and Scandinavia-related contacts of Jørgensen and Logeman-Van der Willigen, and the 'virtual' contact Bjørnson, who was not included in further network analyses. Jørgensen and Logeman-Van der Willigen, for their part, were also in contact with several members of the *DWB* staff. It becomes apparent that the Scandinavian network, except for the publishing house Van Langenhuysen, coincides with a part of the larger *DWB* network, constituting a smaller cluster with a calculated density of 0.30 or 30 percent.[39]

....

38 Jeremy Boissevain, *Friends of Friends: Networks, Manipulators and Coalitions* (Oxford, 1974), p. 148.
39 Density indicates the mean interconnection in a graph: 1 or 100% meaning the interconnection of all the members. John Scott, *Social Network Analysis: A Handbook* (London, 1991), pp. 72-73; Stanley Wassermann and Katherine Faust, *Social Network Analysis: Methods and Applications* (Cambridge, 1994), p. 101.

Dina (Dien) Logeman-Van der Willligen

1. Biography

Much less is known about Logeman-Van der Willligen than about Belpaire because she was not a public figure like her colleague, nor were her activities as widespread. Dina (Dien) Samuela Logeman-Van der Willigen was born on June 18, 1864 in Deventer, the Netherlands. Her parents were Prof. Volkert Simon Maarten (1822-1878) and Susanna Antonietta van der Willigen (1831-1895). Her father, who worked as a Latin teacher and later taught physics at the University of Amsterdam, encouraged her to study.[40]

In 1889 Van der Willigen married Hendrik (Henri) Logeman (1862-1936), who became a professor in the philosophy faculty of the University of Ghent.[41] The young couple soon moved to Ghent, where they lived for the rest of their lives (Dien died in 1925), only leaving Belgium for journeys to Scandinavia and during the First World War. Henri Logeman originally taught English and became a full professor in 1896. In 1903 he was the first person to introduce a class in modern Scandinavian philology at the University of Ghent.[42]

Not only her father but also her husband encouraged Dien to study, and she evolved a great talent for languages as an adult, starting with Danish in order to read Andersen's fairy tales in the original.[43] Soon after, in 1902, she began to translate at the age of 38. Over a period of 24 years Logeman-Van der Willigen managed to translate approximately 129 pieces and 16 articles by Scandinavian authors.[44] She also wrote many articles herself on Scandinavian

....

40 Amy Lahousse, 'Dien Logeman-Van der Willigen (1864-1925): Een vertaalster en cultuurbemiddelaarster voor de Scandinavische literatuur met een specifiek Fins effect' (unpublished Master's thesis, Ghent 2003), p. 57; B.H. Estelle, 'Dien Logeman van der Willigen', *Tidens kvinder: Damernas illustrerede ugeblad* (Copenhagen, February 28, 1924), p. 1.

41 Petra Broomans, '"Vertalingen waar haast bij is, boeken die gerecenseerd moeten woorden." Dien Logeman-Van der Willigen (1864-1925)', in: Isabelle Desmidt, ed., *De overzet: Een bundel over vertalen* (Ghent, 2002), p. 49.

42 Lahousse, 'Dien Logeman-Van der Willigen', p. 57.

43 Estelle, 'Dien Logeman van der Willigen', p. 1.

44 Lahousse, 'Dien Logeman-Van der Willigen', p. 58 and attachment pp. 1-2, xiv-xv. Lahousse refers to D. Grit, *Dansk skønlitteratur i Nederland og Flandern 1731-1982: Bibliografi over oversættelser og studier* (Ballerup, 1986); Jos Groen, *250 jaar Noorse literatuur in Nederland en Vlaanderen, 1743-1993: Bibliografie van vertalingen en recensies* (Hoorn, 1994).

subjects such as nature, culture, reports of her journeys and the work of other authors. These articles appeared in Dutch and Flemish journals such as *DWB*, *Onze Eeuw*, *De Lelie*, *Vrouwenleven* and *De Vlaamsche Gids*.[45]

As a result of her many journeys, her husband's academic contacts and her great eagerness to work, Logeman-Van der Willigen managed to build up a vast network of Scandinavian contacts and colleagues. Some of them even became close friends. She dedicated a large part of her life solely to the transmission of Scandinavian literature and culture and was highly respected by her colleagues and other authors. Furthermore, she was officially recognised by different governments, receiving the award of the Knight of the White Rose[46] from Finland, the Danish medal *Ingenio et arti*[47] and the Knight of the Order of the Belgian King, Leopold II.[48]

2. Literary activities

Logeman-Van der Willigen's journalistic oeuvre comprises 48 articles, published in fifteen magazines. In addition to the above-mentioned travel reports and descriptions of nature and culture, she also dedicated some articles to individual authors. Among these are articles about Viggo Stuckenberg (1863-1905), Holger Drachmann (1846-1908), Johannes Jørgensen, Saint Birgitta of Sweden (1303-1373), the Finns Werner Söderhjelm (1859-1931), Juhani Aho (1861-1921) and Johannes Linnankoski (pseudonym of Vihtori Pelvonen 1869-1913), and the Norwegian Johan Bojer (1872-1952). Herman Bang (1857-1912) seemed to have held a special interest for Logeman-Van der Willigen as she devoted four articles to the Danish writer. Logeman-Van der Willigen also worked with her husband and her Dutch colleague Margaretha Meyboom (1856-1927) as editors of the literary magazines *Scandia* and *Scandinavie-Nederland* in 1904-1905.[49]

....

45 Lahousse, 'Dien Logeman-Van der Willigen', p. 58.

46 She received this award on March 3, 1923. Lahousse, 'Dien Logeman-Van der Willigen', p. 102.

47 Letter from the Danish consul in Belgium to Logeman-Van der Willigen on September 23, 1924 (Sint-Amandsberg), Archive of the University Library Ghent, Sign. HS III 118.

48 Letter from Belgian Minister for Foreign Affairs to Logeman-Van der Willigen (Brussels), Archive of the University Library Ghent, Sign. HS III 118; N. N., 'Mevrouw Logeman-Van der Willigen', *Onze Eeuw* XII/1 (1926/2); Ingeborg Maria Sick, 'In Memoriam: Professorinde Logendal v. d. Willigen', *Berlingske Tidene*, s.d.

49 Lahousse, 'Dien Logeman-Van der Willigen', p. 70.

Taking a closer look at Logeman-Van der Willigen's translations with respect to the various countries and languages she was familiar with, the following distribution emerges:

Danish authors:
Danish was her first Scandinavian language and she began by translating *Inga Heine*[50] by Jenny Blicher-Clausen (1865-1907). Of the 129 pieces mentioned, 65 were Danish, and they were written by 20 different authors. Ranking as her probable favourites on the basis of the number of translations of their works, one should mention Ingeborg Maria Sick (1858-1951) (18), Herman Bang (9) and Jørgensen (7).

Swedish authors:
Logeman-Van der Willigen translated 21 works by 15 authors. Among them are three pieces each by Ellen Key (1849-1926), Verner von Heidenstam (1859-1940) and Anna Lenah Maria Elgström (1884-1968).

Norwegian authors:
Logeman-Van der Willigen translated the works of 14 Norwegian authors, totalling 34 books. Here again one can distinguish certain favourites, such as Barbra Ring (1870-1955) (8), Johan Bojer (1872-1952) (7) and Bjørnstjerne Bjørnson (2).

At this point I should allude to the language situation in Norway. At the beginning of the nineteenth century, written Norwegian was practically identical with Danish, since Norway had been under Danish rule for centuries. As nationalism grew in the mid-nineteenth century, a movement for the establishment a more authentic Norwegian developed (the *landsmaal* movement). The final result of this movement is still present today in the form of two official Norwegian languages, Bokmål and Nynorsk.[51] Most of the works by Norwegian authors that Logeman-Van der Willigen encountered were presumably written in Danish.

Finnish authors:
The eight pieces by Finnish authors were written by Juhani Aho, Werner and Torsten Söderhjelm (1880-1908), Johannes Linnankoski, Ester Ståhlberg

....

50 Jenny Blicher-Clausen, *Inga Heine* (Utrecht, 1902).
51 Harald S. Naess, ed., *A History of Norwegian Literature*, p. xv. See also the contribution of Van Elswijk in this volume.

(1870-1950) and Henning Söderhjelm (1888-1967). The language question here is even trickier. In some letters to colleagues, such as Belpaire for example, Logeman-Van der Willigen reported that she was busy studying Finnish:

> I am very busily studying Finnish and I have to master it this winter. Not only for the pleasure, the glory and the consciousness that I am still able to work, but also because my income shall rise.[52]

However, there is no proof that she actually acquired sufficient knowledge of the language to translate. Furthermore, all of the works she chose were available in Swedish translation, while the authors Söderhjelm wrote in Swedish anyway.[53]

3. Logeman-Van der Willigen's role in transmitting Scandinavian literature and culture

Logeman-Van der Willigen not only translated from different languages, she also translated authors from very different literary currents. Among them were the modern progressive Herman Bang, the conservative Blicher-Clausen and the Nobel Prize winner Sigrid Undset (1882-1949).

Thus, there is no primary tendency to be discovered in her choice of texts. She managed to transmit contemporary Scandinavian literature and culture in all its different facets. Of course one notices a bias towards certain authors, as seen in the overview of her translations. Also, Logeman-Van der Willigen was very fond of Scandinavian nature and folk customs, which becomes obvious from several articles. Moreover, towards the end of her life she developed a great affection for Finland and even translated political articles[54] because she felt great sympathy for the people and the country.

....

52 'Ik studeer heel ijverig Finsch en moet het deze winter onder de knie hebben, niet alleen om het genot maar, de glorie en het bewustzijn, dat ik nog tot werken in staat ben, maar ook om mijn inkomsten te verhogen'. Cf. Letter from Logeman-Van der Willigen to Belpaire, Ghent, October 16, 1912, Archive and Museum of Flemish Cultural Life in Antwerp.

53 Lahousse, 'Dien Logeman-Van der Willigen', p. 63.

54 For example, Eirik Hornborg, 'De Finsche kwestie', *Onze Eeuw* (1911), pp. 355-372; Henning Söderhjelm, *Het roode oproer in Finland 1918: Volgens officiële Documenten* (Utrecht, 1920).

Dien Logeman-Van der Willigen, March 1923. University Library Ghent

In letters to Belpaire you can read that the two women, who were amicable colleagues, shared a passion for Catholicism and Johannes Jørgensen. However, in contrast to her Belgian colleague, Logeman-Van der Willigen seemed to have no problem in dealing with modern, realistic and socially critical literature. For example, she wrote about Herman Bang that:

> In the small, he saw the great and he heard so much where others remained deaf. He did not limit himself to a certain area, he found motivation everywhere, from all classes of society. His horizon was infinitely vast, his motives were most diverse. He did not practise any particular genre.[55]

Clearly, ideologies such as strong religious belief also played a part in Logeman-Van der Willigen's transmission work. However, this was certainly not to the same extent as in Belpaire's case or some other contemporary transmitters described by Broomans.[56]

....

55 'In het kleine zag hij het groote, en hij hoorde zooveel waarvoor anderen doof bleven. Hij bepaalde zich niet tot een zekeren kring, hij haalde zijn motieven overal vandaan, uit alle klassen der maatschappij. Zijn horizont was oneindig uitgestrekt, zijn motieven zijn de meest uiteenlopende. Hij heeft nooit een bepaald genre beoefend'. Cf. Dien Logeman-Van der Willigen, 'Herman Bang', *Dietsche Warande en Belfort* (1912), pp. 305-321.
56 Broomans, 'Reception and Ideology', pp. 107-120.

Whether her broader choice of literature was really due to her open-mindedness and tolerance of artistic expression is not certain. One issue that was never a concern for Belpaire dogged Logeman-Van der Willigen throughout her life – a lack of money. This problem is mentioned in many of her letters, in which she also states that she is happy to be working on several translations at the same time because of the money. She did not have the luxury to be very particular about the work assignments. Notwithstanding this, her taste and interest in Scandinavian literature was much broader than that of Belpaire.

4. Scandinavian network

In contrast to Belpaire, transmitting Scandinavian literature and culture was probably Logeman-Van der Willigen's purpose in life. She loved visiting the countries and meeting the foreign writers, and she stated more than once in her letters how much she loved her work. As this was her main activity over 24 years, she naturally managed to establish a huge network. Counting every contact she had concerning her work, including authors, publishers, colleagues and friends, I found 81. Of course, the intensity of those contacts varied broadly. For many authors she only translated one piece, and this might have happened completely without the knowledge of the author.[57] In the case of the Finnish author Juhani Aho, she used the Swedish translations of his works.[58]

I decided to exclude all those with whom only one contact was made in the form of a translation or an article about the author and where there was no proof of personal interaction. Subsequently, a network of 23 members emerged. The material I used in this case consisted of letters, articles and translations, as well as Amy Lahousse's Master's thesis, which provides a good overview of Logeman-Van der Willigen's work. The time period ranges from her first translation in 1902 until her death in 1925. Diagram 2 shows the Scandinavian network established by Logeman-Van der Willigen. As in Belpaire's case, the colours of the dots indicate the nationalities of the network members: white=Dutch, light grey=Belgian, grey =Danish, dark grey =Swedish, dots=Norwegian, cross=Finnish, and black indicates the central member.

....

57 Letter from Logeman-Van der Willigen to Marie Bregendahl, Ghent, February 14, 1906, Danish Royal Library Copenhagen.
58 Letter from Logeman-Van der Willigen to Werner Söderhjelm, Ghent, October 13, 1912, Archive of the University Library Ghent.

Diagram 2

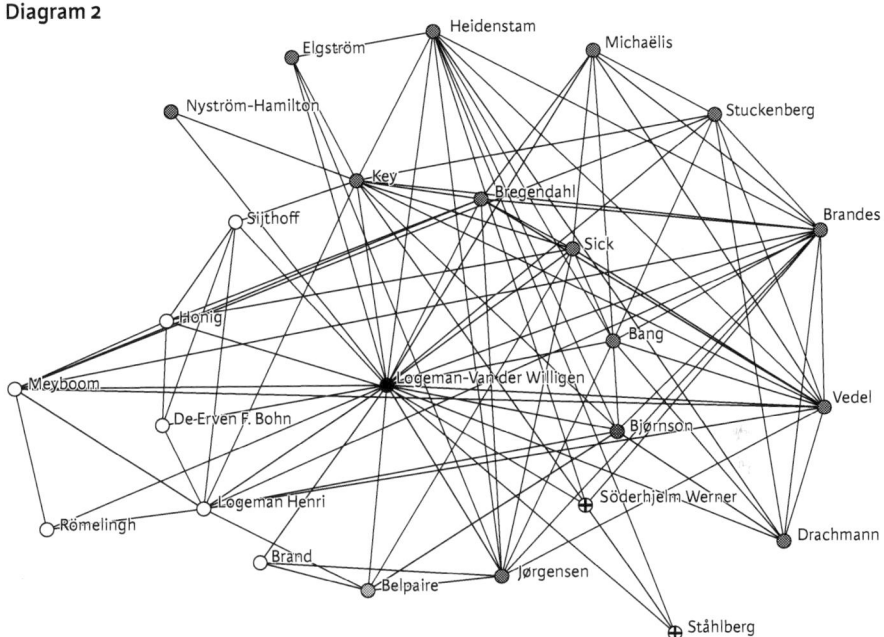

Diagram 2 shows the contacts Logeman-Van der Willigen acquired during her 24-year working life. Her 'Scandinavian' network can more or less be seen as her entire professional network. Although she also had contacts with Dutch publishers and Dutch magazines, this was almost always in connection with a Scandinavian topic. The network includes Scandinavian authors and scholars, editors of magazines, translator colleagues, publishers and her husband.

Parallel to Belpaire's case, a division into two categories on the basis of closeness was made. It differs slightly from Belpaire because of the nature of Logeman-Van der Willigen's contacts. Belpaire's contacts were fewer but more intense as she was the unofficial head of an important Flemish journal for decades and, furthermore, an outstanding figure in Antwerp cultural life, which meant she was engaged in various other networks. Logeman-Van der Willigen in contrast seems almost like a hermit, spending much time alone at home translating and maintaining her main contacts via letters. Thus, in Logeman-Van der Willigen's case I determined that significantly close contact meant ten or more contacts (via letters, personal encounters, translations and articles). The inner circle thus established consists of Marie Belpaire, Bjørnstjerne Bjørnson, Marie Bregendahl, Johannes Jørgensen, Ellen Key, Henri Logeman, Werner Söderhjelm and the publishing houses De Erven F. Bohn, Honig and Sijthoff. The remaining contacts form the outer circle. In Boissevain's terms, Logeman-Van der Willigen can be called a broker because she disposed of knowledge and strategic contacts but not her own capital.

Several clusters or subgroups can also be distinguished in this case; for example, a Danish group, a group of modern authors and so on. There is not enough space here to discuss all of these groups specifically; however, it is striking that the interconnection between the Scandinavian authors – and the Danish authors especially – was particularly strong, while the contacts with Dutch/Belgian members was quite weak. The strong inter-Scandinavian connection can be traced back to the pan-Scandinavian movement which started in the mid-nineteenth century as a reaction to rising German nationalism and because the countries were going through similar social, political and cultural changes. Together with its 'successor', the Modern Breakthrough, this movement enhanced alliances in the Scandinavian countries.[59]

The density of the whole network amounts to 0.23 or 23 percent, which is clearly less than that of Belpaire.

Conclusion – Comparing the networks

Comparing two people's networks might seem audacious for reasons I have already mentioned above. However, in this case it seems possible, as both worked in the same geographical and temporal space, transmitting culture from the same countries and, at the very least, are of interest with respect to their positions in the literary field and their respective agendas in transmitting literature and culture.

As this comparison of the networks of cultural transmitters is part of an ongoing PhD research project, the development of the most appropriate categories for comparison has not yet been finalised. The table below (Table 1) shows a selection of possible categories for comparison.

....

59 Birgitta Steene, 'Liberalism, Realism and the Modern Breakthrough: 1830-1890', in: Lars G. Warme, ed., *A History of Swedish Literature* (=Vol. 3 of A History of Scandinavian Literatures) (Nebraska, 1996), p. 234; H. Stang, 'Nordism', in: Byron J. Nordstrom, ed., *Dictionary of Scandinavian History* (Westport/London, 1986), pp. 417-419.

Table 1

	Belpaire	Logeman-Van der Willigen
Nationalities	Dutch/Flemish	Scandinavian, Dutch, Flemish
Density	30%	23%
Position/role in network	Central 'patron'/'broker'	Peripheral 'broker'
Choice of Literature	Limited	Broad, money as issue
Agenda	Promoting 'good', Christian art	Spreading knowledge about Scandinavia

The difference concerning member nationalities is prominent. Belpaire's contacts were almost exclusively Flemish/Dutch, while Logeman-Van der Willigen made various contacts from four Scandinavian countries. Belpaire's network is also denser than Logeman-Van der Willigen's, which means that the members of the network are more interconnected. This might be due to the fact that Logeman-Van der Willigen's network numbers a few more contacts – the bigger a network, the lower the interconnection rate. However, it seems more logical that the density is higher in Belpaire's network because almost all of the members were working colleagues from the same journal.

Also, their respective roles/positions inside their networks differ significantly. Due to her fortune and influence, Belpaire had a central position in her own network and the Catholic Flemish literary field. Logeman-Van der Willigen, however, seems not to have been the centre of any network, rather it appears that she might be better located on the periphery of a vast, densely interconnected Scandinavian network.

The two colleagues also differ in their choice of literature. Belpaire could afford to limit her choice of what she would translate or promote. Logeman-Van der Willigen on the other hand translated and promoted literature from Sweden, Norway, Denmark and Finland, written in a great variety of literary styles. Certainly financial insecurity was an issue for her, but notwithstanding this her interests appear to be much broader than those of Belpaire. A certain agenda in transmitting different traits of a foreign culture coincided with the choice of literature each made. It is more than obvious that Belpaire cared much more about Christian art, 'good' art, as she called it, than about Scandinavian literature in particular. Moreover, she tried to disguise her moral values as typical Scandinavian traits where it suited her. Logeman-Van der Willigen, in contrast, had a more tolerant and open view of Scandinavia. She happily embraced most of the works she translated and expressed positive views about Scandinavian culture and literature in her essays. In addition to earning a living, spreading knowledge about her beloved Scandinavia was without doubt her main agenda.

Despite their geographical and personal closeness, their great affinity for certain Scandinavian authors – their mutual interest coincided in relation to Jørgensen and Bjørnson – and their occasional working relationship, with Logeman-Van der Willigen writing several articles for *DWB*, the areas of interest of the two women were quite divergent. For most of her life Belpaire was primarily involved in Flemish cultural life and politics, never spending long periods abroad, and therefore the literary field she engaged in mainly comprised members of conservative Belgian/Flemish Catholic circles. Logeman-Van der Willigen, however, came into contact with and maintained relationships with many Scandinavian authors over the decades. Thus, she not only came into contact with various literary circles in different Scandinavian countries, but she also became part of what could be called an inter-Scandinavian[60] literary field. Furthermore, Logeman-Van der Willigen was also engaged in Dutch and Flemish circles due to her contacts with Dutch publishers and her work for different Dutch and Flemish magazines, as mentioned above. As we have seen, not only was Belpaire's involvement in the transmission of Scandinavian literature quite limited, she was also active solely in a refined literary field. In contrast, Logeman-Van der Willigen was active in different national and international circles due to her great love of Scandinavian literature and her commitment to her work.

....

60 As seen here in Logeman-Van der Willigen's case, one can assume that there was a very dense network of Scandinavian authors, probably due to the close relationship between the languages, but also due to the fact that similar topics were popular among the authors at the time. Further investigation of such networks is recommended.

Greta Baars-Jelgersma, Cora Sandel and the Dutch Literary Field, 1925-1950

Aspects of Cross-national Literary Transfer

« Janke Klok »

In 1950 the Dutch translation of the novel *Kranes konditori. Interiør med figurer* (*Krane's Café*) (1945) by Cora Sandel (pseudonym of Sara Fabricius, 1880-1974) was published by the Wereldbibliotheek publishing house. The translation was by Greta Baars-Jelgersma (1911-) and was entitled *Krane's lunchroom*. It is one of many translations by the cultural transmitter Baars-Jelgersma, who translated an extensive body of work from Nordic languages into Dutch, spanning various genres. That Baars-Jelgersma chose a novel by Cora Sandel is not so surprising, as Sandel's novels and short stories had been published in Dutch by several publishing houses and in different literary magazines between 1928 and 1934 and were thus known to the Dutch public. What is more surprising is that Baars-Jelgersma did not start with the third part of Sandel's classic triptych on the painter Alberte Selmer, *Bare Alberte* (*Alberta Alone*) (1939), when she selected a text by Cora Sandel, the first two parts having already been published in Dutch in 1928 and 1934.[1]

In this article I will discuss both the translation oeuvre of Baars-Jelgersma and the Dutch reception of the works of the Norwegian author Cora Sandel. I will focus on the period 1925-1950, which is distinct in the history of the literary relationship between the Netherlands and Scandinavia, as during this time the image of Scandinavian literature in the Netherlands changed radically. From being regarded as an inspiring, engaged, modern literature, it came to be seen as rather conservative and boring, and it was linked to regional trilogies and at times to the ideology of

....

1 Cora Sandel, *Levenshonger* (Amsterdam, 1928), translation of *Alberte og Jakob* (1926) from Norwegian by W. Quanjer-Steltman; Cora Sandel, *Alberte en de vrijheid* (Santpoort, 1934), translation of *Alberte og friheten* (1931) from Norwegian by W. Quanjer-Steltman. In fact a Dutch translation of *Bare Alberte* has still not been published.

National Socialism.[2] What can the Dutch reception of Cora Sandel and the translation oeuvre of Baars-Jelgersma tell us about their positions within the literary field in the Netherlands? Could these positions shed light on the timing of the changing image of Scandinavian literature in the period 1925-1950? In turn what can they tell us about the Dutch literary field in this period? Which impulses could the outcomes of these findings give to the knowledge of cross-national literary transfer?

The translation oeuvre of Greta Baars-Jelgersma in the period 1925-1950
When Greta Baars-Jelgersma translated Cora Sandel's *Kranes konditori* into Dutch in 1950, she already had a long career as a translator of Scandinavian literature behind her. Amongst her works we find novels and stories by Knut Hamsun, Magnhild Haalke, Eyvind Johnson, Pär Lagerkvist, Haldór Laxness, Tora Nordström-Bonnier and Aksel Sandemose, to name but a few. In other words, Baars-Jelgersma translated literary works from Norwegian, Danish, Swedish and Icelandic. How does *Krane's lunchroom* fit within this translation oeuvre, and what were Baars-Jelgersma's motives for her cultural transmission in general? Below, I will describe Baars-Jelgersma's profile as a translator, that is, as a cultural transmitter.

Baars-Jelgersma started her translation career in 1936 with *Een vluchteling kruist zijn spoor*, a translation of *En flyktning krysser sitt spor* (1933) by Aksel Sandemose (1899-1965), a fascinating novel in which the protagonist, Espen Arnakke, through an introspective self-analysis, attempts to understand why he became a murderer. It was regarded as a scathing attack on the herd instinct and small-town beliefs. These Sandemose most famously formulated into ten rules on how to cut someone down to size, later referred to as the Jante Law. The novel is also seen as the main work by Sandemose, with the

---

2 See A. Van Marken, 'Inn i kampen mellom ideologiene', in: Grøndahl, C.H., ed., *Dyade. Sigrid Undset vurdert i utlandet* 2 (1982), pp. 7-8; D. Grit, 'Bestaat de receptie van "de" Deense literatuur in Nederlandse vertaling, 1731-1990?', in: Grit, D., *Driewerf zalig Noorden. Over literaire betrekkingen tussen de Nederlanden en Scandinavië* (Maastricht, 1994), pp. 120-129; P. Broomans, 'Hur skapas en litteraturhistorisk bild? Den nordiska litteraturens "fräschhet" i Nederländerna och Flandern', in: Dahl, P. and Steinfeld, T., eds.,*Videnskab og national opdragelse. Studier I nordisk litteraturhistorieskrivning. Del II* (Copenhagen, 2001), pp. 535, 536; P. Broomans, 'Scandinavische literatuur in Nederland: verslonden, verzuild en verguisd', in: Braber, H.M. van den and Gielkens, J.A.W., eds., *In 1934. Nederlandse cultuur in internationale context* (Amsterdam/Antwerp, 2010), pp. 411-413.

Norwegian scholar of literature Yngvar Ustvedt considering Sandemose's attack on the narrow-mindedness of humanity one of the most important themes in Norwegian literature.[3] The translation, *Een vluchteling kruist zijn spoor*, appeared in the same year as the English version, *A Fugitive Crosses his Tracks* (New York, 1936). Both the Dutch and the English translation contain a foreword by the Norwegian author and Nobel Prize winner Sigrid Undset (1822-1949). The book would become the most successful Norwegian book in the US at the time, after *Markens Grøde (The Growth of the Soil)* (1917) by Knut Hamsun and *Kristin Lavransdatter* (1920-1922) by Undset.[4]

Thus, with Sandemose's novel, Baars-Jelgersma started her translating career with a modern text from mainstream Norwegian literature. In 1936, Aksel Sandemose was not unknown to the Dutch public. As early as March 19, 1929 Dr Annie Posthumus (1881-1964) had discussed Sandemose's novel *Ross Dane* (1928), which was about 'colonists in Canada', in the evening edition of the *Nieuwe Rotterdamsche Courant*, singling out the theme of 'the psychology of the immigrant'.[5] It took two more years before *Ross Dane* (1931) appeared in Dutch translation with the same title 'naar het Deensch' (from Danish) by M.J. Molanus-Stamperius and published by the Utrecht publisher Bruna. *En flyktning krysser sitt spor* (1933) was the first novel that Sandemose, who immigrated from Denmark to Norway in 1930, published in his new homeland.[6] In 1936 Baars-Jelgersma and the Dutch publisher Bijleveld positioned Sandemose explicitly as a Norwegian author, for example, by printing a map of Norway on the book's cover.

....

3   He made this statement in a radio portrait, *Sånn er livet* (Such is life), NRK P2, September 17, 2001. Published on September 12, updated September 14, 2001 as *NRK Portretter. Aksel Sandemose (1899-1965)* http://www.nrk.no/nyheter/bakgrunn/ portretter/1284705.html, accessed November 8, 2010. Sandemose's inventory of intolerance in his Jante Law became a standard in social psychology, see http://www. bokkilden.no/SamboWeb/produkt.do?produktId=142473, accessed June 27, 2010.

4   According to Philip Houm in *Norges litteratur fra 1914 til 1950-årene* (1955), vol. 6 of Bull, Paasche, Winsnes and Houm, eds., *Norsk litteraturhistorie* (Oslo: Aschehoug, 1924-1955), p. 428.

5   *Nieuwe Rotterdamsche Courant*, March 19, 1929, evening edition, p. 18 http:// kranten.kb.nl/, accessed November 8, 2010. Posthumus introduced Sandemose as a young Danish author in the 'Deensche Letteren' (Danish literature) section.

6   Sandemose's mother was Norwegian, he was born in Denmark, where he would also die in 1965, in 1930 he immigrated to Norway where he would live and work until around 1955. His oeuvre is commonly presented in the framework of Norwegian literary history.

EEN VLUCHTELING
KRUIST ZIJN SPOOR

Baars-Jelgersma's first translation, 1936, showing
her fascination for the Norwegian coastline.

From the two meetings I had with Baars-Jelgersma, it became clear that the cover of *Een vluchteling kruist zijn spoor* also tells us something about her reasons for concentrating on literature from Scandinavia as she told me she was fascinated by the extensive Norwegian coastline.[7] However, she also had, one could say, a romantic longing for the unique and the exotic. In the spring of 2010 she explained that she had not chosen German or English when she decided to become a translator because she did not think they would be sufficiently satisfying. She wanted 'something special, which no one had done before'. These desires led her to focus on Scandinavian languages after secondary school in Enkhuizen, and alongside the job she took with Nederlandse Post (Dutch postal services) in Utrecht at the age of eighteen to support herself, she started private education in Norwegian.

....

7   In the search for information about Baars-Jelgersma (1911), who no Dutch scholar of Scandinavian Studies could tell me much about, I tried to make contact with the literary agency that she had founded at the beginning of the 1950s and which was still mentioned in the *Writers' & Artists' Yearbook 2006*. Very surprisingly, at the end of 2007, I found the name Greta Baars-Jelgersma in the telephone book of the town where the literary agency was also listed. A first telephone contact resulted in a meeting with Baars-Jelgersma herself. On November 29, 2007 I found myself in nearby Utrecht in a off-white apartment, filled with books and papers and photographs of her husband Herman and Knut Hamsun side by side on the piano. The door was opened by a short woman with a walking stick, Greta Baars-Jelgersma, who at that time had just turned 96. This first interview was followed by a second on June 14, 2010 – the day that the Netherlands-Brazil World Cup football match in South Africa turned the country orange. In both interviews Baars-Jelgersma confirmed that her fascination with the Norwegian coastline was one of her reasons for focusing on Scandinavia when she decided to become a translator.

Critical and innovative mainstream literature

Baars-Jelgersma's first translation set the tone of her translation oeuvre, which she would maintain throughout the 1930s and 1940s, translating critical and progressive mainstream literature. Her oeuvre comprised novels, short stories and non-fiction (for example, a book written in journalistic style about Black America in the 1930s), mainly from the Norwegian-language area,[8] and she regarded the introduction of an author from one language area into another to be one of her particular tasks.

The story about the murderer Espen Arnakke was the first of three translations of work by Sandemose that Baars-Jelgersma would publish, the former arguing in his work that every human being has a primitive and a civilised side and that environment determines which predominates. *Een vluchteling kruist zijn spoor* was followed by *Er stond een bank in 't groen* (1939), a translation of *Der stod en benk i haven* (1937), and *De teerhandelaar* (1947), the translation of *Tjærehandleren* (1945). The cover of the third translation, Sandemose's *De teerhandelaar*, indicates that Baars-Jelgersma – and the publishing house – consciously chose to counter the image of Scandinavian literature which was commonplace at the time: that of singing forests and sentimentality. The front cover states: 'No Norwegian pine-tree mystique but rather a stick of psychological dynamite' and the back cover refers to the fact that Sandemose's book does *not* match the idea of Scandinavian literature 'as a kind of standard dish which some love and others hate, a mixture of waving pine trees, alcoholic ministers, crazy old ladies, tragic like the dark pine forests'.[9] Each of the three titles was published by a different publisher, the first in Utrecht by Erven J. Bijleveld, the second in Amsterdam in the Arbo series (Arbeiders Roman Bibliotheek Ontwikkeling) by Arbeiderspers, and the third by De Driehoek in 's-Graveland.

That a foreign author was published by multiple publishers was not strange in the Dutch literary landscape of the first decade of the twentieth century. Many authors were well travelled through the world of Dutch

....

8   See for a complete survey of Baars-Jelgersma's translations during the period 1936-1950, Appendix I.

9   On the front cover of *De teerhandelaar* ('s Graveland, 1947): 'Geen Noorse pijnwouden-mystiek, maar een brok psychologisch dynamiet'; on the backcover the Dutch author Jef Last is quoted: 'als zo'n soort standaardgerecht, waar de een dol op is en waar de ander een hekel aan heeft; een mengsel van ruisende pijnbomen, aan de drank geraakte dominees, gekke oude vrouwtjes, tragisch als donkere dennebossen'.

publishing, including Sandemose and August Strindberg (1849-1912), as well as Nobel Prize winners such as Selma Lagerlöf (1858-1940) and Sigrid Undset. The same can be said of Cora Sandel and Knut Hamsun (1859-1952) – the latter also a Nobel Prize winner and whose work Baars-Jelgersma also translated between 1935-1950.

In the case of the latter, in 1936, the year of Baars-Jelgersma's Scandinavian translation debut, Hamsun's pro-Nazi attitude in relation to the Ossietzsky case had led to intellectuals in Norway and the Netherlands publicly protesting against his stance.[10] However, this did not lessen the interest of the Dutch press in his works. In the years 1936-1940, announcements about Hamsun's new books, film versions of his work, discussions of his novels, references to his work, notices of anniversary events and anecdotes about his unapproachableness continued to appear in newspapers such as *Het Vaderland, Nieuwe Rotterdamsche Courant* and *Wetenschappelijke bladen*, without a word about Hamsun's political point of view.[11] In 1940 Baars-Jelgersma's translation of Hamsun's last novel *De cirkel gesloten (Ringen sluttet*, 1936) was published by Salm publishing house in Amsterdam, and in 1944 Strengholt in Amsterdam published her translation of *Maar het leven leeft (Men livet lever*, 1933).[12] At that point Hamsun's sympathy for the Nazis had repercussions which not only affected him personally – in the sense that he lost his property, was temporarily put under psychiatric observation, was forced to pay compensation for his membership of the Nasjonal Samling (NS) in 1947 and spent his last years in poverty – but also had literary consequences.

....

10 In the evening edition of *Het Vaderland* from February 12, 1936, a notice was dedicated to the discussion at the Noorsche schrijfersvereeniging (The Norwegian Authors' Union) on the occasion of Hamsun's stand against the nomination of Carl von Ossietzky for the Nobel Peace Prize. The discussion had resulted in a condemnation of Hamsun's attitude ('optreden in het geval Ossietzky') by a great majority of Norwegian authors, *Het Vaderland*, February 12, 1936, evening edition, p. 9. On February 26, *Het Vaderland* reported that the Norwegian action had been followed in the Netherlands, where a group of intellectuals – including former translators of Hamsun, Jan Romein and Annie Romein-Verschoor – also protested against Hamsun's stance, *Het Vaderland*, February 26, 1936, evening edition, p. 9.

11 See for example, *Het Vaderland*, July 10, 1936; March 20, 1938; August 5, 1939; November 3, 1939.

12 The latter was published simultaneously by the Belgian publisher De lage landen in Brussels.

In Norway and many other European countries his work was no longer published or reprinted and after the publication of *Maar het leven leeft* in 1944, silence also fell around Hamsun in the Netherlands.[13]

Travels through the Dutch publishing landscape

Other authors whose works were translated by Greta Baars-Jelgersma in the 1930s and 1940s reveal a similar journey through the world of Dutch publishing. Her translation of *Allis sønn* (1935), by Magnhild Haalke, was released in 1937 by Stols in The Hague. *Gurianna* (a translation of Haalke's *Åkfestet*, 1936) appeared in 1939, published by Windroos in Amsterdam, *De dag is zoo kort* (*Dagblinket*, 1937) was published in 1947 by Salm in Amsterdam and two short stories by Haalke appeared in the collection *Noorderlicht over de lage landen* in 1941, published by Ad. M. C. Stok/Zuid-Hollandsche Uitgevers Maatschappij in The Hague. According to Greta Baars-Jelgersma, publishing this anthology was the 'last good deed' done by Stok before the publisher changed to 'rubbish, romances and the like'.[14] The anthology includes work by a varied group of outstanding, innovative and progressive Norwegian authors, including Johan Falkberget, Ingeborg Refling Hagen, Sigurd Hoel, Arnulf Øverland and Nini Roll-Anker. The stories chosen are accompanied by short biographies written in the third person or at times in the first person – all probably by the authors themselves.

In the anonymous presentations written in the third person, such as those about Johan Falkberget, Johan Bojer and Sigurd Kvåle, it is of note that the texts contain many references to Norwegian nature and the Norwegian landscape.[15] The large number of authors who present themselves in the first person illustrates the fact that Baars-Jelgersma had good contacts

....

13 No further translations of Hamsun's work were published in the Netherlands until 1961, when *De koningin van Sheba*, two short stories, again translated by Greta Baars-Jelgersma, was published by Gaade in The Hague.

14 As Baars-Jelgersma stated on November 29, 2007.

15 Baars-Jelgersma, *Noorderlicht over de lage landen* (The Hague, 1941), examples are to be found in the short biographies of Johan Falkberget (p. 26): Johan Bojer (p. 136) and Sigurd Kvåle (p. 166).

with 'her' authors.[16] Cora Sandel's presentation of herself is also evocative. With self-irony she writes that she 'recently published a trilogy, which, as commonly known, is a necessity of life for a Scandinavian author'.[17] The cliché of the Scandinavian trilogy was obviously also familiar in Scandinavia around 1940. In her preface Baars-Jelgersma writes that she wanted the collection to be 'a harmonious unit', with the aim of 'the gradual blending of opposing colours and forms'. The second edition of the anthology appeared in 1948. The diversity of texts was strengthened by the wide range of illustrations by Toon van Ham.

In 2007 Baars-Jelgersma stated that the collection was the result of a long process – she had to 'read and discard' much before she made her final selection. This was also how she would generally chose books to show a publisher. In 2010 she added that early on she had travelled to Scandinavia with the little money she had and had bought books there. After having read and considered the novels, she would then contact the publishing house that she thought most suitable with a business proposition. This indicates a professional approach to her activities as a literary agent, which she formalised in 1951 by founding the literary agency Auteursbureau Greta Baars-Jelgersma.

Baars-Jelgersma gained her knowledge of Scandinavian literature from the university library in Utrecht where she could borrow the books in their original language, as well as access other resources. Later she received literary magazines such as *Vinduet* (Norway) and *BLM* (Sweden) from the Scandinavian publishers with whom she had contact. Baars-Jelgersma only chose books that she liked herself. Since she used highly recognised literary magazines as one of her sources of information, she must have chosen mainly from a corpus of authors with so-called high cultural capital. Nevertheless, her own judgement was her most important criterion. In that sense, Greta Baars-Jelgersma can be regarded as one of the translators who 'met zorg en naar hun beste weten hun werk uitzoeken' (picked their work

....

16 The impression was confirmed by Baars-Jelgersma in June 2010. She had good contact with her Scandinavian authors and remembers that Sandemose once borrowed money from her. The Swedish woman Marika Stiernstedt, whose work, *Aanslag in Parijs* (*Attentat i Paris*, 1942), she translated in 1946, was a good friend.

17 Baars-Jelgersma, *Noorderlicht over de lage landen*: 'onlangs een trilogie [publiceerde], wat zo men weet voor een Scandinavische auteur een levensbehoefte is', p. 240.

The stand of literary agency Greta Baars-Jelgersma at the Frankfurter Buchmesse in 1957, the display showing many of her Scandinavian authors.

carefully and to their best knowledge), as her predecessor Margaretha Meyboom had described them.[18] She based her choices on the material she had at her disposal, or in response to a request from a publisher who was looking for a book for his list. Baars-Jelgersma was surprised that she could interest so many publishers and looking back in 2010 concluded that her enthusiasm must have been very infectious.

Changing image in the 1940s

After her focus on Norwegian authors in the 1930s, in the 1940s Baars-Jelgersma also translated work by Swedish and Danish authors. The first Swedish author whose work she translated was Eyvind Johnson (1900-1976), one of the Swedish literary innovators from the interwar period. After 1945 he would dedicate himself to subjects from Classical Antiquity and the European Middle Ages, attempting to demonstrate how the past could be a mirror to the present. Baars-Jelgersma translated Johnson's four-part

....

18 Margaretha Meyboom, 'Skandinavische literatuur in Nederland', in: H.E. Greve, ed., *Boekzaal*, vol. 5 (Zwolle, 1911), p. 49. For more information about Meyboom, see also the article by Ester Jiresch 'title' and the introduction by Petra Broomans and Marta Ronne in this volmue.

autobiographical cycle *Romanen om Olof* (The novel about Olof), a series which presents the developmental history of young Olof Persson, who after being a jack of all trades and master of none decides to become an author. The works are characterised by the alternation of realistic and fairy tale-like styles in the tradition of Selma Lagerlöf. Baars-Jelgersma's translation of the cycle was published in two volumes in the Arbo series by Arbeiderspers.

The titles of the Dutch translations reflect a specific phenomenon. The Swedish titles tell readers that they are going to read a developmental novel about a young man, which is exactly the case.[19] However, the Dutch titles, *Olof lacht tegen het leven* (Olof smiles to life) and *De weg naar onzekerheid* (The road to uncertainty), evoke immediate associations with the Dutch phenomenon of *streekliteratuur* ('regional literature').[20] The Arbo series was apparently intended to promote reading among the working class by publishing accessible literature. In addition, the pastoral rural environment represented in a number of these novels may have been intended to counterbalance the rough daily life of the working class. If this was the case, Johnson's novels did not belong in the series and this may explain why they were not reprinted, unlike many other books in the Arbo series. Of course, the Second World War also played an important role in publishing policy during the 1940s.[21]

Baars-Jelgersma also translated more than one novel from two other Swedish authors: Tora Nordström-Bonnier and Peter William Nisser (1919-1999). She translated Nisser's *Hunger* (1942) and *De försvunna* (1945), which appeared under the titles *Honger* (1946) and *Vermist* (1949) respectively, both published by Van Holkema & Warendorf. Of the works by journalist and author Tora Nordström-Bonnier (1895-1991), Baars-Jelgersma translated *De vrouwen van Bisslingegaard* (1946), published

----

19   The Swedish titles were, *Nu var det 1914* (1934); *Här har du ditt liv!* (1935); *Se dig inte om!* (1936); *Slutspel i ungdomen* (1937). For more information on translated Swedish literature into Dutch, see: P. Broomans and I. Kroon, *Zweedse Literatuur in Nederland en Vlaanderen en supplement Fins–Zweeds in vertaling* (Groningen, forthcoming, 2011).

20   Present-day readers will not immediately associate the genre of regional literature with the Arbeiderspers. In the 1930s and 1940s, the Arbo series by Arbeiderspers also included original Dutch novels which are now considered regional literature. An example is J.P. Zoomers-Vermeer, *De grijze hoeve* (1947).

21   See Adriaan Venema, *Schrijvers, uitgevers & hun collaboratie. Uitgevers en boekhandelaren* (Amsterdam, 1992) for more information on this subject.

by Van Holkema & Warendorf in Amsterdam (translation of *Uppländsk kvinnospegel*, 1941) and *Een nacht in Juni* (1948), published by Stols in The Hague (translation of *Juninatten*, 1940).[22] The latter novel, about a tragic love, had been made into a film starring Ingrid Bergman in 1940. The phenomenon observed with respect to the titles of Johnson's cycle repeats itself here with regard to the works of Nordström-Bonnier, where the translation of the title changes the genre of the work. *De vrouwen van Bisslingegaard* reminds us of historical novels such as *De vrouwen van het Leycestersche tijdvak* by Anna Louisa Geertruida Bosboom-Toussaint (1812-1886) or *De vrouwen van Tannó*, a novel by Ernst Zahn (1867-1952), which is categorised as regional or peasant literature, while the original, *Uppländsk kvinnospegel*, is in fact a modern novel centred around a women's collective. It is almost as if the Dutch publishing houses had made up their minds about the nature of Scandinavian literature and adjusted the titles, presentation and covers of their translations accordingly.

Alienating translation and genre omnivore

Regarding Baars-Jelgersma's translation strategy, in 2007 she commented that a translation should not 'harm the text'. In her eyes it was not acceptable to adjust or leave out certain elements simply because 'the things happening in those countries are quite different from the things happening here'. That this was not something that goes without saying can be illustrated by translations of novels by Lagerlöf and Undset, for example, where smaller or larger fragments were omitted.[23] Baars-Jelgersma stated in 2007 that if omissions could not be helped one had to use footnotes or an explanation at the back of the book. In 2010 she further emphasised

....

22   The latter novel was translated in cooperation with Rolv Ravn, with whom Baars-Jelgersma would often work in the future.

23   Amy van Marken mentions a chapter about Doris in Sigrid Undset's novel *Vaaren* which has been omitted in the Dutch translation. Van Marken assumes that the chapter contained too many 'strong' passages, see Van Marken, 'Inn i kampen mellom ideologiene', *Dyade* 2 (1982), p. 5. She also argues for a thorough investigation of translations in this regard and states that translators and publishers in the 1920s tended to censor more or less due to moral considerations, *ibidem*, p. 9. A random sample from *Gösta Berling* (1898), Margaretha Meyboom's translation of Selma Lagerlöf's *Gösta Berlings saga* (1891), shows that sentences and passages have also been omitted here.

her strategy and explained that she found the process of 'searching for the right word, trying to bring across someone's thoughts in a way that person himself wanted it' to be fascinating: 'I've always engrossed myself in that – what was behind it'. She considered that translating should attempt to bring the original and translation 'as close together as possible'. This translation strategy focuses on the source text, bringing the reader to the source. Within translation studies such a strategy is called 'alienating translation', in contrast to a more adaptive translation strategy.

As a translator, Baars-Jelgersma was an omnivore regarding genre, translating novels, short stories, folk tales and non-fiction. Of the latter, over the period discussed here, two works were originally in Norwegian, one Danish and one Swedish. Her choice of non-fiction also included a diverse range of subjects, although the quality and critical tone of the works were similar. Her first non-fiction translation was a popular introduction to medical psychology and psychiatry by Trygve Braatøy, published by Erven J. Bijleveld of Utrecht. The second was *Ook ik ben Amerika* (*Nederst ved bordet*, 1936) by journalist Odd Hølaas (1898-1968), a good friend of Nordahl Grieg (1902-1943). In his book, Hølaas exposes, among other things, the practices of the Klu Klux Klan, and he later included his experiences in a volume of essays entitled *Livstegn og speilinger* (1966), which resulted in a nomination for the Nordic Council Literature Prize. However, strangely enough, he is relatively unknown in the Norwegian literary establishment. Upon the posthumous publication of a second volume of his essays, *Livstegn og speilinger 2: Storm og Lys*, edited by Gordon Hølmebakk and published by Aschehoug in 2001, Arne Skouen (1913-2003) called it a 'literary scandal' that Hølaas was not included in the standard work, *Norsk litteraturhistorie – sakprosa fra 1750-1995*.[24]

The Dutch media, however, did cover the book by Hølaas in the 1930s with a remarkable full-page article in *Het Nieuws van den dag voor Nederlandsch-Indië* in July 1938. The book also provoked an article about the situation facing the black population in America. The critics called Hølaas's book the 'epos der zwarte Amerikanen' (epic tale of the black Americans) and praised it as 'een journalistieke prestatie van ongewoon formaat' (a journalistic presentation of unusual length) and a 'cultureel document van wetenschappelijke waarde' (cultural document of scientific value), with the aside that perhaps not all the aspects of the multifaceted 'black question'

....

24 Skouen, 'Lysende skrivekunst', *Dagbladet*, September 29, 2001, http://www.dagbladet.no/kultur/2001/10/29/291260.html, accessed July 30, 2010.

had been covered.[25] The final two non-fiction books translated by Baars-Jelgersma in this period were travel books. These included a Danish book about the journey of a healthcare officer to the Dutch East Indies, written by Johan Wøller, and a Swedish book with accounts of seal hunting in the Arctic Ocean and expeditions to Panama to find the Kuna and Choco Indians, written by Per Høst. The first book was published by Bijleveld, who specialised in non-fiction, the second by De Tijdstroom.

In summary, Baars-Jelgersma translated almost 40 works in the period 1936-1950. This amounts to almost three titles per year and is evidence of enormous translation activity. She would later call this period 'de goede tijd' (the good times).[26] An analysis reveals that in the 1930s and 1940s most of the Norwegian works she translated were by modern, innovative authors, most of whom held centre stage in the Norwegian canon. It is clear that neither Baars-Jelgersma nor her publishers were afraid to take on controversial Scandinavian literature. Quite the contrary, in fact. The selection of authors, the foreword to *Noorderlicht op de lage landen* and the cover texts for Sandemose's *De teerhandelaar*, all indicate that Baars-Jelgersma wanted to demonstrate the literary diversity of Scandinavian literature. Her choice of Odd Hølaas's book, which challenged racism, was highly progressive. This trend partially continued in the 1940s. Novels by Grieg, Skouen, Kåre Holt (1916-1997) and Sandel certainly do not reflect the stereotype of Scandinavian literature emerging at the time, despite Sandel's ironical reference to this in her short autobiography in *Noorderlicht op de lage landen*, mentioned above. The works by Johnson, Nisser and Nordström-Bonnier, the translations of which were published by a wide range of Dutch publishers in the 1930s and 1940s, do not fit this stereotype either. In other words, in the period 1936-1950 it was possible to publish translations of works by very different kinds of Scandinavian authors in the Netherlands.

Baars-Jelgersma regarded the introduction of an author from one language area into another to be one of her tasks and she fulfilled this task in many ways. She introduced her authors to the Dutch publishing world, editing anthologies and writing forewords and introductions to some of her translations. As mentioned above, as a translator she chose the strategy of alienation, keeping the texts as close to the original as

....

25   *Het Nieuws van den dag voor Nederlandsch-Indië,* July 19, 1938, vol. 43, morning edition, p. 22.

26   From the interview on June 14, 2010.

possible, and after 1950 she would extend and further professionalise her activities in the field of transmitting culture by founding the literary agency Auteursbureau Greta Baars-Jelgersma (1951).

Cora Sandel in the Netherlands

Cora Sandel's works were published very early in the Netherlands, beginning with *Levenshonger*, the translation of *Alberte og Jakob* (1926) by Willemke Quanjer-Steltman (1879-1966), published by Becht in 1928. In the decade that followed, Sandel's literary work received a fair amount of attention in the Netherlands, with literary magazines publishing parts of *Levenshonger* and some of her short stories. *Alberte en de vrijheid*, the translation of *Alberte og friheten* (1931), was published in 1934. In the following we will look at what happened to Sandel's work in the Netherlands after 1935, as well as discuss which texts were translated and how they were received by Dutch literary critics. Was her work canonised by the literary critics of Scandinavian literature in the Netherlands?

Sandel made her novelistic debut in 1926 in Norway with *Alberte og Jakob* (1926), which immediately convinced the Norwegian literary critics, and it did not take long for her work to find its way to the Netherlands.[27] Quanjer-Steltman became an important introducer of her novels and short stories, and her translation, 'naar het Noorsch' (after the Norwegian), of Sandel's debut appeared in 1928 with 'Eenige beoordelingen van de Noorsche Pers' (Some assessments from the Norwegian press) from the *Oslo Avondblad, Avondpost, Stavanger Avondblad,*

Cora Sandel (1880-1974) in 1926, the year that she published her novel Alberte og Jakob. *Photo courtesy of Gyldendal Norsk Forlag, Oslo.*

---

27 Sandel made her literary debut in 1922 with the short story 'Rosina', which was published in the newspaper *Social-Demokratens* Saterday's Supplement *Lørdagskveld.*

Noorwegens Handels and *Zeevaartblad, Noorwegens Kommunistenblad* and *Arbeidercourant*.[28] There was also a review by Dr Annie Posthumus published in the *Nieuwe Rotterdamsche Courant* before the Dutch translation was available. Here Posthumus states that *Levenshonger* is an important book for 'alle optimisten in de vrouwenbeweging' (all the optimists in the feminist movement). Mindful of the novel's lack of optimism concerning the possibilities for a young woman in a small provincial town, Posthumus no doubt considered it would have been misplaced and that Sandel's novel could be read as a warning.

In 1934 *Levenshonger* was followed by *Alberte en de vrijheid*, again translated by Quanjer-Steltman, and this time published by C.A. Mees in Santpoort. *Alberte og friheten*, the second part of Sandel's trilogy about Alberte Selmer, had been published by Gyldendal in Oslo in 1931. Before the full translation of the second part appeared, large sections had been published in *Groot-Nederland* in 1933.[29] Quanjer-Steltman – or perhaps her publisher – seems to have followed a strategy of attempting to excite the curiosity of the public by pre-publishing parts of the novel and thereby recruiting potential readers for the entire work. The strategy was also followed by others, sometimes successfully, sometimes not, for example, the author Siegfried Emanuel van Praag (1899-2002), who early on dedicated himself to a translation of Marcel Proust's work, had attempted to attract attention to his work through pre-publications in literary magazines.[30]

Quanjer-Steltman not only used the literary magazines for pre-publications of Sandel's novels, but also published some of Sandel's short

....

28 Sandel, *Levenshonger* (Amsterdam, 1928), pp. 3-5.

29 Chapters of the novel were published in part I of vol. 31 (1933, pp. 507-514) and in part II of vol. 31 (1933, pp. 32-46, 111-122, 123-128 and 434-451). In Part II we also find another Norwegian author: a translation by B.A. Meuleman of two fragments of *Peer Gynt* by Henrik Ibsen, *Groot-Nederland* vol. 31 (1933, pp. 391, 484).

30 Siegfried Emanuel van Praag published on French culture of the eighteenth century and wrote a bibliography of Julie de Lespinasse (1934). Sophie Levie discusses the works and selling strategy of Van Praag based on an analysis of the letters between him and his wife Hilda van Praag-Sanders and authors, editors and publishers, in S. Levie, 'De contacten van Siegfried E. van Praag met zijn uitgevers', in: Braber, H.M. van den and Gielkens, J.A.W., eds., *In 1934. Nederlandse cultuur in internationale context*, pp. 173-182. It should be noted that another Siegfried van Praag (1888-1958) was active as a translator in the same period, an expert on Slavic languages, who translated Knut Hamsun, as did Baars-Jelgersma.

stories there. For example, in February and July 1929, a year after the publication of Sandel's first novel in Dutch, Quanjer-Steltman's translations of two of her short stories, 'De Larsens' and 'Moeder', were published in the *De Groene Amsterdammer. Weekblad voor Nederland*.[31] The stories had been published in Norway in 1927 in Sandel's first compilation of short stories, *En blå sofa* (A blue sofa), and had been a success in Norway to the surprise of the Norwegian publisher, who considered that the author should stick to writing novels. However, the edition sold 5,000 copies and was well received by important critics such as Sigurd Hoel.[32] The publications in *De Groene Amsterdammer* are translations of complete stories, not 'feuilletons' (serials) as the newspaper's list of contents suggests.[33] Quanjer-Steltman also published a translation of the title story from *En blå sofa* in *Groot-Nederland*. It appeared in the front section of the magazine in 1932,[34] suggesting that the Norwegian author appealed to both the editors and the readers of the magazine.

In short, between 1928-1934 there seems to have been a small boom in Sandel's popularity in the Netherlands. Prominent publishers such as Becht and Mees published her novels, while a broadly based, independent literary magazine such as *Groot-Nederland* and the smaller weekly topical magazine *De Groene Amsterdammer* also published her short stories. *Groot-Nederland* profiled itself as a monthly magazine in which contemporary literature was judged critically, and which together with *Den Gulden Winckel* and *Critisch Bulletin* are considered to be a good text corpus for research into the way in which foreign literature is received by Dutch literary critics.[35] After 1934, the year that Sandel's *Alberte en de vrijheid* was published, Dutch interest in her work declined. As mentioned

....

31 *De Groene Amsterdammer*, Saturday, February 9, 1929, No. 2697, p. 18.
32 See http://www.snl.no/.nbl_biografi/Cora_Sandel/utdypning, accessed June 27, 2010.
33 *De Groene Amsterdammer*, Saturday, February 9, 1929, No. 2697, p. 1.
34 *Groot-Nederland. Letterkundig maandschrift voor den Nederlandschen stam*, vol. 30, part I, 1932, pp. 256-273.
35 See Mathijs Sanders, 'Het buitenland bekeken', in: Braber, H.M. van den and Gielkens, J.A.W., eds., *In 1934. Nederlandse cultuur in internationale context*, p. 305. In this article, *Groot-Nederland* is presented as not attached to a literary or ideological programme, nor is it considered the mouthpiece of a group or generation. Also beyond the sphere of influence of the religious pillars (*zuilen*), its aim was to review large numbers of books for the general public, *ibidem*, p. 305.

Krane's Lunchroom's cover illustration by R. Snapper, 1950.

above, another of her novels, *Kranes konditori*, published in Norway in 1946, was translated by Greta Baars-Jelgersma and published in the Netherlands as *Krane's lunchroom* in 1950. The edition was published by Wereldbibliotheek of Amsterdam and Antwerp with an expressive cover and decorated title page by R. Snapper.

A year later, Veenman in Wageningen published the translation of a collection of short stories by Sandel under the title *Mijn dieren en ik, een verhaal voor jong en oud*, again translated by Quanjer-Steltman. The collection had been published in Norway in 1945 under the title *Dyr jeg har kjent: historier for ung og gammel*. With the exception of five years of war, there is no proper explanation for the fifteen-year lapse in Dutch interest in Sandel's oeuvre. Of course the Second World War broke out shortly after the third part of the trilogy about Alberte Selmer, *Bare Alberte* (*Alberta Alone*), was published in Norway in 1939, making the literary landscape unstable. However, Sandel's collection of stories *Mange takk doktor* (Thank You Doctor), which had been published earlier, in 1935, was also not published in the Netherlands during the 1930s. The lack of interest is curious and it would be worthwhile examining Sandel's reception in the 1930s more thoroughly using the digital historical newspaper archive at http://kranten.kb.nl/ when it has completed its digitalisation of other media publications from the 1930s besides *Het Vaderland*, as will be the case in 2011.

It was not until 1967 that a Dutch translation of one of the stories from *Mange takk doktor* was published in the anthology *Moderne Scandinavische verhalen* by Prisma in Utrecht/Antwerp. This was 'Haar Constance', translated by Richard F.M. Boshouwers (1936). In this anthology of short stories, Sandel represents modern Norwegian literature alongside Knut Hamsun, Sigurd Hoel, Johan Borgen and Torborg Nedreaas. According to the cover text, Boshouwers focused on stories which express 'modern life feelings', or in other words psychoanalytical literature – 'littérature engagée' – dealing with social problems which eradicated the 'instinct to nature, the romance of the escape into dream and legend' and created space for 'existential analysis' and 'eroticism'.[36] In a short introduction, Boshouwers places the authors he has chosen in the context of Western culture, suggesting that he did not look for typically Scandinavian texts, but did not avoid them either. He describes

....

36 R.F. M. Boshouwers, ed. and transl., *Moderne Scandinavische verhalen* (Utrecht/ Antwerp, 1967), inside front cover.

Sandel's work as having 'warm humanity, humour, realism, psychological empathy' and 'overwhelming nature'. In his short introduction to the story, he mentions the main character's restlessness, caused by 'the light, the foaming of the mountain stream under the half-frozen coating of snow, the smell of wet dirt in field and meadow'.[37]

In addition to Boshouwers, other Dutch scholars also studied the work of Cora Sandel after 1950. One of the first discussions appears in Frisian in the form of a themed journal edition on Norwegian literature, *De Tsjerne. Noarwegennûmer* (1956). Here Amy van Marken discusses Sandel as one of the two great women of Norwegian literature in the twentieth century.[38] Sandel is praised for her psychological analyses, her style and her 'virtuous' work *Kranes konditori*. It is a characterisation which does more justice to the innovative novel by Sandel than the fairly expressionless discussion of the Dutch edition in *Arsenaal* a year after publication. The critic writes of 'geen opzienbarende, maar toch wel sympathieke roman' (not a staggering, but at least a sympathetic novel) in a 'vlotte Nederlandse vertaling' (smooth Dutch translation).[39] In the relatively extensive *Scandinavische letterkunde* by Alex Bolckmans from 1984, the quality of Sandel's oeuvre is briefly discussed with special attention paid to her 'precieze, glasheldere stijl vol dramatische spanning' (precise, crystal-clear style full of dramatic tension).[40] Despite this praise, appearances of Sandel in Dutch works on Norwegian literature in the twentieth century did not go without saying. None of her works are included in *De Tweede ronde*, which published a special edition on Norwegian literature in autumn, 1985, nor in another special edition of *Bzzlletin* on Norwegian literature from the same year.[41]

....

37 'Warme menselijkheid, humor, realisme, psychologisch inlevingsvermogen (...) de alles overweldigende natuur (...) het licht, het bruisen van de bergstroom onder de hardbevroren sneeuwkorst, de geur van natte aarde in veld en beemd', *ibidem*, p. 9.
38 Van Marken, 'Panorama fan it noarske proaza', *De Ttsjerne. Noarwegennûmer* 1, vol. 11 (Leeuwarden, 1956), pp. 10-11.
39 Rene Metzemaekers, 'Cora Sandel: "Krane's lunchroom" – Uitg. Wereldbibliotheek N.V. – Amsterdam-Antwerpen – 1950 – 231 blz. – Uit het Noors vertaald door Greta Baars-Jelgersma', *Arsenaal. Tijdschrift voor letterkunde* 3, vol. 6 (1950), pp. 46-47.
40 A. Bolckmans, *Scandinavische letterkunde* (Utrecht/Antwerp, 1984), pp. 281-282.
41 Gryte van der Toorn-Piebenga and Feico Houweling, eds., *Bzzlletin*, 130 (The Hague, 1985).

Even so, to date, the third part of Sandel's Alberte trilogy has still not been translated into Dutch. In 2010, I asked Baars-Jelgersma why she chose *Kranes konditori* rather than the third part of *Alberte* and she responded that she did not know the third part existed at the time. Why Quanjer-Steltman did not translate the third novel in the series is not known, though perhaps an archival study of the publisher's records might provide the answer. After 1950, Sandel's novels were not reprinted and today her works can only be found with some difficulty in a few public libraries.

In summary, the works by Cora Sandel translated into Dutch were popular in the decade 1925-1935. The level of attention in the Netherlands was fairly remarkable, as the first translations of her work did not appear in German and English until the 1960s. However, after her initial success, Sandel disappeared from the Dutch scene for fifteen years, with only a brief revival at the beginning of the 1950s which did not lead to significant renewed interest. For experts she represented the new and modern in Norwegian literature, as is shown by Boshouwer's anthology *Moderne Scandinavische verhalen* and Van Marken's presentation of her oeuvre in *De Tsjerne*. The latter fits with the early Norwegian reception of Sandel as one of the great innovators in Norwegian prose. Her international breakthrough came with *Kranes konditori*, which has now been published around the world, from Helsinki (1949), Amsterdam (1950) and Riga (1965) to London (1984) and Tallinn (2000). It could be suggested that the Netherlands has run counter to international developments with regard to the canonisation of Sandel's work. Despite the fact that Dutch critics of Scandinavian literature gave her work a prominent place within Norwegian literature in the twentieth century, Sandel's Dutch oeuvre is hard to come by in 2010. From a flying start in 1928, her work is now virtually unknown.

Scandinavian literature in the Netherlands 1925-1940 – a 'dominant partner' in the literary field

Contrary to Baars-Jelgersma's assumption that at the beginning of the 1930s only a few people were active in the area of Scandinavian languages – for her a reason to focus solely on these 'special' and 'unknown' languages – innovative Scandinavian literature was well represented in the Netherlands in the 1920s and 1930s. Consequently, Baars-Jelgersma's remark says more about her knowledge of the world of translation in the Netherlands in the first decades of the twentieth century than about the actual situation. It was a time that a colourful and extensive collection of Scandinavian literature was translated into Dutch. An publicity offensive in the *Kleine Courant* from

Het Nieuws van den Dag by the publisher Becht – a medium-sized publisher in Amsterdam – at the beginning of the century illustrates this quite nicely. Of the total of 20 titles on the publisher's list, nearly three-quarters (14) were written by Scandinavian authors.[42] In the following years, Becht continued its Scandinavian list, in which all sorts of authors can be found.[43]

A review of Cora Sandel's *Levenshonger* from December 3, 1928 shows that Becht had managed to make a name for itself. The reviewer Tony de Ridder, praises the publisher 'die reeds zooveel schoonheid uit Scandinavië hier importeerde' (that has already imported so much beauty from Scandinavia).[44] Other publishers also took an interest in literature from the North. These works were published by many different publishers and were not seldom reprinted. They appear with larger publishers such as Van Loghum Slaterus in Arnhem and Strengholt and Van Holkum & Warendorf in Amsterdam, medium-sized publishers such as Arbeiderspers in Amsterdam, Bruna in Utrecht, Kruseman in The Hague and smaller publishing houses such as Meulenhoff in Amsterdam.[45]

....

42 In 1905, the year of Norwegian independence, Becht undertook a publicity offensive in the Dutch 'Sinterklaas' period from November 16 to December 4 in *Kleine Courant of Het Nieuws van den Dag*. Many of the authors are Scandinavian. The offensive culminated on November 30 and December 1, 2 and 4 when titles by Knut Hamsun, Karl Larsen, Herman Bang, Gustaf af Geijerstam, Selma Lagerlöf, Svend Leopold, Karl-Erik Forsslund, Arne Garborg, Anna Wahlenberg, Sophie Elkan and H. van Melsted were given full-page treatment, which provided readers with a good indication of the extensive presence of Scandinavian authors in the lists of this publishing house, something which continued into the first decades of the century.

43 Becht's publishing politics regarding Scandinavian authors, in having an open house for all kind of authors, can also be seen in the same period when it comes to Dutch authors. The relatively young publishing house Meulenhoff (1895) for example published works by Lodewijk van Deyssel, R.N. Roland Holst, Anna van Gogh-Kaulbach, Marie van Zeggelen and Jo van Ammers-Küller in the period 1895-1938. See Laurens van Krevelen, 'Een huis tussen markt en moed. Biografische schets van het literaire fonds van uitgeverij J.M. Meulenhoff 1906-2000 met een epiloog over de jaren 2001-2005', in: Gillis J. Dorleijn and Kees Van Rees, eds., *De productie van literatuur. Het literaire veld in Nederland 1800-2000* (Nijmegen, 2006), pp. 143-146.

44 *Nieuwe Rotterdamsche Courant*, evening edition, December 3, 1928, p. 2.

45 For a survey of the most important publishing houses before the Second World War, see Venema, *Schrijvers, uitgevers & hun collaboratie*, p. 499. Regarding the size of the publishing houses, I base my qualifications on the turnover figures which are mentioned here (see Appendix IV, pp. 499, 500).

Shortly after the publication of the original text, translations were published by authors who were known for their working-class literature, such as Johan Falkberget (1879-1967) and Nini Roll Anker (1873-1942) or experimental authors such as Sigurd Christiansen (1891-1947), and were translated by different generations of translators. The group of translators who were active in the area of Scandinavian literature and who were also praised in the media for their translations included Margaretha Meyboom, Claudine Bienfait, M.J. Molanus-Stamperius, J.E. Gorter-Keyser, D. Logeman-Van der Willigen, Agnes Röntgen, Siegfried van Praag, Betsy Nort, W. Smeding, N. Basenau-Goemans, W. Quanjer-Steltman, Jan Romein and Annie Romein-Verschoor. Noteworthy is the gender of this large group of cultural mediators. With the exception of Hamsun translators, Siegfried van Praag and Jan Romein, they were all women. However, contrary to the image that Johan Schotman paints in one of the first editions of *Vertalen. Orgaan van de Vereeniging Nederlandsche Vertalingen* they cannot be described as 'women with a lot of free time, who thanks to a pliable husband, or no children, or their own servant, have oceans of time, and for whom some pocket money can come in handy'.[46] These were working women, both married and unmarried, who had made translating and/or cultural mediation their profession, as is illustrated here by the cases of Greta Baars-Jelgersma and Annie Posthumus.

Literary critique
All of the books that were published in the Dutch market due to the efforts of the professionals in the translation trade were announced and reviewed in the Dutch newspaper press. Among others, *Het Vaderland*, the *Nieuwe Rotterdamsche Courant* and the *Algemeen Handelsblad* published reviews, while the table of contents of Dutch literary and academic magazines, also found in these national newspapers, show that Scandinavian literature was also often on the agenda. Annie Posthumus, Tony de Ridder, L. Lacomblé

....

46 'dames met veel vrijen tijd, die dank zij een gemakkelijken man, of geen kinderen, of een zelfstandig werken kunnende dienstbode, zeeën van tijd hebben en wien een speldegeld te pas komt'. Schotman is quoted from Ton van Kalmthout, 'Vertalen, het orgaan van de Vereeniging Nederlandsche Vertalingen', in: Braber, H.M. van den and Gielkens, J.A.W., eds., *In 1934. Nederlandse cultuur in internationale context.* (Amsterdam/Antwerp, 2010) p. 67.

and Augusta de Wit are some of the reviewers who discuss literature from Scandinavia in the *Nieuwe Rotterdamsche Courant*. In *Het Vaderland*, the reviewers are often identified by their initials, such as K. de R., whose review of *Levenshonger* in the evening edition of January 9, 1929 was full of praise, or M.t.B., who presents a review of *Nora* in the morning edition of March 20, 1938. Annie Romein-Verschoor also wrote about Scandinavian literature in the *Algemeen Handelsblad*, as well as other media.[47] However, it was Posthumus who became the first female 'privaat-docent in de moderne Deensch-Noorweegsche philologie' (private university lecturer in modern Danish-Norwegian philology) at the University of Amsterdam, who gave the *Nieuwe Rotterdamsche Courant* a Scandinavian flavour. She started her work as a literary critic in 1923, with a discussion of *Cimbrenes Tog* by Johannes W. Jensen under the heading 'Deensche Letteren' in the evening edition of the *NRC* of March 10. This was followed by reviews of 'Skandinaafsche' (Scandinavian) or 'Deensche' (Danish) literature once or twice a year. From 1926 onwards the reviews appeared more frequently. Works by Scandinavian authors were discussed by Posthumus on almost a monthly basis, while the space allocated to Posthumus also increased, with the reviews generally placed under headings such as 'Deensche', 'Noorsche', 'Zweedsche', 'Skandinaafse' or 'Scandinavische letteren' (Danish, Norwegian, Swedish or Scandinavian literature).[48]

Posthumus apparently had *carte blanche*. She reviewed a wide variety of books, sometimes translations, sometimes on the occasion of the release of the original, with some of them being later translated into Dutch, others not. The Dutch reader obtained a broad image of Scandinavian literature: as well as books, Posthumus discussed literary phenomena, such as the emerging idea of a book club created in Denmark by the Gyldendal publishing house, or reflections on literature from a national perspective

....

47 The information on L. Lacomblé, Augusta de Wit and Annie Romein-Verschoor comes from the article by Van Marken, 'Inn i kampene mellom ideologiene', *Dyade* 2 (1982), p. 15.

48 It is not unlikely that the increase of Posthumus' review activities is connected with a development in Dutch papers in the 1910s and 1920s. It is in this period that papers were forming their professional art sections. See Nel van Dijk, 'Tussen professionalisering en verzuiling. Kunstkritiek in de Nederlandse dagbladpers tijdens het interbellum', in: Gillis J. Dorleijn and Kees Van Rees, eds., *De productie van literatuur*, pp. 141, 142.

in relation to the Danish scholar Jørgen Bukdahl's (1896-1982) study of Norwegian literature. Posthumus referred to many different translated and untranslated Scandinavian authors and movements in her book reviews, illustrating that it was also a well-known canon for Dutch readers. She differentiated between oeuvres and referred to earlier articles she had written on Scandinavian authors. The tables of contents of the literary and academic magazines show that she also published on Scandinavian literature there.[49] In time, publishers started using quotes from Posthumus in their publicity. She had clearly made a name for herself as an expert on Scandinavian literature.

However, it was not only the *Nieuwe Rotterdamsche Courant* that found space for Scandinavian literature during these years. In his article 'Het buitenland bekeken' (Looking abroad), Mathijs Sanders discusses the interest in foreign literature amongst Dutch publishers and critics connected to the literary magazines *De Gulden Winckel, Critisch Bulletin* and *Groot-Nederland* in 1934. He demonstrates that as well as the large language areas a few smaller language areas were also being discussed, among them Norwegian and Danish,[50] which when combined meant that Scandinavia, as a small language area, received the most attention after Hungary and Czechoslovakia.

Small language areas in the Dutch literary landscape 1925-1940
When Baars-Jelgersma decided to dedicate herself to Scandinavian literature, especially Norwegian literature, she had many predecessors in the Netherlands. In fact, Scandinavia seems to have been a so-called 'dominant partner' in the literary field in the Netherlands in the first

....

49 For example in *De vrouw in haar huis*, where she published an article on Sigrid Undset and one on Hulda Lütken (February 1931), as can be learned from *Het Vaderland*, February 11, 1931, evening edition.

50 Mathijs Sanders, 'Het buitenland bekeken', in: Braber, H.M. van den and Gielkens, J.A.W., eds., *In 1934. Nederlandse cultuur in internationale context*, pp. 301-312.

three decades of the twentieth century.[51] The translation oeuvre of Baars-Jelgersma emphasises this position. It shows us a colourful variety of publishers who were interested in and published Scandinavian authors. Baars-Jelgersma's translation oeuvre in the 1930s shows a preference for innovative, engaged, mainly Norwegian literature, which was opposed to the Scandinavian literary stereotypes and was from a country which had fascinated her from the start. With regard to her motives, approach and translating strategy, Baars-Jelgersma fits the transmitter profile that begins with Meyboom in 1911: as a translator who 'wants to immerse herself completely in the life of another'.[52]

Baars-Jelgersma's alienating translation strategy also indicates that the Dutch literary climate during the first decade of her work was open and receptive. It was a field in which, in the words of Even-Zohar, translated literature could take a primary position.[53] It is a translation strategy that points to the fact that the publishing houses she approached looked upon Scandinavian literature as innovative. According to Even-Zohar, translations focusing on the source language only occur if the literature in the receiving language area is weak – which was hardly the case in the Netherlands in the 1920s and 1930s – or if the 'other' literature was seen as an enrichment. In this environment, translators such as Baars-Jelgersma could choose to work with their focus on the source language. In addition, Baars-Jelgersma seems to have had a good eye for innovative literature in her choice of texts. The literature which she introduced, together with an early Dutch susceptibility to a ground-breaking author such as Cora

....

51 See Reine Meylaerts, 'The study of cultural transfer in the literary fields of small language communities: some preliminary thoughts', paper at the workshop 'Peripheral autonomy? Longitudinal analyses of cultural transfer in the literary fields of small language communities', Ghent, December 1-2, 2006, p. 1, see http://www.peripheralautonomy.org/files/proposal%20Reine%20Meylaerts.doc, accessed October 29, 2010.

52 'zich geheel in 't leven van een ander wil hebben ingeleefd'. Margaretha Meyboom, 'Skandinavische literatuur in Nederland', *Boekzaal* 1911, vol. 5, p. 49.

53 Itamar Even-Zohar, 'The position of translated literature within the literary polysystem', in: Holmes, James S., Lambert, José & van den Broeck, Raymond, *Literature and translation: new perspectives in literary studies* (Leuven, 1978), pp. 117-127.

Sandel, reveal that the Dutch literary field was open to new trends from abroad in the period 1925-1940. The translation oeuvre of Baars-Jelgersma, together with the Dutch reception of Cora Sandel also point to a difference from the preceding period. Both illustrate the way that Dutch publishers dealt with authors from a small language area such as Scandinavia in the period 1925-1940. Their texts were translated by many different translators and published by many respected publishers with different publishing profiles. This was a change from the period before 1925, when authors such as Bjørnson and Ibsen were mostly published by only one publisher, in their case Meulenhoff. However, the Becht publishing house also shows that at the turn of the century some publishers followed the career of a particular author.[54] While this publishing policy was adopted once again in the second half of the twentieth century, with many publishers launching an author and attempting thereafter to publish all of his or her work, between 1925-1950 this policy does not appear to have been in vogue, at least not for the Scandinavian authors.

The narrowing of an open and colourful literary landscape?
Baars-Jelgersma's choice of books and the way the texts were presented to the Dutch reader changed in the 1940s. Her translation oeuvre becomes more varied, and alongside the works of innovative, mostly Norwegian authors, a number of translations of works by mainly Swedish authors emerged, whose work tended to be portrayed as rural, provincial literature. It was a classification that was unjust and incorrect – as we have seen – in the case of Eyvind Johnsson and Tora Norström-Bonnier. Based on the covers, titles and presentations of the Dutch translations, a reader might be inclined to classify their works as provincial literature, a conservative

....

54 Another example of publishers following 'their' authors in the period 1900-1925 is
    W. Versluys in Amsterdam who was the regular publisher of Arthur van Schendel.
    Van Schendel only went to another publisher when Versluys rejected a piece. See
    Laurens van Krevelen, 'Een huis tussen markt en moed. Biografische schets van
    het literaire fonds van uitgeverij J.M. Meulenhoff 1906-2000 met een epiloog over
    de jaren 2001-2005', in: Gillis J. Dorleijn and Kees Van Rees, eds., *De productie van
    literatuur*, p. 145.

genre consisting of popular, often sentimental, predictable, romantic-realistic stories set in rural society. In Scandinavia, the genre of regional or provincial literature had different connotations in the first half of the twentieth century. Provincial literature could be universal, innovative and canonised as high quality literature, which also makes a less well-known aspect of a particular country visible

In the Netherlands, Scandinavian authors were affected by a Dutch trivialisation of their genre.[55] My case study of the translation oeuvre of Baars-Jelgersma and the reception of Cora Sandel confirms and seems to illustrate the consequences of changing the image of Scandinavian literature from an innovative, engaged, fresh literature to one which was considered rural and predictable. Baars-Jelgersma's translations of respected Scandinavian authors increasingly seem to have been incorrectly labelled, and it looks as if it became more difficult to find publishers for innovative literature. Sandel's experimental literature, including *Kranes konditori*, did not reach the Dutch public until 1950, suggesting that a change must have taken place in the second half of the 1940s. The early enthusiasm of the Dutch publishing houses and reviewers for innovative literature from Scandinavia and new literary trends and tendencies from the North was replaced by a new image at the end of the 1930s, as evidenced in the ironical reference by Cora Sandel to Scandinavian trilogies mentioned above. It appears that a

....

55 See Annemarie van Buuren, *De taal van het hart. Retorica en receptie van de hedendaagse streekroman* (Groningen, 2005), pp. 30-42. Van Buuren discusses how this genre came and went in waves throughout the literary history of the Netherlands. There was a booming period for the genre in the transition from romanticism to realism and naturalism, when, for example, Stijn Streuvels (1871-1969) and Felix Timmermans (1886-1947) wrote small 'literaire hoogstandjes' (literary masterpieces). This was followed by a 'generatie van kleiner formaat' (a generation of smaller stature). In the interwar period, the genre gained new popularity, until Menno Ter Braak condemned the genre for being provincial (or narrow-minded) and even made the connection with 'Blut- und Boden' ideologies. Both Ter Braak and his opponents used the genre to position themselves in the polemics about cosmopolitism versus provincialism in the 1930s in the Netherlands. See also Arne de Winde, Tom Sintobin, 'Theun de Vries versus Menno ter Braak: provincialisme versus internationalisme', in: Den Braber and Gielkens, eds., *In 1934. Nederlandse cultuur in internationale context*, pp. 55-64. Following this discussion the genre was almost exclusively linked to trivial, sentimental, popular and predictable literature in the Netherlands.

clash between published literature and the image of this literature occurred at this time, with the image seeming to have won the 'battle'. It is almost as if the image of Scandinavian literature as consisting of predictable stories set in the countryside amidst rough natural landscapes, was so persistent that translators and publishing houses who attempted to publish other styles could not succeed, with this tendency seeming to grow stronger in the 1950s. This leads to the conclusion that on their own, good translations of good literature – which we assume to be the case for Baars-Jelgersma, whose translations were well received by reviewers[56] – do not guarantee a good reception for translated literature.

Another observation is that the consequence of such a change in image may be that many worthwhile literary texts are relegated to oblivion. The image of a country's literature almost seems to be a stronger factor than the quality of the literature, as has been shown in the case of Cora Sandel. However, a further issue is that the changing image of Scandinavian literature in the Netherlands coincided with a Dutch trivialisation of the regional literature genre, with both events affecting the reception of Scandinavian literature. Furthermore, considering the analyses of the literary system by Even-Zohar and Reine Meylaerts, the 'rejection' of Scandinavian literature or the 'depowerment of this literature' also tells us something about the literary landscape in the Netherlands at the end of the 1940s and during the 1950s. Less space is available for innovative foreign literature, and when it is published it is given an 'innocent', secondary status and labelled 'safe' and conservative, thus making it possible for literature from the receiving language area to be presented as innovative and high profile. This situation, where the dominant position is reserved for the literature of the receiving country, seems to point to a society tending towards insularity.[57]

....

56 For example, by Metzemaekers, 'Cora Sandel: "Krane's lunchroom"', *Arsenaal. Tijdschrift voor letterkunde* 3, vol. 6 (1950), p. 47.

57 This assumption is supported by the observations of Kees van Rees and Gillis J. Dorleijn. In 'Het Nederlandse literaire veld 1800-2000', they state that the Netherlands was a rather closed nation during large parts of the nineteenth and twentieth centuries, not only politically, economically and socially, but also culturally and institutionally, Dorleijn and Van Rees, eds., *De productie van literatuur*, p. 28. My research reveals a more open society in the 1920s and 1930s.

Transmission and aspects of canonisation

For the continued success or canonisation of a translated author in a different language area, a major image change appears to have great consequences. In 'Reception and Ideology. "Wild Volcanism" and Other Varieties on Strindberg', Petra Broomans describes five phases in the process of cultural transfer.[58] In the case of Cora Sandel all five phases were completed: Sandel's work was introduced (phase 1), several Dutch publishers became interested (phase 2), her work was translated (phase 3), her books were read and discussed (phase 4), and the introduction was followed by reviews, articles and books (phase 5). In terms of these phases, the process of the cultural transfer of Cora Sandel's works to the Netherlands can be considered to have been 'successful'. However, Sandel's case shows that there are other aspects to the cultural transfer of an author. My suggestion would be to add a sixth phase: the continuation and canonisation of the translated author in a different language area. As we have seen, Sandel did not become part of the Scandinavian canon in the Netherlands. Aspects of the sixth phase should aim to define how continued success and canonisation occurs, addressing questions such as: Are the books of the author still available? How do readers in the receiving country learn more about authors from specific language areas? Are there literary histories in the field? What about new sources provided by the internet? What kind of interaction is there with international or European literary histories that are available in the receiving country? A response to the latter could also provide new insights into the construction of the 'autonomous (peripheral) literary field', as Meylaerts states in her essay, 'The study of cultural transfer in the literary fields of small language communities: Some preliminary thoughts'.[59]

....

58 Broomans, 'Reception and Ideology. "Wild Volcanism" and Other Varieties on Strindberg', in Ton Naaijkens, ed., *Event or Incident – Evénement ou Incident. On the Role of Translation in the Dynamics of Cultural Exchange. Du rôle des traductions dans les processus d'échanges culturels*. Series: *Genèses de Textes – Textgenesen* Volume 3 (Bern, 2010), pp. 107-120.

59 Reine Meylaerts, 'The study of cultural transfer in the literary fields of small language communities: some preliminary thoughts', paper at the workshop 'Peripheral autonomy? Longitudinal analyses of cultural transfer in the literary fields of small language communities', Ghent, December 1-2, 2006, p. 1, see http://www.peripheralautonomy. org/files/proposal%20Reine%20Meylaerts.doc, accessed October 29, 2010.

As to the cases of Baars-Jelgersma and Sandel presented in this article, my analysis provides information about a change in the Dutch literary climate over the period 1925-1950. It seems to indicate a specific development in the reception of foreign literature during this period. From the open literary landscape of the 1920s and 1930s, where there was room for new impulses from abroad, there is a 'closing' of the literary borders to other than conservative foreign literature, which starts in the 1940s and probably continues in the 1950s. This had a great impact on the labelling and status of such literature. In addition, the genre issue – in this case, the changing image of 'regional literature' (*streekliteratuur*) – is also worth further investigation. Both developments suggest that a new literary self-definition occurred, which is illustrated by the way foreign literature in the cases presented interacted with the Dutch literary field. It would be interesting to investigate if these developments only occurred in relation to the Dutch – the receiving country's – interaction with Scandinavian literature or if there was a more general trend. The case studies show the influence of factors such as the image of a foreign literature and/or the changing literary status of a genre in the receiving country. As well as the specific image of Scandinavian literature, the image of regional literature in general also changed, perhaps as a consequence of the increasing divide in the perception of urban and rural existence and culture. It is clear that the literary status of Scandinavian literature, which was readily classified as non-urban, regional or provincial literature, was negatively influenced by this development. I would suggest that the changing image of regional or provincial literature which took place in the Netherlands in the 1930s not only affected Scandinavian literature. This points to another interesting topic for further investigation: how the 'ranking' of genres and the changes in this ranking is related to the appreciation or the primary or secondary position of other literatures. It would be of interest to test these assumptions using further case studies from other small language areas.

The research presented here demonstrates how diverse this type of research into literary relationships can be. It can range from historical archive research to translation criticism, from content analysis of reviews and longer essays on literature to in-depth interviews with actors within the literary world, from comparative analyses of the literary landscape in countries with very different publishing landscapes and profiles to the processing of this information in theoretical models related to literary evaluation, the literary climate and canonisation. The cases that are described in the article also demonstrate the importance of taking the three dimensions distinguished by Heilbron and Sapiro into account,[60] these being cross-national transfer (here Broomans' phases are illuminating), distinguishing between political, economic and cultural dynamics on the various levels of exchange, and the structure of the space of reception and the position of the intermediaries in the field.

....

60 Johan Heilbron and Gisèle Sapiro, 'Outline for a Sociology of Translation: Current Issues and Future Prospects', in: Michaela Wolf and Alexandra Fukari, eds., *Constructing a Sociology of Translation* (Amsterdam, 2007), pp. 93-107.

Appendix I:
Translation oeuvre by Greta Baars-Jelgersma in the period 1936-1950,
in chronological order

1. Aksel Sandemose (N), *Een vluchteling kruist zijn spoor*,
   Bijleveld, Utrecht, 1936.
2. Magnhild Haalke (N), *Alli's zoon*, Stols, 's Gravenhage, 1937.
3. Odd Hølaas (N), *Ook ik ben Amerika*, Bijleveld, Utrecht, 1938
   (non-fiction).
4. Trygve Braatøy (N), *Uit de praktijk van een psychiater:*
   een populaire inleiding tot de medische psychologie en de
   psychiatrie, Erven J. Bijleveld, Utrecht, 1939 (non-fiction).
5. Aksel Sandemose (N), *Er stond een bank in 't groen*,
   Arbo, De Arbeiderspers, Amsterdam, 1939.
6. Magnhild Haalke (N), *Gurianna*, Amsterdam, Windroos, 1939.
7. Knut Hamsun (N), *De cirkel gesloten*, Salm, Amsterdam, 1940.
8. Eyvind Johnson (S), *Olof lacht tegen het leven*, Arbo,
   De Arbeiderspers, Amsterdam, 1940.
9. Eyvind Johnson (S), *De weg naar onzekerheid*, Arbo,
   De Arbeiderspers, Amsterdam, 1940.
10. Per Chr. Asbjørnsen en Jørgen Moe (N), *Noorse volkssprookjes: uit*
    de verzameling van Asbjørnsen en Moe, W. De Haan, Utrecht, 1941.
11. Greta Baars-Jelgersma (selection and translation) (N) *Noorderlicht*
    over de lage landen: zeventien Noorsche schrijvers, Ad. M.C. Stok/
    Zuid-Hollandsche uitgevers maatschappij, Den Haag, [1941].
12. Bjørn Rongen (N), *Nacht der nachten*, Leiter-Nypels,
    Maastricht, 1941.
13. Johan Wøller (D), *Als officier van gezondheid naar Nederlands-*
    Indië, Bijleveld, Utrecht, 1943 (non-fiction).
14. Gunnar Gunnarsson (D), *Koningszoon*, Holle, 's Gravenhage,
    1943 (novella).
15. Kåre Holt (N), *Speelman en ceremoniemeester*,
    Strengholt, Amsterdam, 1943.
16. Arthur Omre (N), *Harmonie*, Kemink en Zoon, Utrecht, 1943.
17. Per Chr. Asbjørnsen en Jørgen Moe (N), *Noorse volkssprookjes:*
    uit de verzameling van Asbjørnsen en Moe: nieuwe bundel,
    W. De Haan, Utrecht, 1944.
18. Knut Hamsun (N), *Maar het leven leeft*, Strengholt,
    Amsterdam, 1944.

19. Gustaf Ullman (S), *Kerstin Thotts ring*, De Pelgrim, Eindhoven, 1944.
20. Else af Trolle (S), *Ylva: een Laurentiusnachtdroom*, Het Hollandsche Uitgevershuis, Amsterdam, 1946 (with Rolv Ravn).
21. Tora Nordström-Bonnier (S), *De vrouwen van Bisslingegaard*, Van Holkema & Warendorf, Amsterdam, 1946.
22. Peter William Nisser (S), *Honger*, Van Holkema & Warendorf, Amsterdam, 1946.
23. Marika Stiernstedt (S), *Aanslag in Parijs*, Bijleveld, Utrecht, 1946.
24. Eva Berg (S), *Lokroep in de lente*, Het Hollandsche Uitgevershuis, Amsterdam, 1946.
25. Aksel Sandemose (N), *De teerhandelaar*, De Driehoek, 's-Graveland, 1947.
26. Jens Andreas Friis (N), *Lajla, een verhaal uit Lapland*, Scheltens & Giltay, Amsterdam, 1947.
27. Ingrid Christiansen (D), *De dood op Rossnaesholm*, Kemink en Zoon, Utrecht, 1947.
28. Magnhild Haalke (N), *De dag is zo kort*, Salm, Amsterdam, 1947.
29. Nordahl Grieg (N), *De wereld moet nog wel jong zijn*, Ten Brink, Meppel, 1948 (with Rolv Ravn).
30. Tora Nordström-Bonnier (S), *Een nacht in juni*, A.A.M. Stols, 's Gravenhage, 1948 (with Rolv Ravn).
31. Per Høst (S), *Wat de wereld mij toonde: robbentochten in de Ijszee, expedities naar de Cun- en Choco-Indianen*, 2e druk De Tijdstroom, Lochem, 1948 (with Rolv Ravn).
32. Peder Sjögren (S), *Zwarte palmkronen*, Leopold, 's Gravenhage, 1949 (with others).
33. Tora Dahl (S), *Der Mysteriën Bron*, De Driehoek, 's-Graveland, 1949 (with Rolv Ravn).
34. Arne Skouen (N), *Feest op Réunion*, Stols, 's Gravenhage, 1949 (with Rolv Ravn).
35. Peter William Nisser (Z), *Vermist*, Van Holkema & Warendorf, Amsterdam, 1949 (with Rolv Ravn).
36. Cora Sandel (N), *Krane's lunchroom*, Wereldbibliotheek, Amsterdam, 1950.
37. Frithjof E. Bye (N), *De grote eenzaamheid*, Callenbach, Nijkerk, 1950 (with Rolv Ravn).
38. H.C. Branner (D), *De ruiter*, Leopold, 's Gravenhage, 1950 (with Rolv Ravn).

Appendix II:
Cora Sandel in the Netherlands

Cora Sandel, *Levenshonger* (Amsterdam, 1928), translation of *Alberte og Jakob* (Oslo, 1926) from Norwegian by W. Quanjer-Steltman.

Cora Sandel, 'De Larsens', *De Groene Amsterdammer. Weekblad voor Nederland*, Saturday, February 9, 1929, No. 2697, p. 18, translation of 'Larsens' from *En blå sofa* (Oslo, 1927) from Norwegian by W. Quanjer-Steltman.

Cora Sandel, 'Moeder', *De Groene Amsterdammer. Weekblad voor Nederland*, July 27, 1929, No. 2721, p. 18, translation of 'Mor' from *En blå sofa* (Oslo, 1927) from Norwegian by W. Quanjer-Steltman.

Cora Sandel, 'Een blauwe sofa', *Groot-Nederland*, part I of vol. 30 (1932, pp. 256-273), translation of 'En blå sofa' from *En blå sofa* (Oslo, 1927) from Norwegian by W. Quanjer-Steltman.

Cora Sandel, Chapters of *Levenshonger*, *Groot-Nederland*, part I of vol. 31 (1933, pp. 507-514).

Cora Sandel, Chapters of *Levenshonger*, *Groot-Nederland*, part II of vol. 31 (1933, pp. 32-46, 111-122, 123-128 and 434-451).

Cora Sandel, *Alberte en de vrijheid* (Santpoort, 1934), translation of *Alberte og friheten* (1931) from Norwegian by W. Quanjer-Steltman.

Cora Sandel, 'De vlucht naar Amerika', in: Greta Baars-Jelgersma (ed. and transl.) *Noorderlicht over de lage landen: zeventien Noorsche schrijvers*, Ad. M.C. Stok/Zuid-Hollandsche uitgevers maatschappij (1941), translation of 'Flykten til Amerika' from *Mange takk doktor* (Oslo, 1935) from Norwegian by Greta Baars-Jelgersma.

Cora Sandel, *Krane's lunchroom* (Amsterdam/Antwerp, 1950), translation of *Kranes konditori* (Stockholm, 1946) from Norwegian by Greta Baars-Jelgersma.

Cora Sandel, *Mijn dieren en ik, een verhaal voor jong en oud* (Wageningen, 1951), translation of *Dyr jeg har kjent: historier for ung og gammel* (Oslo, 1945) from Norwegian by W. Quanjer-Steltman.

Cora Sandel, 'Haar Constance', in: *Moderne Scandinavische verhalen* (Utrecht/Antwerpen, 1967), translation of 'Ho Konstance' from *Mange takk doktor* (Oslo, 1935) from Norwegian by R.F.M. Boshouwers.

'There is Always an Invisible Reader ...'

The Swedish Critic Margit Abenius and the Making of a Female Cultural Transmitter

« Marta Ronne »

This contribution presents the work of Margit Abenius (1899-1970), one of the most prominent Swedish literary critics of the twentieth century, who also worked as a translator and cultural transmitter. Having earlier discussed Abenius' work, introducing the French philosopher Simone Weil in a previously published essay, my focus here will be on Abenius' entire oeuvre as a cultural transmitter.[1] The first part of the article examines how Margit Abenius began her academic and her literary career. In this regard, I draw on Toril Moi in speaking of the 'making' of Abenius as a female critic, something I see as a process of production and self-construction. I also see Abenius as a product of 'different discourses and determinants', such as gender, social origins, the literary canon of the time, and her early preference for literary studies.[2]

The second part of the article explores Abenius' oscillation between different audiences, with the aim of discussing whether and in what way this movement might have had a negative impact on her position in the field of literary criticism or on her posthumous reputation. I will also examine her ability to move between different fields (here understood both in Bourdieu's sense of meaning and as different fields of action), such as research, literary critique in magazines and on Swedish Radio, translations, lectures and book circles, not to mention informal contacts with other members of the Swedish cultural elite.

....

1   Marta Ronne, 'Decoding a Genius Mind. The French Philosopher Simone Weil (1909-1943) and the Swedish Critic Margit Abenius (1899-1970): a Case of Cultural Transmission', in: Petra Broomans, ed., *From Darwin to Weil* (Groningen, 2009), pp. 139-157. I am currently working on a biography of Margit Abenius as a prominent Swedish critic of the post-war period.
2   Toril Moi, *Simone de Beauvoir. The making of an intellectual woman* (Oxford UK/ Cambridge US, 1994), p. 6.

According to Petra Broomans, the central issue of cultural transmission is to transmit elements of another national literature and its cultural context into one's own national literary and cultural context. Cultural transmitters can include translators, critics, literary historians and publishers working in a particular language area. Their motives may be purely aesthetic, ideological or even political. As Broomans states, '[t]ransmission often reflects a bilateral situation' whereby transmission of one's own national literature can also take place.[3] According to Broomans, transmitters can be regarded as 'the pillars of the process of cultural transfer', which she further defines as a five-stage process, consisting of introduction, translation and several stages of reception.[4]

As pointed out by Johan Heilbron and Gisèle Sapiro, an interpretative or an economic approach is not the most effective way of approaching the complex process of translation. Instead, they argue for a sociological analysis which 'embraces the whole set of social relations within which translations are produced and circulated' and which puts the focus on how translations function:

> (...) in their contexts of production and reception, that is to say, in the target culture (Holmes/Lambert/Lefevere 1978; Even-Zohar 1990; Toury 1995). The question of the relation between the contexts of production and reception also underpins the historical study of 'cultural transfers', which investigates the role of the agents in these exchanges, both institutions and individuals, and their inscription in the political and cultural relations between the countries.[5]

....

3   Petra Broomans, 'Literary Fields: Battles and Borders'. Opening lecture at *Cultural Transfer and Minor Language Areas*, University of Groningen, November 5-6, 2008. Broomans, 'Introduction: Women as Transmitters of Ideas', in: Broomans, ed., *From Darwin to Weil*, p. 2.

4   Broomans, 'Reception and Ideology. "Wild Volcanism" and Other Varieties on Strindberg', p. 4-5.

5   Johan Heilbron and Gisèle Sapiro, 'Outline for a Sociology of Translation: Current Issues and Future Prospects', p.2, in: Michaela Wolf and Alexandra Fukari, eds., *Constructing a Sociology of Translation*, (Amsterdam, 2007), pp. 93-107.

According to Heilbron and Sapiro, '[i]nternational cultural exchanges are organised by means of institutions and individual agents, each arising from different political, economic and cultural dynamics'. However, they also stress the importance of single transmitters, as 'literary exchanges also depend on a set of specific agents in the literary or scientific field (authors, translators, critics, academics, and scholars, for whom work founded on linguistic and social resources procures specific benefits)'.[6]

Drawing on both Itamar Even-Zohar's Polysystem Theory of Translations (PST) and Gideon Toury's Descriptive Translation Studies paradigm (DTS), Reine Meylaerts has, for her part, suggested a combination of, on the one hand, an 'analysis of the critical discourse on "other" literatures and cultures' and on the other an 'analysis of the roles and positions of the different institutions and actors (translators, critics, authors, editors, publishers, magazines, publishing houses, translation policies) in these intercultural contacts'.[7]

As to the latter, Meylaerts poses several questions that are of importance to my own study:

> Which are the leading publishing houses, magazines, subvention organisms etc. promoting (or censoring) intercultural contacts? Who are the leading translators and critics, from a quantitative point of view or with reference to symbolic prestige? Do they take on any other functions (e.g. author) in the literary field and do they publish in various languages? All the data on translators/authors/critics as biographical individuals, as literary and cultural agents in specific institutions and contexts will allow both to fine-tune the interpretations of specific translation strategies and/or discursive practices and to concretise specific mechanisms and instances of interculturality.[8]

....

6   Heilbron and Sapiro, 'Outline for a Sociology of Translation', pp. 9 and 10.
7   Reine Meylaerts, 'The study of cultural transfer in the literary fields of small language communities: Some preliminary thoughts', proposal presented at the first workshop of the project: *Peripheral autonomy? Longitudinal analyses of cultural transfer in the literary fields of small language communities*, in Ghent – December 1-2, 2006, p. 4 and 5.
8   Meylaerts, 'The study of cultural transfer', p. 5.

Abenius' way of switching between critique and translation on the one hand, and highbrow and popular literature on the other, not to mention her way of using different channels of literary transmission, evokes the questions above. This approach also indicates that transmitting foreign writers into the home literary market can be done on many different levels, in different contexts, and by addressing many different groups of readers simultaneously. However, what neither Heilbron and Sapiro nor Meylaerts mention is that the transmitter's ability to act as a cultural agent in so many different contexts can also be considered from a gender perspective. On this basis, we can ask whether Abenius' way of acting in the field of cultural production can be seen as similar to that of her female predecessors, or is it typical of female intellectuals of her time?

Margit Abenius – a making of a female critic
Born in 1899 as the eldest of four children in a well-educated middle-class family in the provincial town of Örebro, Margit Abenius developed a very early interest in literary history and language studies. From her early teens she was a devoted reader and the family's shared passion for reading and discussing literature was mentioned daily in the diaries she kept from the age of sixteen.[9] As the literary preferences at home were typically middle class, Abenius was brought up reading the Nordic literary canon of the time. Her diaries were thus full of comments on the Swedish Romantics Carl Jonas Love Almqvist (1793-1866) and Per Amadeus Atterbom (1790-1855), as well as Viktor Rydberg (1828-1895) and some of the most famous Nordic male writers from the Modern Breakthrough and late nineteenth century, such as Ola Hansson (1860-1925), Henrik Ibsen (1828-1906), Jonas Lie (1833-1908), Oscar Levertin (1862-1906) and Verner von Heidenstam (1859-1940). The poets Gustaf Fröding (1860-1911) and Carl Axel Karlfeldt (1864-1931) are also often mentioned, as well as the worshipped Adolph Törneros (1794-1839), Abenius' absolute literary idol in her teens. Later on, suffering from increasing depression and anguish during her secondary school years in Uppsala 1917-1919, she chose the symbolist poetry of Bo Bergman (1869-1967) as her closest companion.

....

9   Margit Abenius' diaries are kept in Margit Abenius 1, Dagböcker 1916-1932, Uppsala University Library (UUL), Uppsala.

As to women writers in Abenius' early readings, the diaries mention few except Romantic *femme savante* Malla Silfverstolpe (1782-1861), Anna Hamilton-Geete (1848-1913) and – briefly – the *grande dame* of Swedish literature and Nobel Prize winner, Selma Lagerlöf (1858-1940). There are no traces, for example, of Victoria Benedictsson (1850-1888) or Anne Charlotte Leffler (189-1892) in Abenius' diaries, although both authors were included early in Swedish literary manuals and remained a part of the Swedish literary canon even after 1916 when many other women writers were omitted.[10] Abenius seems as uninformed about contemporary women writers as she is about the suffrage movement occurring after 1910. This was probably not unusual for the well-educated but conservative middle classes, but it is still an interesting detail to bear in mind when discussing her work as a critic.

As already mentioned, Abenius' passion for belles-lettres was not the only interest that suggested a life as a scholar and critic. The eager study of manuals in literary history and of contemporary Swedish literary critique, which she voluntary devoted herself to from the age of sixteen, is also very significant. From January 1916 she notes readings Henrik Schück and Karl Warburg's newly edited *Illustrated Swedish Literary History (Illustrerad svensk litteraturhistoria)*. She also spent many afternoons and Sundays at home or in the Örebro Public Library studying the works of influential critics such as Fredrik Böök (1883-1961) and the literary historian Martin Lamm (1880-1950), as well as reading literary magazines. At the age of sixteen, she was already a self-critical reader, and also clearly shows that she was bored by school and preferred to study on her own. On January 2, 1916, she notes:

At first such a quiet and peaceful 'morning full of reading', of which there have been plenty during this unusually peaceful and nice Christmas. It is so seldom one gets a chance to read and learn

....

10 Anna Williams, *Stjärnor utan stjärnbilder. Kvinnor och kanon i litteraturhistoriska översiktsverk under 1900-talet* (Uppsala, 1997) pp. 59-62 (Stars Without Constellations. Women and Canon Formation in Twentieth century Literary Historiography). Swedish text with a summary in English. As Williams observes, speaking in quantitative terms, women writers were well represented in literary manuals before 1916. Many male writers were also excluded from the manuals after 1916. Nevertheless, there was a strong gender bias in the way of presenting women writers, as their works were often treated as peripheral to the mainstream and judged in moral terms, Williams, *Stjärnor utan stjärnbilder*, pp. 62-63.

something. During the semester one only wastes energy. Now I am
reading, undisturbed, Schück and Warburg, both in order to get the
highest mark in this subject and because of my personal interest.
And also *Essays and Critics* by Fredrik Böök, and Shakespeare, and a
couple of other novels and short stories. Not to mention Liedgren's
The Swedish Book of Psalms.[11]

On April 20 that year she observes:

> In the evening I went to the library. I took a thick *Ord och Bild* from
> the shelf and sat down at an empty table and read. I got a little bit
> dizzy from it all, no matter whether it was a sketch of a short story
> or a causerie by Laurin, an essay by Böök or a paper by Warburg.
> Impressions overwhelmed me. I often notice that I, more or less
> willingly, take up the author's opinions while reading a text. And my
> 'education' is yet so imperfect. But those two things, judgement
> and education, might increase when I get older. In any case, I am
> only sixteen and thus have to have patience.[12]

In assessing the young Abenius' route to literary education, one could say
that from her teens she started gathering the cultural capital that would

....

11 'Först en sådan där lugn, fridfull "läsförmiddag", som det har varit så gott om under
detta ovanligt stillsamma och trevliga jullov. Det är så ovanligt att få läsa och lära sig
något, under terminerna bara splittrar man sina krafter. Nu läser jag, i all sköns ro,
Schück och Warburg för att förtjäna mitt a i detta ämne och för att det intresserar
mig kolossalt, Fr. Bööks Essayer och Kritiker, Shakespeare samt flera romaner och
noveller. Och Liedgrens Den svenska psalmboken icke att förglömma', Margit
Abenius' Diary, January 2, 1916 (Margit Abenius 1, Dagböcker 1916-1932, UUL).
Unless stated, all translations from Swedish into English are my own.

12 'På kvällen gick jag på biblioteket. Tog en diger Ord och Bild från hyllan, satte
mig vid ett ensamt bord och läste. Jag blev något yr i huvudet av allt, än var det
ett novellistiskt utkast, än ett Laurinskt kåseri, än en uppsats av Böök eller en
vetenskaplig avhandling av Warburg, som fängslade min tanke. Intrycken stormade
på mig, jag märket ofta att jag med eller mot min vilja får den författares åsikter, vars
alster jag läser. Och att min "bildning" är så ytterst bristfällig. Men dessa två saker,
omdöme och bildning kanske möjligen kunna [sic!] komma med åren. Jag är ju bara
sexton vårar än, och jag får väl ge mig till tåls', Margit Abenius' Diary, April 20, 1916
(Margit Abenius 1, Dagböcker 1916-1932, UUL).

later on provide access to the Swedish literary field and to highbrow literary magazines. Even if it were anachronistic to claim that Abenius was a conscious agent, making an investment in a certain kind of 'symbolic good', she was not wholly insensitive to what we might call the 'cultural' and 'social capital' that ruled different parts of the social field her family moved in.[13] She was thus very much aware of her family's social position and of different intellectual interests within the local middle class. As her father Wilhelm Abenius (1864-1956) was an associate professor of chemistry and the director of the Technical College in Örebro, the family's acquaintances were mostly other tertiary teachers, officials and the local upper-middle class. Her mother Maria Westholm's (1868-1935) family represented a traditional idea of *Bildung*, based on a solid humanist education. Nevertheless, full of her own juvenile literary and academic ambitions, Margit Abenius regarded her family, with its typical middle-class interests, as being inferior to a number of local humanists who – as she saw it – were far more sophisticated in their interests and less conventional in their social life. On this point one might say that she perceived the existence of different kinds of 'symbolic capital'.[14]

....

13 Here I use the term 'cultural capital' as equivalent to education and literariness and 'social capital' as synonymous with class and social acquaintance. Speaking in Bourdieu's terms is not unproblematic, as one might be given the wrong impression that the agent herself was aware of terms such as 'cultural capital' and 'investments in the field'. Hoping to avoid any such anachronisms, here I have put these terms in quotation marks. A broad definition of different kinds of symbolic capital is given by Donald Broady in his *Sociologi och epistemology. Om Pierre Bourdieus författarskap och den historiska epistemologin* (Stockholm, 1991), pp. 169-179 (Sociology and Epistemology. On Pierre Bourdieu's Work and the Historical Epistemology). Nevertheless, it may be assumed that the cultural capital that Abenius in fact gathered later on had an impact on her choices as an agent in the field of literary translation and literary critique. As Meylaerts puts it, this is the kind of biographical data that can 'fine-tune' the understanding of her strategies in these fields, Meylaerts, 'The study of cultural transfer', p. 5. According to Heilbron and Sapiro, '[t]he *habitus* of the translator, the mode of acquisition of linguistic competence, the type of education and training, the publishing norms, the national tradition with respect to translation norms – all contribute to orienting linguistic and stylistic choices (Gouanvic 1997, 2002; Simeoni 1998, Sapiro forthcoming)', Heilbron and Sapiro, 'Outline for a Sociology of Translation', pp. 12-13.

14 Margit Abenius' Diary, February 15, 1917 (Margit Abenius 1, Dagböcker 1916-1932, Uppsala University Library).

From autumn 1916 onwards, young Abenius was so preoccupied with
literature and with her own inner life that her diaries say almost nothing
about the First World War, apart from noting a food crisis affecting the
family's daily life. Her self-centred inner life, not unusual for teenagers,
would generate many critical comments from her parents and contribute
to an ever-present sense of guilt and a growing tendency towards self-
punishment.

Despite this, it seems that her plans to study met no resistance from the
family. In fact, it seems that she was acknowledged as a very good pupil,
and that her further education, including university, was taken for granted,
especially by her father, who encouraged this course. In May 1916, when Margit
Abenius graduated from the girl's junior secondary school in Örebro, Swedish
women had been admitted to university for more than thirty years, and their
number had increased to about nine percent of the total student population
in Sweden.[15] From the late nineteenth century, women's professional
training, including academic professions, was an accepted solution to the
growing number of unmarried middle-class women who had to earn a living.
However, women's access to higher education remained a political issue and
women students, still a clear minority at Swedish universities, were often
alienated and marginalised and had no access to public employment.[16] Thus,
in relation to Abenius' dreams of becoming an academic, it was thus notable
that her family took for granted that she would take a university degree, as
would her two younger brothers.

....

15 According to the Swedish university historian Tord Rönnholm, 471 (or 9.3%) of a total
    of 5,078 students registered at Swedish universities in 1911-1915 were women, Tord
    Rönnholm, *Kunskapens kvinnor. Sekelskiftets studentskor i motet med den manliga
    universitetsvärlden* (Umeå, 1999), p. 38 (Swedish text with a summary in English).
16 As the Swedish university historian Hanna Markusson Winkvist has observed, even
    when women were lawfully admitted to all public employment in 1925, the reform was
    believed to be unnecessary. Many authorities claimed that the job market for academics
    was 'self-sanitising', as women would not take employment which they were not suitable
    for 'by nature', Markusson Winkvist, *Som isolerade öar. De lagerkransade kvinnorna
    och akademin under 1900-talets första hälft* (Stockholm/Stehag, 2003), pp. 85-87 (*As
    Isolated Islands. Female Post-Graduates and Academia During the First Half of the 20th
    Century*). Swedish Text with an English summary. The parallel between Williams' term
    'lonely stars' for women writers without admittance to the literary field, and Winkvist's
    'isolated islands' for women academics without legitimacy in the job market is striking.
    Both address the same phenomena although within different intellectual professions,
    see Williams, *Stjärnor utan stjärnbilder*; and Winkvist, *Som isolerade öar*.

Margit Abenius in the early 1930s, photo by the renown Swedish photographer Gunnar Sundgren in Uppsala. (Original in Uppsala University Library)

In the autumn of 1916, Margit Abenius was taking private lessons in French and Latin, as well as piano lessons and courses in sewing and housekeeping. It is clear that the family was preparing her for future studies, but without abandoning their efforts to make her a good housewife. Abenius herself chose to devote most of her time to extensive reading and voluntary literature studies. Örebro suddenly felt boring and provincial, while Uppsala symbolised a place of wisdom and higher learning, so in spring 1917, she left home and moved to Uppsala, which would become her home for the rest of her life. She was admitted to the esteemed Humanist Secondary School where she gained her baccalaureate in May 1919. The years at this secondary school, where she boarded with some of her female classmates far from home, were in many ways crucial to her future career. Her daily reports in her diaries indicate that she was an outstanding pupil with a clear preference for literary history and English, two subjects taught by Olof Gjerdman (1883-1965), who later became professor of Nordic languages in Uppsala, and who quickly recognised Abenius' outstanding language skills. He encouraged her to strive for the best results in all subjects, while tutoring her in English and stylistics. Their friendship would lead to a lifelong informal relationship, but in secondary school Abenius was still only a sensitive teenager, sometimes dreaming of conquering the academic world, and at other times fighting worsening insomnia and decreasing self-confidence.

Full of plans and eager to study Nordic languages, she was accepted into Uppsala University in the autumn of 1919, aiming to start at once. However, due to her psychological condition and her insomnia, she was forbidden by her family to start until the autumn of 1920, when she was finally enrolled in the Arts Faculty. Abenius' own reports from her student years are surprisingly brief, compared to the detailed day-to-day – and sometimes almost hour-by-hour – diaries from her teens. In her last preserved diary, from 1921, she hardly ever mentions her studies, and elsewhere there are only short notes concerning exams, health and weather. Both from her diary and from her memoirs we know, however, that her first year was mostly devoted to a struggle with growing depression, an illness that would have a great impact on her whole career.[17]

In fact, her depression arose with great intensity during her student years in Uppsala, which might have contributed to her sudden disinterest in documenting her daily life. Nevertheless, we do know that she became friends with Karin Boye (1900-1941), as well as others, during this time. Boye was a young but already acknowledged poet and a literary authority among the student population in Uppsala and would soon become the most famous literary personality of Swedish modernism. Both she and Abenius were habitués of a private household which served dinner to students. Such

....

17 Margit Abenius' Diary, dated 'September 25, 1920-February 18, 1921' (in reality until March 10, 1921) (Margit Abenius 1, Dagböcker 1916-1932, Uppsala University Library). Adopting Moi's terms, in my forthcoming biography I propose that textuality (Abenius perceived as a 'body of texts') and subjectivity (Abenius perceived as a 'speaking subject') should be seen as constantly overlapping in Abenius' life, Moi, *Simone de Beauvoir*, pp. 4-5.

small student 'diners' were a very common way of making acquaintances at the university,[18] and Abenius' and Boye's dinner companions called themselves 'the Round Knights of the Table' (a humorous take on the legend of King Arthur) or 'the Reformatory Dinner Group'. Within the group, Abenius' nickname became Melanchton.

Despite her growing health problems, in April 1925 Abenius gained her Master's in Nordic languages, English and literary history and continued her postgraduate studies. In 1928 she passed her *filosofie licentiatexamen*, and in May 1931 defended her thesis, *Stilstudier i Kellgrens prosa* (Studies in stylistic elements in the prose of Johan Henric Kellgren), which was published the same year in Uppsala.[19] The subject of the thesis illustrates very well Abenius' interest in combining language and literary studies, although the actual choice of subject may not have been her own.[20] As a

....

18 These 'diners' (*matlag*) were a very popular way of making a living among Uppsala's working class and lower middle class, as most students needed at least one warm meal a day and they could not afford to dine at restaurants. The habitués usually became more or less permanent groups of intellectuals who not only shared the same table, but also became small discussion clubs and factions. Many lifelong friendship started at such diners.

19 The Swedish *filosofie licentiatexamen* can be passed half-way to a doctorate. Until about the 1960s, it was still much esteemed so many academics, women in particular, did not proceed to a doctorate after obtaining a 'lic'. On the other hand, to the majority of postgraduate students the exam was only a step to a doctoral dissertation, as a licentiate thesis could, after a small reworking and after passing a couple of necessary exams, be defended as a doctoral thesis.

20 Of the first eleven Swedish women, including Abenius, who obtained their doctoral degrees in literary history between 1909 and 1948, ten wrote their dissertations on male writers. For a list of these, including their dissertation subjects, see Anna Nordenstam, *Begynnelser. Litteraturforskningens pionjärkvinnor 1850-1930* (Stockholm/Stehag, 2003), p. 231 (Beginnings. The Pioneering Women in Swedish Literary Historiography from *1850 to 1930*). Swedish Text with a summary in English. Nordenstam does not count Abenius among them, while I have chosen to do so, as Abenius is mentioned in some earlier sources as having a PhD in literary studies. See John Tuneld, *Akademiska avhandlingar vid Sveriges universitet och högskolor läsåren 1910/11-1939/40. Bibliografi* (Lund, 1945), pp. 271-271 and Urban Dahllöf, *Akademiska avhandlingar vid Sveriges universitet och högskolor 1890-1939. En kompletterande sammanställning* (*Pedagogisk forskning i Uppsala*, no. 73.) (Uppsala 1987), p. 61. Also, the very subject of her dissertation can be seen as belonging both to research in stylistics and to literary research.

journalist, a critic and rhetorician, Johan Henric Kellgren (1751-1795) was one of the most prominent and versatile literary personalities of the Swedish Enlightenment, an époque in which French influences on Swedish were very strong. To Abenius, both his various literary productions and the situation of Swedish in the eighteenth century made Kellgren a very interesting subject of both rhetorical and linguistic studies. In her thesis, she thus studied Kellgren's lexicon and typical rhetorical elements in his prose, as well as rhythm and syntax, and placed all these in relation to the literary Swedish of the Enlightenment. However, it is important to remember that as a result of her studies she also became familiar with the early tradition of Swedish literary criticism and its aesthetics.

Abenius' thesis received a high mark, but not an associate professor's grade (a *docent* grade). Although it was possible at that time to become an associate professor on the basis of a doctoral thesis, the option hardly existed for women academics.[21] It is difficult to say what ambitions Abenius might have had regarding continuing her research. Devoted as she was to studies in style and rhythm, she was in fact a promising pupil of three prolific scholars in Nordic languages and in stylistics, Olof Gjerdman, Nils Svanberg (1902-1939) and Bengt Hesselman (1875-1952). However, at

....

21 Of the first eleven women PhDs in history of literature, only three became associate professors. Among the seven who left the academy after obtaining their PhDs, Margit Abenius and Elisabeth Tykesson (1906-1962, PhD in 1947) would become literary critics. Kerstin Hård af Segerstad and Hilma Borelius were admitted as university teachers. Kerstin Hård af Segerstad (1873-1955) (PhD in French literature 1906), was appointed to lecture in literary history 1907-1908, becoming the first Swedish woman to lecture on the subject at the university. She was active both as a scholar and as an essayist and she became a member of Samfundet de nio in 1912. In my study of pioneer women students of literary history I have argued that both Abenius and Hård af Segerstad should be considered as scholars of literary history, with respect to both their dissertation subjects and their careers. It would make Hård af Segerstad the very first female PhD in the history of literature and a predecessor of Hilma Borelius (1869-1932), PhD and associate professor of literature in 1910, often considered as the absolute Swedish female pioneer in the discipline. Marta Ronne, 'Kvinnliga studenter I litteraturhisoria 1900-1940. Studier, examina och kunskapssyn' (Women students of literary history at Swedish Universities, 1900-1940: Their Achievements and Their View of the Literary Canon), in: Bengt Landgren, ed., *Universitetsämne i brytningstider. Studier i svensk akademisk litteraturundervisning 1947-1995* (A University Discipline in Transition: Studies in Swedish Academic Literature Instruction 1947-1995) (Uppsala, 2005), p. 629.

the time of her dissertation she had already taken her first steps towards literary critique. In 1926 she reviewed *Det speglade livet* (The mirrored life) by the famous critic Klara Johanson (1875-1948, usually known as 'KJ'), a review that would bring them both together. Shortly after obtaining her doctorate, Abenius started publishing literary critiques and essays on literary theory, reception and literary history. In 1933, she published her first essays in the newly established *Bonniers Litterära Magasin* and in the prestigious *Ord och Bild* (established in 1892). Within a decade she would become an influential voice within the field of literary criticism and by the early 1950s she was one of the most versatile cultural transmitters in Sweden of the mid-twentieth century.

Between the highbrow and the popular

Abenius' debut in *Bonniers Litterära Magasin* and *Ord och Bild* can be seen as her entrance into the Swedish literary establishment. Both magazines represented highbrow middle-class literary taste and academic literary critique.[22] She debuted in *Bonniers Litterära Magasin* in 1933 with an essay on the reception of modern poetry. Her next essay, published in 1934, was on Emily Dickinson, followed by another on Norwegian author Cora Sandel and a later one on Lord Byron, both in 1936. In 1938 Abenius introduced Franz Kafka's *Letters to Milena*, also translating fragments of the work.

One could say that at the beginning of her career as a critic and translator she made a series of strategic moves in order to augment her cultural capital. According to Heilbron and Sapiro, '[b]eginners or authors who have a relatively marginal position, are often tempted to translate promising but still unknown authors: one thinks of Larbaud translating Joyce's *Ulysses*, to name one canonical example'.[23] However, Heilbron and Sapiro strongly suggest that the very activity of translation should not only be studied 'as a field governed by a logic of competition for the monopoly of legitimacy founded on the accumulation of symbolic capital', but also in relation to both international space and the space of reception.[24] This

....

22 *Bonniers Litterära Magasin* was established by Bonniers publishing house and it had a purely literary profile, while *Ord och Bild* (more conservative) was also devoted to art, architecture and culture. In the 1930s, both took a firm stand against Nazism and after 1968 *Ord och Bild* became a pronounced left-wing cultural magazine.

23 Heilbron and Sapiro, 'Outline for a Sociology of Translation', p. 12.

24 *Ibidem*, p. 11.

statement is in my opinion also relevant to literary critique, which often introduces foreign writers in translation and is therefore ruled by similar principles. As to Abenius' choice of the subject, this cannot be attributed to her alone, as it also had to fit the ambitions and interests of the magazine.

Abenius' introduction and translation of *La pesanteur et la Grace* by the French philosopher Simone Weil is a very good example of how cultural transfer can emerge from literary critique when the critic becomes established within the literary field. It also indicates that '[a]t the level of mediators, (...) the uses of translation vary from the consecration of the translated author to the self-consecration of the translator'.[25]

When interest in Simone Weil's works on Catholicism and philosophy developed in Sweden in the late 1940s, Abenius was already an esteemed contributor to literary magazines and an established collaborator with Bonniers publishing house. In fact, it was the chief editor of the magazine who gave Abenius the mission to introduce Simone Weil to the Swedish literary market. In a way, Abenius was 'consecrated' by this, as the notion of Weil's posthumous authority had already reached some of the Swedish literary elite. Alternately, it might be claimed that Abenius possessed significant literary capital to consecrate Weil by translating and introducing her.[26] The very phenomenon of the French and Catholic Simone Weil posthumously reaching Sweden in the Cold War years of the early 1950s also shows that '[t]he value of translation does not depend only on the position of languages, but also on the positions of both translated authors and their translators, and each of them in both the national literary field and the global literary space'.[27]

After publishing her own translation of *La pesanteur et la grace* in 1951, Abenius remained the chief authority on Weil in Sweden and she cooperated with the translators of Weil's other works, writing her own introductions to subsequent volumes.[28] Due to her contacts with the

....

25 *Ibidem*, p. 12, after Kalinowski, 2001.
26 Ibidem, p. 12.
27 *Ibidem*, p. 11. Their reference is to Pascale Casanova, 'Consécration et accumulation de capital littéraire. La traduction comme échange inégal', *Actes de la recherche en sciences sociales* 144:2002, pp. 7-20.
28 Speaking in general terms of Abenius' contribution, the introduction of Weil to Sweden followed the five phases of cultural transfer listed by Broomans: introduction, the selected author being 'in quarantine', translation, the author and the translated work being 'in quarantine again', and finally a second reception (i.e. reviews, lectures, books, etc.), Broomans, 2006, p. 2-3.

Weil family, she was also in a position to decide which of Simone Weil's essays were to be published in Sweden.[29] In the meantime, her image as a critic primarily dealing with questions of ethics, spirituality and religion became more or less fixed due to her preoccupation with Weil's Christian philosophy. Abenius willingly contributed to this image of herself, describing her encounter with Weil's writings as an answer to her own inner crisis.[30] The effect was that some of her intellectual acquaintances started perceiving her as biased and far too orthodox in her interpretations of Weil's philosophy. Due to some critical reviews of her translation of *La Pesanteur et la Grâce*, as well as her own interest in religion, a conflict arose in 1954 between Abenius and some of her oldest friends in Uppsala. Among them were the philosopher Ingemar Hedenius (1908-1982), the writer Tora Dahl (1886-1982) and the renowned critic Knut Jaensson (1893-1958). As a result, in 1958 Abenius broke definitively with some of her most important intellectual acquaintances.[31]

Abenius cooperated closely with *Bonniers Litterära Magasin* and occasionally with *Ord och Bild* until the early 1960s, publishing both literary criticism and essays on literature. Over the course of thirty years she would not only write on eighteenth-century English literature and Virginia Woolf, Kafka and Weil, but also on modern Russian and Latvian authors. In addition she published essays on the Swedish modernist poet Karin Boye and the writer Per Lagerkvist (1891-1974), as well as on her friends Stina Aronson (1892-1956) and Tora Dahl, and in the late 1950s on Sara Lidman (1923-2004). Three of her few essays in *Ord och Bild* were devoted to the Romantic poet Carl Jonas Love Almqvist (1793-1866) and to the poet Birger Sjöberg (1885-1929), but her most important contributions to the magazine were reflections on reading and on the very nature of literary critique. It was in one of these essays that she formulated the famous expressions 'the invisible reader' and 'a text always has to find its reader', which would become part of her professional image – and of her literary heritage.

---

29 Ronne, 'Decoding a Genius Mind', 2009, p. 156.

30 In her memoirs, Abenius claimed that Weil's works led her to discover 'the transcendental' and find an answer to the question of the conflict between good and evil, Abenius, *Memoarer från det inre* (Stockholm, 1963), pp. 201-204.

31 The conflict was as much a result of the philosopher Ingemar Hedenius's unwillingness to compromise with other philosophical standpoints. In this case, he disliked Abenius' interest in Weil's view of Christian ethics. Svante Nordin, *Ingemar Hedenius. En filosof och hans tid* (Stockholm, 2004), pp. 98-100, pp. 245-250.

Before devoting herself to Simone Weil, in 1950 Abenius published *Drabbad av renhet* (Struck by purity), a voluminous literary biography of Karin Boye, who at the time of her tragic death was already a famous poet and an acknowledged literary figure in Swedish modernism.[32] According to Abenius herself, writing on Boye was both a professional challenge to her as a critic and a kind of a personal obligation.[33] The book was to become the most important of Abenius' literary works and would mean her name was remembered both among literary historians and ordinary readers. It was also quite controversial, and despite positive reviews and a broad response from readers throughout Scandinavia, from the start the biography drew strong reactions from many of Boye's acquaintances who did not agree with Abenius' portrait.[34] It was hardly surprising – widely acclaimed as a poet,

....

32 As Meylaerts points out, when studying translations and cultural transfer it is important to investigate whether the agents take on other functions in the literary field. Abenius is a very good example of a cultural transmitter who both gathered and used her cultural capital in various ways: as a critic, a translator and an author. 'In addition, an attempt has to be made to analyse the structured and structuring dimensions of the (translation and intercultural) *habitus* (Bourdieu, 1992) of these actors. How do they internalise institutional and discursive structures and how is this expressed in perceptions and practices regarding their intercultural activities? Each individual is a complex product of multiple socialisation processes spread over an array of situations. An analysis using the *habitus* concept is an essential part of the study of cultural transfer', Meylaerts, 'The study of cultural transfer', p. 5.

33 'Second to Klara Johanson, she has meant most to me in my work – a brightly shining soul! But Karin B. was also my friend, and the best, the finest, the most intelligent person you could imagine' ('Näst Klara Johanson är hon den som betytt mest för mig som yrkesvarelse – en strålande ande! Men Karin B. var ju dessutom min vän och den bästa, finaste, intelligentaste människa man kunde tänka sig.'), Abenius wrote to her father shortly after Boye's suicide, Abenius' Letter to Wilhelm Abenius, April 29, 1941, G1n:19, Uppsala University Library.

34 Abenius' colleague, the critic Sven Stolpe, partly disagreed with her picture of Boye's relationships. A letter from Sven Stolpe to Margit Abenius, December 5, 1950. Letters to Margit Abenius, G1n:14, Uppsala University Library. Abenius was not alone in glorifying Boye and her death. The poet and member of the Swedish Academy Hjalmar Gullberg (1898-1961) wrote his famous poem 'Död Amazon' (The dead amazon) shortly after Boye's death. However, many literary personalities of Boye's acquaintance, such as the poet Gunnar Ekelöf (1907-1968) and the critic Olof Lagercrantz (1911-2002), wrote about her with ambivalence, or even hostility. Camilla Hammarström, *Karin Boye* (Stockholm, 1997), pp. 248-251.

but also a complex and controversial personality, a gay left-wing activist and finally a suicide at the age of forty-one, Boye continued to excite and provoke even after her death.

While praised by her reviewers for her stylistic brilliance and brave interpretations, Abenius' approach to Boye's poetry was at the same time characterised as 'intuitive, rather than strictly academic'.[35] Her way of characterising Boye's literary generation was found to be both moving between professional critique and fiction, and partly to be writing her own literary manifesto.[36] Even regarding Abenius' own comments about the emotional aspects of her work, the epithet 'intuitive' is striking. Until very recently, the traditional division of literary history into writers and 'female writers', as well as critics and 'female critics' has meant that women writers and academics have traditionally been characterised in terms of intuition and emotions rather than professionalism and a critical approach. Ultimately, many were erased from the manuals of literary history.[37]

However, for contemporary feminist research, and for scholars dealing with Boye, Abenius' book is also controversial, not in the least because of her way of writing about Boye's homosexuality in terms of guilt and planned conversion.[38] Some of the biographical information on Boye has

....

35 Birger Christofferson, *Svenska kritiker och deras metoder* (Stockholm, 1962), p. 70.

36 *Ibidem*, pp. 70-71.

37 The Danish critic Georg Brandes is often mentioned as the main influence on literary historians seeing women writers as emotional. In his *Den unge Tyskland* from 1890, he stated that women writer's primary goal was to create an emotional contact with their readers and that their works usually lacked originality, which was necessary in all artistic creation (and typical of male writers), see Williams, *Stjärnor utan stjärnbilder*, pp. 191-193. Women students of literary history during the first half of the twentieth century were often judged in the same way: they were seen as naïve and brisk, rather than original and creative, Margaretha Fahlgren, 'Från periferin till centrum. Edith Södergran och kvinnorna i 1900-talets litteraturhistoriska seminarierum', in: Marta Ronne, ed., *Mot normen. Kvinnors skrivande under 1900-talet* (Uppsala, 2007).

38 See for example Paulina Helgesson, 'Karin Boye: Posthumous Excuses', *Scandinavica. An International Journal of Scandinavian Studies* 1 (2001), pp. 71-95. Abenius' standpoint on this issue was not unique. After Boye's death her nearest acquaintances did their best to erase the memory of her homosexual relationship with Margot Hanel, Hammarström, *Karin Boye*, pp. 247-248.

also been contradicted in the past two decades.[39] Regardless of the criticism, Abenius' book still remains the only existing biography of Karin Boye that is based on primary sources and on information coming from Boye herself and her acquaintances, and it is still the most voluminous work on Boye, which makes it an indispensible, albeit problematic reference.

Despite mixed reactions to the book, in the early 1950s Abenius was already an established member of the Swedish literary elite and an esteemed arbiter of taste. Since 1949 she had been a member of the prestigious literary society Samfundet De nio (Society of the nine).[40] In 1944, Bonniers publishing house had edited a collection of her essays entitled *Kontakter* (The contacts). Most of them had been previously published in *Bonniers Litterära Magasin*, but the volume also included three lectures and the title essay, 'Kontakter', especially written for the book in the summer of 1943. The fact that her essays were reprinted in a separate volume indicates that at the time she had become established as a critic within the Swedish literary field. Apparently, she was even becoming interesting to a broader audience, among whom her popularity was also fuelled by lectures and radio appearances.

It is in the context of the radio broadcasts that Abenius' ability to oscillate between highbrow critique and a more popular approach to literature should be analysed. Here I am talking of both her ability to bring esteemed writers to an audience outside highbrow literary magazines, and of her interest in less established authors whom she found worth popularising. In the mid-1930s, Abenius had started reviewing books and giving short talks on literature on Swedish Radio (at that time known as the Swedish Radio Service). The radio started broadcasting cultural programmes in 1925 and in 1927 there was a separate literary criticism programme, called 'Literaturkrönikan' (Talking about literature) which was broadcast when the radio only had one channel and was later replaced by various programmes on literature, literary critique and reading. The

....

39 Anette Arnell, 'Margit Abenius som Karin Boyes biograf', in: *Karin Boyes liv och diktning IV* (Huddinge: Karin Boye Sällskapet, 1988); Gumilla Domellöf, *I oss är en mångfald levande – Karin Boye som kritiker och prosamodernist* (Umeå, 1986) (*Within Us a Multiplicity is Living. Karin Boye as a Critic and a Modernist Novel Writer*); Camilla Hammarström, *Karin Boye*, p. 9; Helgesson, 'Karin Boye', p. 71.

40 She was not the only member among the first women literary historians. Kerstin Hård af Segerstad (1873-1955, PhD of French literature) was elected in 1913, and the critic Elisabeth Tykesson (1906-1962, PhD in literary history) in 1956.

period from 1930 to 1950, which was also the era in which the Swedish welfare state was being created, can be seen as the programme's 'golden age'. Book reviews and talks on literature were given by some of the most prominent poets, critics and translators, such as Margit Abenius, Gunnar Mascoll Silfverstolpe (1893-1942), Ivar Harrie (1899-1973) and Sten Selander (1991-1957), while other parts of the programme were devoted to literary debate and interviews. Literature played a very important part in the radio's educational project. According to the Swedish ideal of *Bildung*, book circles and cultural activities were to be promoted to a broad audience with different social backgrounds.[41]

Between 1931 and 1967 Abenius gave eighty talks, of which eighteen were short lectures on various literary subjects and sixty-two book reviews.[42] Despite her radio appearances being quite rare, from two to six times a year, with a couple of longer breaks in between, she soon became a well-known radio voice.[43] Here she started moving between highbrow literature on the one hand, be it Swedish or foreign, and more popular literature on the other, adapting herself to the new medium and its ambitions. The radio became a very important part of her work as a cultural transmitter, as it enabled her to reach a very broad audience, to whom she not only presented contemporary literature of the Western world, but also a popularised version of literary history. The subjects of her talks included

41 Solveig Lundgren, *Dikten i etern. Radion och skönlitteraturen 1925-1955* (Uppsala, 1994), pp. 18-19 (Literature on the Air. Poetry and Prose on the Swedish Radio 1925-1955), Swedish text with an English summary.

42 Abenius gave about one lecture a year between 1931 and 1966 and approximately six book reviews a year between 1933 and 1952 but a total of only four between 1955 and 1962. The list and two additional drafts that have not been listed are stored in Margit Abenius 25, Biographica, Uppsala University Library, Uppsala. Solveig Lundgren lists 62 reviews by Abenius 1955, a list that is based on manuscripts preserved in the Swedish Radio's archive. Apparently, she does not count all lectures, while two of them she counts as reviews. Solveig Lundgren, *Dikten I etern. Radion och skönlitteraturen 1925-1955*, p. 225.

43 Professor Lars Furuland (1928-2009) at the Literature Department in Uppsala mentioned to me in 2008 that the amateur cultural circle *Scri-scri-di-di-di*, founded 1946, that he belonged to during his secondary school years, sometimes compared their most ambitious members to Margit Abenius' critical voice on the radio. See also Lars Furuland, *Mina dagsverken. Minnen från folkhögskolor, folkbildning, universitet och möten med arbetarförfattare* (Uppsala, 2009).

'The Child as a Motive in Swedish Poetry', 'The Brontë Sisters', 'The Big Tradition' and 'Dante and Us'. She also made longer presentations of authors such as the German theologist Dietrich Bonhoeffer (1906-1945), Nelly Sachs (1891-1970), the German-Jewish writer who was to receive the Nobel Prize for literature 1966, Simone Weil and Karin Boye.

Each programme lasted about 30 minutes, at the beginning broadcast between 7 a.m. and 9 a.m., and from the mid-1930s and sometimes even from 7 p.m. to 9 p.m. Abenius reviewed about five titles per programme, including canonised and esteemed writers and poets, both Swedish and foreign, alongside Swedish working-class writers and contemporary European and American authors, many of whom are barely remembered today. Both the books she reviewed and the subjects of her radio lectures were suggested to her and – sometimes – imposed on her by the editor-in-chief Hjalmar Gullberg and the editorial staff:[44] 'Let's see what I can do with the talk on the art of reading a book. The alternative subject I received was not especially inspiring', Abenius wrote concerning a coming presentation on February 10, 1942. She added, '[s]ometimes they send me books with an excuse, when the publishing house, etc. wishes *partout* to be mentioned. In such cases I do not know whether I should do as they wish or refuse. – "You just have to mention it, that's all", Gullberg appealed to me, and so I agreed, be it right or wrong'.[45]

Her manuscripts were sent to the editor in advance.[46] Still it seems that she was quite free to plan her broadcasts. In the autumn of 1937 for example, she was asked to speak on epistolary art and to read letters from

....

44 The poet Hjalmar Gullberg, later on a member of the Swedish Academy, was the editor of the radio theatre 1936-1950 and programme editor-in-chief at Swedish Radio 1949-1950. Abenius and Gullberg also cooperated outside the radio. Abenius' Letter to Wilhelm Abenius, January 29, 1942, G1n:19, Uppsala University Library.

45 'Ibland lämnas en eller annan bok med ursäkt – det är förlaget eller något sådant som partout kräver att bli uppmärksammat. Jag vet inte om man ska vara lojal i sådana fall eller vägra – 'behövs bara lite, så den kommer med', sa Gullberg vädjande och jag sa ja, om det nu var rätt eller orätt', Abenius' Letter to Wilhelm Abenius, January 29, 1942, G1n:19, Uppsala University Library.

46 The manuscripts, a few of them incomplete, are preserved in Margit Abenius 18: Litteraturkrönikor 1933-1940 and Margit Abenius 19: Litteraturkrönikor 1941-1967 och andra författares manuscript, both in Uppsala University Library.

well-known historical figures.[47] The programme entitled 'Swedish letters' was broadcast on October 10 that year. According to her letter to the critic Klara Johanson, her friend and mentor, she also planned to talk on eighteenth-century Swedish women writers, such as Agneta Horn (1629-1672) and Hedvig Charlotta Nordenflycht (1718-1763).[48] A radio manuscript called 'Swedish Women: Hedvig Charlotta Nordenflycht, a Shepherdess of the North' has been preserved but it is uncertain when the programme was broadcast.[49] The title 'Swedish Women' might indicate that Abenius planned a series of talks on the subject of women's literature and women's history, but no other manuscripts have been preserved.[50]

As a critic, Abenius' work on disseminating literature and the art of critical reading to a broader audience was not limited to her radio appearances. Along with some of her fellow women literary historians, she lectured to women's societies and clubs, such as Sällskapet Nya Idun (The Nya Idun Society) or Akademiskt Bildade Kvinnors Förening (Professional Women's Society) of which Abenius was a member.[51] These activities helped her create new networks and obtain more engagements. In 1944, she was asked to lead a women's book circle in Uppsala which had started in 1943 within the Professional Women's Society, whose members were all middle-aged, middle-class women of different professions. To Abenius, accepting the proposal meant that she succeeded the former

....

47   The manuscript was 12 pages, including fragments of quoted letters, dated October 10, 1937, the day the programme was broadcast on the radio, Margit Abenius 16, Manuskript till föredrag i skilda ämnen, Uppsala University Library.

48   A letter from Margit Abenius to Klara Johanson ('KJ'), September 5, 1937, L 2 suppl, The Royal Library, Stockholm.

49   The manuscript of about 31 A4 pages is stored in Margit Abenius 25, Biographica, Uppsala University Library. It is not mentioned in the list of Abenius' literary reviews written for the radio, but not all her manuscripts for the radio are, which makes it difficult to place them in any chronological order. Only a few recordings of Abenius on the Swedish Radio have been preserved by the radio archive (SVTR). Some additional information on her radio contributions comes from her own letters and diaries.

50   In any case, promoting women's literature or women's culture for its own sake, the way early women academics did from the late nineteenth century and onwards, was never high on Abenius' agenda. Nor did she claim any relationship with the women's movement.

51   Winkvist, *Som isolerade öar*, p. 156 and pp. 288-289.

chair Elsa Norberg, a legendary historian of literature and one of the very few women associate professors in literature in Sweden at the time. It also meant a new kind of audience, and a new challenge to her as a critic, as she 'had never studied in a circle before, nor chaired one', as she stated in her memoirs twenty years later: 'The members arrived, and I suddenly realised I was the chair, a very shy one and in no possession of any method, principles or suggestions'.[52] In the beginning, the circle met in cafés or in a member's home. The number of participants varied and readings were chosen randomly.

Between 1944 and 1948 the group read about 40 titles, according to their own list.[53] Abenius seems to have perceived herself as one of the members, rather than as the chair of the circle. She wrote to her father on March 3, 1944:

> The day before yesterday I attended the Society reading circle together with fifteen other ladies. We discussed *Ordet*. The first speaker had no success with her chaotic introduction, but a lively discussion followed and the party enjoyed themselves anyway. A couple of very intelligent ladies were present (...). I made animated comments myself. Struck by a sudden megalomania, I invited the circle to my place on March 30, when I am supposed to deliver an analysis of Aurell.[54]

It is striking how self-critical Abenius was, despite being an academic, a well-known radio voice and an acknowledged arbiter of literary taste.

> The day before yesterday I had my big battle in the Professional Women's reading circle. I was as much afraid as if I were defending my dissertation. It was very good that I had prepared so carefully. Fourteen people came and we discussed Tage Aurell's abridged novel *Martina*. I am of course not used to leading a discussion and I could have done a better job, but most participants asserted they were very much satisfied with the meeting. A black sheep was

52 Margit Abenius, *Memoarer från det inre* (Stockholm, 1963), p. 139.
53 *Litterära cirkeln 1944-1984 (Literary Circle 1944-1984)*, an unpublished memorial booklet by Gertrud H.[?] and Ingrid Ingelman, a copy in my possession.
54 Letter from Margit Abenius to Wilhelm Abenius, March 3, 1944, G1n:19, Uppsala University Library.

present, the wife of the great sculptor Bror Hjorth. She seemed to try to spoil the whole discussion by moving to a very trivial and ridiculous level and I almost lost the thread (...).[55]

A few years later Abenius introduced a more strict reading method: the participants received questions to prepare in advance, the meetings started with short introductions by some of the members and notes were taken at every meeting. Also, a treasurer and a secretary were elected. The official name of the circle was now The Spiritual Club (Andliga Klubben). Among the members were the Uppsala artist Märta Hummel-Gumaelius, who also painted a portrait of the circle, Ragna Ofvandahl, the owner of the famous Ofvandahl's Tea Room in Uppsala where the circle sometimes met, and the exiled Latvian writer Zenta Maurina (1897-1978). Abenius remained the leader until her death in August 1970, and during those thirty-six years the members read some two hundred titles, both poetry and prose, and arranged a number of discussions on literary issues, not to mention attending plays together. The circle was devoted entirely to highbrow literature, both the classics and new works, with the readings exceeding the canon of the West, with Chinese and Japanese literature also on the list. The discussions dealt with ethical and existential matters, two subjects that were of particular interest to Abenius, but in general her contribution to the circle can be defined as transmitting foreign literature to Swedish middle-class readers, whom she, in the meantime, tutored in critical reading and literary history.

....

55   'I förgår hade jag mitt stora slag I yrkeskvinnornas läsecirkel. Jag var lika rädd som om jag skulle disputera. Och nog behövdes mina grundliga förberedelser. Det var fjorton som kom och vi diskuterade Tage Aurells komprimerade roman Martina. Jag är ju inte van att leda någon diskussion och det kunde nog ha gjorts bättre, men de flesta förklarade sig dock synnerligen nöjda med aftonen. Ett svart får var med, Bror Hjorths fru, den store bildhuggarens. Hon ville tydligen sabotera hela diskussionen genom att föra över den på ett trivialt och löjligt plan, och jag höll på att alldeles komma av mig i portföret (...)', letter from Abenius to Wilhelm Abenius, April 1, 1944, G1n:19, UUL. In the original text, Abenius refers to Aurell's novel as 'komprimerad', which I have chosen to translate as 'abridged', rather than 'compressed', although the meaning might be twofold. Abenius sent detailed reports and comments on her daily work to her father, not in the least on the Circle's meetings and their readings. This letter was almost entirely devoted to the Circle's meeting in her own home on March 30, 1944.

According to the circle's booklet, the last meeting she participated in took place on 'an evening in June' in 1970 in her summer home outside Uppsala, where the circle read poems about birds chosen by some of the members.[56] According to the members, it was to a great extent due to Abenius' influence that the Spiritual Club survived after her death, until 1984, with the members being deeply involved in the meetings to the very end, despite their own careers and family duties: 'Margit liked playing with words, but there was always a seriousness hidden behind them. She knew that literature was the link that chained us together, despite the differences in interests, temperaments and views. We were joined in a circle of mutual understanding, joy and friendship'.[57] Abenius herself took her own membership of the circle as seriously as all her professional engagements, which had to do with her interest in the very process of the reception of a literary work: 'There is always an invisible reader, and the art of writing is the art of finding him', she declared in her opening essay in *Kontakter*, while in her literary critique she always regarded herself as speaking to the 'invisible reader', an expression that became her motto.[58]

Abenius' way of oscillating between highbrow literary magazines and book projects, and radio appearances and an amateur book circle indicates that she had the ability to address many different groups of readers simultaneously. However, considering that she had started with an academic career only to leave academia after gaining her PhD, this oscillating movement as a critic and a cultural transmitter can be seen as a part of a certain gender pattern. As gender research has observed, many early twentieth-century women academics who did not have the chance to stay within academia were often forced to develop certain strategies in order to be able to survive within their professions and to publish their historical and literary research, albeit in a more popular form. That is why many of them continued their work within the so-called 'women's cultural field', a cultural production for a broad middle-class audience outside prestigious cultural institutions and on the margins of the literary field.[59]

....

56 Ingelman, *Literary Circle 1944-1984*, p. 19.
57 'Margit lekte gärna med ord, men det fanns ett allvar under. Hon visste, att litteraturen är länken som binder oss samman, trots olikartade intressen, temperame toch åskådningar, till en cirkel av förståelde, glädje och vänskap', Ingelman, *Litterära cirkeln, 1944-1984*, p. 13.
58 'Det finns alltid en osynlig läsare, och konsten att skriva är konsten att finna honom.' Margit Abenius, 'Den osynlige läsaren', *Kontakter* (Stockholm, 1944), pp. 9-25, p. 9.
59 Anna Nordenstam, *Begynnelser*, p. 21-22, pp. 214-217.

Such career choices – as it is in my opinion wrong to speak of deliberate career 'strategies' as does Nordenstam – were not only typical of the first women pioneer academics, but also of Abenius' own generation of female academics and academically trained women who were still a minority within a male-dominated academic world.[60]

Between the foreign and the local

Abenius' work on introducing foreign writers to Sweden was by no means limited to translations, essays in literary magazines or book reviews. In fact, she found her own way of moving between the foreign and the local. As a cultural transmitter, her motives were seldom purely aesthetic, but rather a mixture of the aesthetic, ideological and sometimes political.

Many of Abenius' professional relationships led to private friendships, which again was a form of cultural transfer. Among these were her relationship with the Weil family, where Abenius as the Swedish editor of Simone Weil's writings also became an ambassador for Swedish literature and culture. After publishing her biography on Karin Boye and editing a collection of essays on her, Abenius received comments on her book and on Karin Boye's life and oeuvre from both single readers and literary personalities throughout Scandinavia. This means that she helped popularise Boye's literary heritage even outside Sweden.

Also, Abenius' lifelong friendship with the Norwegian writer Cora Sandel (Sara Fabricius) can be seen as both a private attachment and a kind of a transnational cultural exchange. Abenius was often in touch with writers whom she intended to study further, and this was the case with Cora Sandel, to whom she wrote, probably in autumn 1935, while preparing an essay on her literary career.[61] Despite her initial reserve, Sandel soon became more personal in her correspondence. As an 'exile' writer, living in

....

60 Nordenstam, *Begynnelser*, pp. 214-217. Similarly to Nordenstam, Markusson Winkvist has also studied academic women's alternative intellectual arenas, Marskusson Winkvist, *Som isolerade öar*.

61 Only Cora Sandel's reply to Abenius' letter has been preserved (January 11, 1936). In her letter, Cora Sandel summarises her life and literary career, probably as an answer to Abenius' questions. Letters from Cora Sandel to Margit Abenius, G1n:18, Uppsala University Library. Abenius' essay 'Herr Salomon är oberörd. Om Cora Sandels författarskap' (Mr. Salomon is unmoved. On Cora Sandel's writings), was published in *Bonniers Litterära Magasin*, 1936:3, p. 213-218.

Sweden and writing in Norwegian, she soon became aware that Abenius' essay had some impact on her position in Sweden: 'I have always been of the opinion that one should not expect anything more from a writer than just writing. His [sic!] private self should be kept outside. So now I have been quite honest with you', she concluded in her first letter. Despite this, shortly after Abenius' essay appeared in *Bonniers Litterära Magasin*, she wrote enthusiastically:

> Dear Dr Abenius, I wish to thank you from all my heart for your essay on my writing in *Bonniers Litterära*. You have so very correctly understood my attitude towards life and people, towards the implacable 'face of the Sphinx' and our 'co-passengers' that it has really done me much good to hear it. (...) To put it briefly, your deep analysis of my work has been all joy and encouragement to me.[62]

Between 1933 and 1951, Abenius reviewed several of Sandel's novels and short stories in Swedish translations on the radio. Notwithstanding their deep friendship, Abenius' professional interest in Sandel's writings helped to popularise the latter's work among Swedish readers and, according to Sandel herself, encouraged her to write.

Sandel was not the only non-Swedish-speaking writer living in Sweden whom Abenius introduced to Swedish readers. From the 1930s, Abenius was a declared critic of both Nazi Germany and the Soviet regime. In her radio talks and lectures, as well as in the daily press, she condemned both the anti-Semitism occurring in Hitler's Germany and Stalin's purges in the

....

62 'Kjära Doktor Abenius. Jag må få lov til hjertlig å takke Dere for Deres studie om mitt forfattareskap i Bonniers Litterära. De har så riktig opfattet min instilling til livet og menneskene, til det obönhörlige "Sfinx-ansiktet" og til vore "medpassasjerers", at det virkelig har gjort mig godt å höre det. (...) Allt i allt har Deres inngående analys av mit arbeide varet en stor glede og opmuntring for mig', Cora Sandel to Margit Abenius, March 8, 1936, Letters from Cora Sandel to Margit Abenius, G1n:18, Uppsala University Library.

Soviet Union.[63] Her interest in helping political refugees, and especially exiled writers, had probably as much to do with literary critique as with her political views. In her essays on and reviews of the exiled Jewish poet Nelly Sachs, she not only spoke of Sachs's literary qualities but also of her Jewish identity in the time of the Holocaust.

Abenius was also personally involved in helping the German-speaking writers Zenta Maurina and Konstantin Raudive, who were Latvian refugees in Sweden from 1946 who had left successful literary careers behind them to escape the Soviet terror in Riga. Abenius became personally acquainted with them in Uppsala and assisted them in several ways using both her own position as a critic and her informal contacts among Swedish intellectuals. Her efforts to encourage the interest of *Bonniers Litterära Magasin* and some of the biggest publishing houses in Zenta Maurina's philosophical and critical works may be seen as the work of cultural transfer, as she attempted to help Maurina to become established in the Swedish highbrow literary market. The mission was of a peculiar kind and did not wholly succeed, as Maurina still perceived herself as the famous philosopher and writer she had been in Riga, and was unable to accept the anonymity of exile. She only wrote in German, expecting her texts either to be published in German or to be translated into Swedish. This and her strong sympathy for Germany and its culture did not make her popular in Sweden in the late 1940s. The few essays she published in Swedish magazines were hardly noticed. Nevertheless, the economic support and the literary scholarships she and Raudive received due to Abenius' intervention enabled her to continue writing and eventually to start publishing in Germany in the 1950s, ultimately making

....

63 Here I refer, for example, to her radio manuscripts, 'En varning. När nerverna sveko under Danmarks ödesnatt', on the German invasion of Denmark, April 9, 1940, and 'Svar på tal om "Europaskydd mot bolsjevismen"' (no date), in Margit Abenius 25, *Biographica', UUL. In the largest Swedish newspaper, *Dagens Nyheter*, on November 9, 1947, Abenius also gave a polemical answer to a group of 31 prominent Swedish authors, (including Lars Ahlin, Werner Aspenström, Jan Fridegård and Ivar Lo-Johanson) who in an open letter to Kreml (*Dagens Nyheter* on November 7, 1947) had praised the Soviet Union and the October Revolution. The debate between Abenius and Jan Fridegård, who represented the authors in question, followed in *Dagens Nyheter* on November 11 and November 12 of the same year. See also Erik Peurell, *En författares väg. Jan Fridegård I det litterära fältet* (Hedemora 1998), pp. 137-138. (A writer's trajectory. Jan Fridegård in the literary field.) Swedish text with a summary in English.

her name there. Konstantin Raudive was also encouraged by Abenius to conduct his studies in psychology at Uppsala University and to write. Thus, to some extent, Abenius' way of promoting them both as writers may be seen as cultural transfer, as she was not only an advocate of these foreign literary personalities in Sweden but also encouraged them as Uppsala-based writers to publish abroad. Her engagement with them led to an interest in the situation of the very small Latvian minority in Sweden, on whom she published an essay advocating their and other refugees' right to become legitimate members of Swedish society.[64]

Conclusion

In this paper, I have focused on several aspects of Abenius' career as a critic and a cultural transmitter. My aim was to analyse her career on the basis of some general ideas on the mechanisms of cultural transmission and its agents, as presented by Broomans, Meylaerts and Heilbron and Sapiro. The 'making' of Abenius as a middle-class intellectual, faithful to the academic literary canon, was important to her work of introducing several highbrow foreign writers to Sweden, such as Franz Kafka, Simone Weil and Cora Sandel. However, Abenius also had an impressive ability to oscillate between highbrow and more popular forms, and between different groups of readers. This had very much to do with her academic interest in literary reception and in teaching the tools of literary interpretation.

Devoted mostly to questions of ethics and human existence, as well as to defending human rights during the Second World War and the Cold War, she became an important and widely recognised voice among her readers and listeners, as well as within the field of literary critique. Among female critics debuting during the first half of the twentieth century, she can be seen as second only to the famous 'KJ' (Klara Johanson).[65] Not least, she was acknowledged for her stylistic brilliance, which is hardly surprising for someone who had devoted her postgraduate studies to stylistics. Many of her contemporaries acclaimed her sensitiveness to literary texts and to her

....

64 Margit Abenius, 'Lettiskt. Några intryck' (Latvian. Some impressions), *Bonniers Litterära Magasin* 4 (1948), p. 276-282.
65 Together with Olof Lagercrantz and Gunnar Ekelöf, Abenius is regarded as one of the leading Swedish critics of the 1940s. Teddy Brunius, 'Fyrtiotalets kritik', in: Teddy Brunius, *Ord och övertygelser* (Stockholm, 1955).

'invisible readers'.[66] Her fellow critic Olof Lagercrantz remembered her as 'one of the best literary critics of our century'.[67] Nevertheless, in manuals on literary criticism Abenius remains in the background, often labelled as both 'intuitive' in her method and possessing what are traditionally perceived as female virtues: sensibility, tenderness and care.[68] She is sometimes mentioned as an outsider to the most important literary movements of her time, such as Swedish modernism in the 1930s and 1940s as well as the so-called 'new simplicity' poets of the early 1960s.[69] Her preoccupation with ethical and existential questions, together with her critical attitude towards the left-wing intellectual movement, also contributed to this conception. Also the fact that she never needed to make a living through writing literary critique in the daily press also suggested she belonged to the more elitist areas of literary critique and had a more peripheral role.[70]

However, Abenius' remote position in literary history also seems to follow a certain gender pattern. In her way of proceeding with her career outside the academia as well as in her interest in transmitting foreign literature to a broad audience, she has much in common with many of her female contemporaries who were academically trained. Each of them became established within the literary field in various ways. In manuals on Swedish literature and literary critique, they became an archipelago of forgotten islands, whose work was placed on the margins of literary research and critique.[71]

....

66 See Artur Lundkvist's review of Abenius' *Drabbad av renhet*, 'Karin Boye', *Dagens Nyheter*, December 6, 1950.; Gerda Antti, 'Så skärper den ena människan den andra. Om Margit Abenius "Memoarer från det inre"', *Ord och Bild* 3 (1964), pp. 254-264; Marta Ronne, '"Så skärper den ena människan den andra". Om litteraturkritikern Margit Abenius och hennes många nätverk', in: Eva Heggestad and Karin Johannisson, eds., *En ny sits. Humaniora i förvandling. Vänbok till Margareta Fahlgren* (Uppsala, 2008), pp. 113-128, p. 248.

67 Olof Lagercrantz, 'Margit Abenius död', *Dagens Nyheter*, August 5, 1970.

68 Sven Stolpe, 'Kvinnorna och litteraturen', in: Ellen Liliendahl, ed., *Svensk yrkeskvinna. En översikt av kvinnornas insats i svenskt näringsliv* (Göteborg, 1950), p. 242.

69 Lars Bäckström, Göran Palm and Sonia Åkesson were some of the Swedish 'new-simple' poets. On Abenius' position as an outsider, see Arnell, 'I takt med tiden? När Margit Abenius möter 40-talet – exemplet Lars Ahlin', *Bokcafés Magasin* 21 (s.d.), pp. 29-33.

70 Per Rydén, *Domedagar. Svensk litteraturkritik efter 1880* (Lund, 1987), p. 484.

71 And so were many women critics before them. Susan Sniader Lanser, Evelyn Tornton Beck, '[Why] Are There No Great Women Critics? And What Difference Does It Make?', in: Julia A. Sherman and Evelyn Tornton Beck, eds., *The Prism of Sex. Essays on the Sociology of Knowledge* (Madison, 1979), pp. 79-91.

Walking the Streets of Helsinki

The Flâneur in Early Finnish Prose Literature

Lieven Ameel

In this article I will trace the appearance of the flâneur – and more broadly, the *topos* of the city walker – in Finnish literature at the turn of the twentieth century and how this was modified within Finland's literary context. I will focus on novels set in Helsinki, written by Eino Leino (1878-1926), Juhani Aho (1861-1921) and Arvid Järnefelt (1861-1932) and will provide a concise comparison with a number of Finland-Swedish writers belonging to the so-called *dagdrivare* generation. I will first briefly introduce the theme of the flâneur as the focal figure for the experience of the modern. After a brief outline of Finnish literature at the turn of the twentieth century, I will analyse passages from works by the above-mentioned authors to determine to what extent peripatetic experiences in literature of this period can be seen as reflections of the *Baudelairean* flâneur. It will be seen that the Finnish and Finland-Swedish traditions differ dramatically in their approaches: in Finland-Swedish literature the theme of the flâneur gave rise to a whole school of *dagdrivare* (that is, 'idler') literature, while in early Finnish prose literature the same theme only appears in scattered references and motifs. I will treat the references to the theme of the flâneur in Finnish literature as examples of how literary traditions are culturally transferred to peripheral literatures.[1]

Ever since the groundbreaking work of Baudelaire (1821-1867) and Poe (1809-1849), the flâneur, the lonely, male city walker, has been connected with the modernist experience.[2] The flâneur does not walk through the

....

1 For more on the cultural transfer in peripheral communities, see Reine Meylaerts, 'The study of cultural transfer in the literary fields of small language communities: some preliminary thoughts.' (Ghent, 2010). Accessible at http://www.peripheralautonomy.org/node/35

2 For the connection between the modern and the metropolis, see Peter Brooker, *Modernity and Metropolis* (New York, 2002); for the flâneur as the archetype of the modernist experience, see also Walter Benjamin, *The Writer of Modern Life. Essays on Charles Baudelaire* (Cambridge, 1935, 2006). For an analysis of the flâneur as a pivotal chronotype connected to the modern, see Bart Keunen, *De verbeelding van de grootstad. Stads- en wereldbeelden in het proza van de moderniteit* (Brussel, 2000).

city in a purposeful way, engaged in errands of an urgent nature, but rather
follows his own impulses on the spur of the moment, listening to the
incessant pulse of the city and the city crowd:

> For the perfect idler, for the passionate observer it becomes an
> immense source of enjoyment to establish his dwelling in the
> throng, in the ebb and flow, the bustle, the fleeting and the infinite.
> To be away from home and yet to feel at home anywhere; to see the
> world, to be at the very centre of the world, and yet to be unseen
> of the world (...).[3]

The peripatetic itineraries of the flâneur (from Poe's *The Man in the Crowd*
to Auster's city walkers in Manhattan) can be seen as ways of writing and
reading the city, scribbling one's experiences onto urban space, or tracing
the palimpsests created by one's fellow city dwellers. The flâneur lives by
the grace of the disorienting city spectacle and its urban crowd, which is, in
Benjamin's famous words, the 'veil through which the familiar city beckons
to the flâneur as phantasmagoria'.[4] In Simmel's analysis, the city dweller,
surrounded as he is by accelerating nerve impulses, is unable to react
emotionally to the people around him but is swept along by the crowd.[5]
The flâneur not only acts in public places such as pedestrian promenades –
in Paris, the Arcades, in Helsinki, the pivotal Esplanade – but also in semi-
public spaces provided by cafés and restaurants, where it is possible to be
seen and to observe the city without being a physical part of the street
spectacle. An eagerness or readiness to be seen and to return the gaze of
the crowd is essential to the nature of the flâneur.[6]

The appearance of the flâneur in the city has been seen as a symptom
of a changing world, one veering towards the modern: the flâneur emerges

....

3   Charles Baudelaire, *Selected Writings on Art and Literature* (New York, 1863, 1972),
    pp. 399-400.
4   Benjamin, *The Writer of Modern Life. Essays on Charles Baudelaire*, p. 40.
5   Simmel argues that one feels nowhere as alone or lost as in the city crowd; the city
    does not allow for extreme individualism, but rather exemplifies 'the atrophy of
    subjective culture through the hypertrophy of objective culture' (George Simmel,
    'The Metropolis and Mental Life', in: Richard Sennett, ed., *Classic Essays on the
    Culture of Cities* [Englewood Cliffs, 1903, 1969], p. 59).
6   Walter Benjamin, *Silmä väkijoukossa; Huomioita eräistä motiiveista Baudelairen
    tuotannossa* (Helsinki, 1986, 1939), p.79.

from the cracks between traditional society and the fragmented, ephemeral modern. As such, the flâneur is the paragon of the modernist experience: in Baudelaire's poems, the city walker's urban experience in the midst of the overwhelming modern spectacle *is* the modernist experience.[7] In the essay 'Le Peintre de la vie moderne' (1986 [1863]), Baudelaire defines the aim of this 'solitary mortal' as follows:

> We may rest assured that this man, such as I have described him, this solitary mortal endowed with an active imagination, always roaming the great desert of men, has a nobler aim than that of the pure idler, a more general aim, other than the fleeting pleasure of circumstance. He is looking for that indefinable something we may be allowed to call 'modernity', for want of a better term to express the idea in question. The aim for him is to extract from fashion the poetry that resides in its historical envelope, to distil the eternal from the transitory.[8]

The flâneur is traditionally a male middle or upper-class figure. As such, the modernist urban experience can be seen to ignore experiences on the margins: the faceless masses, women or minority groups. Since the 1980s, the figure of the flâneur has been increasingly criticised for providing a gender-biased, one-sided reading of the experience of modernity, and attention has been drawn to the figure of the female city walker.[9] Although some of these readings have in turn been criticised for reducing the extremely complex levels of meaning pertaining to the flâneur,[10] these

....

7   Lehan argues that there are two urban realities in literary modernism, that of the city as perceived by the artist and that of the city as perceived by the crowd. The feelings and impressions of the artist embody an urban vision, while the city crowd has a distinct character and meaning (Richard Lehan, *The city in literature: an intellectual and cultural history* [Berkeley, 1998], pp. 71-73).

8   Baudelaire, 'Selected Writings', p. 402.

9   See Janet Wolff, 'The Invisible Flâneuse. Women and the Literature of Modernity', *Theory Culture Society* 2(3) (1985), pp. 37-46; Pollock, G., 'Modernity and the Spaces of Femininity', in: Griselda Pollock, *Vision and Difference: Femininity, Feminism and the Histories of Art* (London, 1988), pp. 50-90; Leonore Davidoff, 'Gender and the 'Great Divide'. Public and private in British Gender History', *Journal of Women's History* 15.1 (2003), pp. 11-27.

10 Elizabeth Wilson, 'The Invisible Flâneur', *New Left Review* I/191 (1992), pp. 90-110.

contributions have provided important means to understand the gendered implications of the flâneur's enquiring gaze, and to take into account the marginalised city walkers who roamed the turn-of-the-century city in addition to the Baudelairean flâneur.

To what extent does the city walker appear in Finnish Literature at the turn of the century, and what conclusions can we draw about a possible advent of the modern in Finnish literature of that period? At the end of the nineteenth century, the realism prevalent in Finnish literature gradually became infused with symbolism and decadence.[11] Finnish society and its literature witnessed a period of turmoil, and central to the new modes of literature were the increasingly nationalist feelings of an emerging nation, the social and political changes in society and the influence of contemporary European literary and cultural movements. Many of the leading Finnish writers and artist at the turn of the century had travelled extensively in Western Europe and, at least to some extent, had resided in Paris, Berlin or Rome. They were well-versed in French and German, rather than Russian, and the cultural elite would speak Swedish, still the language of the elite, as a matter of course. At the same time the Finnish cultural elite had come under the spell of the Kalevala (1835/1846), the extremely influential national epic composed by Lönnrot (1802-1884), and Carelianism, the fascination for the mythical cradle of Finnish culture on the Carelian border between Finland and Russia, with its lakes and forests still largely untouched by modern culture. In the Finnish arts, the turn of the twentieth century is considered the Golden Era of Finnish cultural history, producing an exceptional synthesis of Kalevala mythology, Carelianism and modern foreign influences.[12] The period saw an extensive collaboration between different artistic and cultural fields

....

11   For a study of naturalism in Finnish prose in this period, see Rossi, R., *Le naturalisme finlandais. Une conception entropique du quotidien* (Helsinki, 2007); on decadence in Finland, see Pirjo Lyytikäinen, ed., *Dekadenssi vuosisadanvaihteen taiteessa ja kirjallisuudessa* (Helsinki, 1998). Different terms have been used to describe these Finnish authors connected to European symbolism: they have been called neo-romanticists or national symbolists (Jaako Ahokas, *A History of Finnish Literature* [Bloomington, 1973], p. 146; George C. Schoolfield, *A History of Finland's Literature* (Nebraska, 1998), pp. 99-102).

12   This 'Golden Era' did not go unnoticed in Europe. At the 1900 Paris World Fair, Finland was represented separately from the Russian Empire and its exhibition was widely admired.

(including architecture, fine arts, literature and music). A frequently cited example of productive cross-fertilisation is the theme of the Kalevala hero Lemminkäinen, which was taken up at the turn of the century first by Sibelius (1896) in musical composition and subsequently by Gallén-Kallela (1897) in painting and Leino in poetry (1898).

Towards the end of the nineteenth century, Finnish cultural life became increasingly divided along language and party lines, but there were small circles of artists with both Finnish and Finland-Swedish backgrounds: the circle of Elisabet Järnefelt (1893-1929),[13] for example, and most notably the circle centred around Sibelius (1865-1957) and the painter Gallen-Kallela (1865-1931).[14] In these informal networks, cultural influences could be rapidly diffused: work by Maeterlinck, for example, left its mark on playwrights and prose writers (such as Järnefelt) and composers (Sibelius) alike.[15] Literary and artistic circles, as well as informal networks, were instrumental in spreading knowledge about events and cultural innovations abroad, in addition to travel to Europe.[16] Eino Leino, for example, travelled widely in Europe, staying in Rome and Berlin, and he was familiar with all the influential artists and writers in Finland of his time.

The turn of the century in Finland was a period of social and political upheaval: the Russian authorities exercised an oppressive policy towards their Finnish subjects, cracking down on liberal newspapers, exiling their political opponents (including a number of writers) and enforcing strict censorship. Events in the Russian Empire were immediately felt in Finland: the Great Strike in 1905, for example, brought public life in the Finnish cities to a standstill and eventually culminated in a partial triumph for the Finnish people and in the granting of universal suffrage.[17] In 1906 there was

....

13 Elisabet Järnefelt, although raised in St Petersburg, was the mother of some of the most influential figures in the Finnish cultural scene at the turn of the century: the writer Arvid, the painter Eero, the composer Armas, as well as Aino, who married Jean Sibelius. Juhani Aho was one of the writers influenced by her circle.

14 Including Arvid Järnefelt and Eino Leino.

15 The influence of Maeterlinck can be seen in Järnefelt's play *Death* (*Kuolema*, 1903), for example; Sibelius put Maeterlinck's *Pelleas et Melissande* (1892) to music in 1905.

16 Even though Finland has been a member of the European Union since 1995, people still tend to say they are 'travelling to Europe' when they embark for countries across the Baltic and Finnish Gulf.

17 The 1907 elections in Finland were the first elections with universal suffrage and in which women could also be candidates.

a revolt of Russian sailors at the Helsinki fortress of Viapori (present-day Suomenlinna), escalating into armed violence between the Finnish right-wing civil guard and the left-wing Red Guard in the streets of the capital, a foreboding of the bloody civil war of 1918. It is against this backdrop of turmoil that the first urban novels were written and the advent of the city walker in Finnish prose literature should be read.

In the last decades of the nineteenth century, descriptions of Helsinki in literature were still mostly fragmented. In this period, the typical protagonist of the urban novel is a young man moving from the countryside to the capital who encounters considerable difficulties in adjusting to his new environment. He is lured away from his studies or duties by women and wine, with the city appearing as a biblical cesspit of vice.[18] However, the literary city in this period is lived not just by the young male student; his gloomy experiences are shared by a whole class of in-between people, women and men alike, moving towards the capital and up (or down) in society. Helsinki is described in distinctly dysphoric and biblical terms until at least the 1930s.[19] During the first decades of the twentieth century, the urban experience is largely determined by uneasiness and uprootedness, with Helsinki being seen as a mythical Minotaur, annually demanding new blood, exposing people's instincts and fears, and eventually returning them empty to the countryside from which they came. Despite this, the city is also the mirror of great expectations, a place where it is possible to rise to a higher social status and where the poor masses are infused with an awakening identity.

The negative images attached to the city in cultural representations at the turn of the century, combined with the tense atmosphere of political oppression, had their effect on how literary characters experienced

....

18 Typical examples of these Northern European student novels are Strindberg's short stories *Från Fjärdingen och Svartbäcken* (1877), the Finland-Swedish writer Tavaststjerna's novel *Barndomsvänner* (1886) and in Norway Garborg's novel *Bondestudenter* (1883). Culturally and politically, the role of Finnish students differed somewhat from that of students in other Northern European countries (Jyrki Nummi, 'Between time and eternity. K.A. Tavaststjerna's *Barndomsvänner*', in: Pirjo Lyytikäinen, ed., *Changing Scenes; Encounters between European and Finnish Fin de Siècle* [Helsinki, 2003], p. 100).

19 The city as the biblical Sodom and Gomorra can been seen explicitly in the titles of novels dealing with Helsinki, such as Unto Karri's *Sodoma* (1929) and Maila Talvio's *The Children of Nineveh* (*Niniven lapset* [1915]).

Helsinki and the way in which they moved around in urban public space. The insecurity and uneasiness felt by literary characters towards the city informs all their actions: the way they furnish and inhabit their homes, their topics of conversation and the manner in which they walk the city. In its description of the arrival of a young man at the Helsinki railway station, Juhani Aho's *To Helsinki* (*Helsinkiin*, 1889) sets the tone for later portrayals of disturbing, initial urban experiences: the young student Antti leaves his home town Kuopio, in rural central Finland, to take up his studies in the capital. During the journey, Antti ponders his expectations, his high hopes and feelings of excitement, and he dreams up grand plans about his future greatness. However, when he arrives at the railway station, the slow and easy-going rhythm of the story takes on a frenetic pace and Antti's role is reduced to one of complete passivity as he is taken by a group of students by carriage to the Kappeli restaurant, situated on the Esplanade. The story ends with Antti, severely intoxicated, being dragged in the direction of Helsinki's more infamous districts. Throughout the description, movement in the city is completely devoid of personal initiative or knowledge of the urban environment: the protagonist is lost, unable to navigate the city on his own and dependent on others for orientation.

A similar unsophisticated attitude towards walking and moving around in the city can be seen in most Finnish-language novels of the turn of the century. In Leino's short story *A Day in Helsinki* (*Päivä Helsingissä*, 1905) one of the male protagonists is taken for a nightly ride through Helsinki by a girl from a prominent bourgeois family. The girl wants to elope with him, not inspired by love, but by a sense of boredom and longing for adventure. Eventually the couple simply wander through Helsinki in a carriage, but here again, the passivity and uneasiness of the male protagonist in moving through the city is striking. In Leino's *Jaana Rönty*, the female protagonist is seen wandering the streets of Helsinki during the first days of her stay in the capital. Completely lost, her aimless walks display an utter lack of purpose. In these instances, the feeling of being lost in the city is completely different from that of the flâneur who loses himself in the city streets. There is a lack of purposeful desire to plunge into the metropolitan crowd and, on the contrary, an expression of a genuine feeling of not-belonging and alienation.

Generally speaking then, the characters in turn-of-the-century literary Helsinki do not display an eagerness for the creative, Baudelairean surrender to the city crowd or to the exciting spectacle of urban life. Most of the time, literary characters prefer not to walk at all, instead taking a carriage to travel even the smallest distances. Whenever walking the streets of Helsinki acquires a certain air of self-confidence, peripatetic practices are rigidly regulated and stratified. The Esplanade is a case in point: it is the central walking promenade for the Helsinki bourgeoisie, and the literary characters (for example, in Leino's *Olli Suurpää* [1908] and Aho's *Papin Rouva* [1893]) partaking in the daily routine of the walk along the Esplanade are very much aware of the meaning of their movements. However, the Esplanade channels the movements of these characters rather than offering an invitation to real flânerie.[20] Walking the Esplanade was subject to unwritten rules: the Swedish-speaking walkers would walk along one side of the Esplanade (the sunny side of the street), while the Finnish-speaking middle class would walk along the opposite side, both sides occasionally engaging in shouting obscenities at each other. When night fell, the Esplanade became a hotbed of sin, where every woman might be approached freely, as happens with dramatic consequences in Leino's *Jaana Rönty* and Järnefelt's *Reminiscences from my youth* (*Nuoruuteni muistelmia*, 1919).[21]

Walking the streets of Helsinki was subject to a number of unwritten rules based on linguistic, gender-related, social and political frames of reference within urban public space. One of the novels that most vividly describes the difficulties in navigating turn-of-the-century Helsinki is Eino Leino's novel *Jaana Rönty*. In this novel, walking and moving in the city is described as a cumbersome affair: people trying to move freely in the city have stones thrown at them, bayonets pointed at them, their right to walk in the city is challenged, some characters are even shot and killed, and the protagonist, Jaana, is arrested and raped when she is unable to explain by what right she is walking along the Esplanade. The reasons for this shocking event are manifold and open to different interpretations. One interpretation is that Jaana, clearly a country girl unable to read the city codes, is mistaken for a prostitute, and in this sense, the events described in the novel are a direct indictment of a morally corrupt society. At the same time, there is a political metaphorical level of meaning present, since the aggressor is a Russian-speaking police officer, and in this reading, Jaana can be interpreted as a symbol of the Finnish nation, suffering under the Russian yoke. It is clear, in any case, that for the vulnerable lower-class women the

....

20 In a telling passage in *Olli Suurpää*, the dog of the main character proudly asserts that he is one of those dogs walking along the Esplanade at the proper time.

21 Minna Toikka, 'Kadun peli katupeilin takana; Hilja Kahilan *Nuoruuteni muistelmia*', in: Kaisa Kurikka, ed., *Paikkoja ja tiloja suomalaisessa kirjallisuudessa* (Turku, 1998), p. 162.

The Helsinki Esplanade, here seen in 1892. Helsinki's central promenade features frequently in turn-of-the-century Finnish prose as a pivotal space for walking. The Esplanade, however, channeled the movements of literary characters into a rigidly stratified ritual, rather than offering an invitation to real flânerie.

city is even less a space for carefree walking than for the disoriented young men moving to the capital to take up their studies. The restrictions on lower-class women walking the city streets have been studied extensively in connection to Victorian London,[22] and in the case of Finland, too, much attention has recently been given to the dire conditions in which young working-class women found themselves when moving to the capital in the late nineteenth and early twentieth century.[23] In the case of *Jaana Rönty*, the inability to walk the city is taken to extremes: in the gloomy passage at the end of the novel, Jaana is unable to walk independently; completely degraded, she has to be supported by a helpful priest.

....

22 See amongst many others Lynda Nead,, *Victorian Babylon. People, streets and images in nineteenth-century London* (London, 2000); Simon Gunn and Robert J. Morris, eds., *Identities in Space; Contested Terrains in the Western City since 1850* (Ashgate, 2001).

23 See Antti Häkkinen, *Rahasta – vaan ei rakkaudesta. Prostituutio Helsingissä 1867-1939* (Helsinki, 1995); Toikka, 'Kadun peli'; Pirjo Lappalainen, *Koti, kansa ja maailman tahraava lika. Näkökulmia 1880 - ja 1890-luvun kirjallisuuteen* (Helsinki, 2000).

The characters in Leino's novels are not only incapable of the flâneur attitude in their peripatetic exploits: when they appear in public, they are equally unable to cope with the gaze directed at them – something of considerable importance, since the gaze was a crucial characteristic of the flâneur attitude. In a crucial scene in Leino's *Olli Suurpää* (1908), the protagonist, visiting Helsinki's concert hall, is stared at by an odd-looking lady whose gaze takes him aback so much that it leads him to anxious soul-searching. This triggers his eventual loss of mental balance and consequent flight from Helsinki.[24] The whole scene can be analysed as an appearance of the uncanny (as put forth by Freud [1947] and further explored by Kristeva [1988] and Vidler [1992]) and as such it carries some of the seeds of modernism: the experience of *das Unheimliche* can be seen as a symptom of emerging modernism and the anxieties of an insecure middle class at the turn of the century.[25]

A more vigorous and enterprising attitude towards the city is displayed by the characters in Arvid Järnefelt's kaleidoscopic novel *Veneh'ojalaiset*, but in this case, again, the main protagonists set out as strangers to their environment and their frantic excursions through Helsinki are meant to firmly establish themselves (socially, financially and politically) in the city, rather than to create a home in the fleeting and bustling soul of the city crowd. Hannes, one of the main protagonists in *Veneh'ojalaiset*, even explores Helsinki with the idea of literally conquering the capital's strategic locations, since he is planning revolution. To some extent the image of the city resembles those appearing in French realist and naturalist precursors such as Zola's *La Curée* (1871-1872) or Balzac's *Le Père Goriot* (1835), where the city is seen as something to be captured or looted.[26]

In *Veneh'ojalaiset*, as in many other novels of the turn of the twentieth century, the main protagonists are defined by a rootlessness which can be traced back to their family history: the clan of the *Veneh'ojalaiset* is exiled from their homelands. The spatial imagination in Finnish novels during this time centres more on the fantasy of a house of one's own (in *Veneh'ojalaiset*

....

24 There are interesting resemblances between this passage – and others in Leino's oeuvre – and Baudelaire's poetry. The gaze of animal-like, yellow female eyes is one example; another is the black swamp as an image of the frightening subconscious.

25 See Anthony Vidler, *The Architectural Uncanny; Essays in the Modern Unhomely* (Cambridge, Mass, 1992).

26 Lehan, 'The City', p. 62.

and equally in *Olli Suurpää*) than on a search for the ephemeral modern. To some extent, the wanderings of the Parisian flâneurs can also be traced back to a feeling of homelessness or uneasiness connected to the physical home: problems with landlords or the cramped living conditions in small Parisian apartments might have given rise to a need to establish a home in the crowd through city strolls. These feelings of homelessness, then, stem from completely different backgrounds: Baudelaire was living in an era in which the 'verticality' of the paternal home, as expressed by Bachelard, had already become lost in the metropolis, while in Finnish literature at the turn of the century, the feelings connected to the concept of home were still very much informed by the traditional idea of the country home.[27]

The peripatetic exploits in Helsinki at the turn of the twentieth century, then, seem to lack most of the features of the modern as exemplified by Baudelaire and Poe. The reason for this is not that the Finnish writers at this time were not interested in the *topos* of the flâneur, or unable to render him in prose. Descriptions of urban wanderings, bearing clear marks of flânerie, can be found in works such as Juhani Aho's *Alone* (*Yksin*, 1890; see Nummi 2002), Maila Talvio's *Under the Stars* (*Tähtien alla*, 1910) and V.A. Koskenniemi's *A Spring Evening in the Quartier Latin* (*Kevätilta Quartier Latinissä*, 1912; see Pääjärvi 2006). All these works, however, are set in Paris and it seems that Helsinki, as a provincial town, was unable to offer a fitting surrounding for flânerie. Moreover, most of the Finnish-speaking characters in Helsinki novels in this period belong to the lower and lower-middle classes and have a country background, and would thus fit awkwardly with the image of a self-confident urbanite with plenty of time to spare. When taking into account a number of Finland-Swedish novels from around the same period, the attitude to the city and the modes of walking the city, however, have a dramatically different outlook.

The group of Finland-Swedish authors who made their debut between 1907 and 1917 and became known as the *dagdrivare* are the first group of writers who provide extensive and insightful descriptions of Helsinki and in

....

27 Gaston Bachelard, *La Poétique de l'Espace* (Paris, 1967). For the traditional home as proposed by Bachelard, see also Henri Lefebvre, *Critique of everyday life* (London, 1991, 1947), p. 122.

whose novels Helsinki appears in a rich and natural light.[28] The *dagdrivare* (a name derived from the 1914 novel of the same name by Torsten Helsingius [1888–1967]) cannot be seen as one particular school centred around a particular programme, but rather as a loosely connected group of authors in whose novels we often find similar attitudes towards society, art and the city, which are written about in a refined style with sharp psychological analysis. When it comes to political and social questions – all the turmoil of the age which is present so prominently in Finnish-language literature – these writers remain aloof. The Finland-Swedish lack of interest in political and social questions is directly linked to the dramatic changes that Finland witnessed at the turn of the century: the parliamentary reform of 1906, as well as an active programme to 'finnicise' Finland, set in motion during the nineteenth century, which had diminished the political influence of the Finland-Swedish minority.[29] The former elite, sidestepped in this process, turned away from political and social discussions and concentrated instead on artistic and cultural endeavours.[30]

The protagonists in these novels appear as rebels without a cause, observing their surroundings as detached outsiders. Their attitude towards the city appears strikingly modern, compared to their Finnish counterparts. The Finland-Swedish literature of the first decades of the twentieth century had its roots in a European-oriented group of intellectuals centred around the journals *Euterpe* (1901-1905), *Argus* (1908-1911) and *Nya Argus* (1911-present day), which introduced and published literature from France, Denmark and Norway as well as from elsewhere (for example, the works of Baudelaire, Rodenbach, Oscar Wilde and Anatole France).[31] These influences met with considerable response in contemporary Finland-Swedish literature. It was not only the cosmopolitan climate of Finland-Swedish intellectuals which made these writers apt to depict the city in a more modern light. Their very existence as a small linguistic minority

....

28 For a comprehensive study of this literary movement and its relationship to the city, see Arne T. Pedersen, *Urbana Odysséer. Helsingfors, staden och 1910-talets finlandssvenska prosa* (Helsinki, 2007).

29 One example of this 'finnicising' movement was the massive change of surnames from Swedish to Finnish. In 1906, the year of Snellman's centenary anniversary, some 100,000 Finns changed their surnames.

30 Raoul Palmgren, *Kaupunki ja tekniikka Suomen kirjallisuudessa; Kuvauslinjoja ennen ja jälkeen tulenkantajien* (Helsinki, 1989), pp. 59-75.

31 Schoolfield, *A History*, pp. 400-402.

which had dominated the cultural life of Finnish cities for centuries facilitated a modernist attitude towards the city: the sense of being part of the cityscape while simultaneously having a sense of alienation came relatively naturally easily to the Swedish-speaking upper and upper-middle class. The extensive adaptation of the *topos* of the city walker in early twentieth-century Finland-Swedish literature is important not only in relation to urban experiences in contemporary Finnish-language literature, but also sheds some new light on the appearance of the same *topos* in Sweden itself. After all, the flâneur in Swedish literature proper has often been seen as a symptom of a time which was boring and blasé, defined by a lack of political or military turmoil, whereas an extremely turbulent time on the other side of the Bothnian Gulf saw the rise of equally extensive appearances of the city walker in Finland-Swedish literature.[32]

In many respects, the protagonists in Finland-Swedish *dagdrivare* literature resemble the Baudelairean flâneur in their combination of a sense of alienation and a sense of belonging to the city, their characters' eagerness to indulge in aimless wandering, the nature of the environment in which these characters move about (public spaces, theatres, cafés, streets) and in the fact that they explicitly reflect upon their walks in urban space, something which is far more rare in Finnish literature. In the much-quoted poem *The City*, Ture Janson (1913) relates how it feels '(...) to be a stranger in one's own city', to 'become a brisk flâneur' and to 'journey towards the evening's crowd on the promenade'.[33] Nevertheless, these traces of the flâneur in Finland-Swedish literature are linked more to European *fin-de-siècle* decadence and the figure of the dandy than to a search for the fragmented, ephemeral modern, as cultivated by Baudelaire and Benjamin.[34] The protagonists in *dagdrivare* literature generally lack the urge to search for 'that indefinable something we may be allowed to call "modernity"' or to 'distil the eternal from the transitory', as Baudelaire put it. For the *dagdrivare*, the flâneur attitude was not an ideal – to be a

....

32 See Alf Kjellén, *Flanören och hans storstadsvärld: synpunkter på ett litterärt motiv* (Stockholm, 1985), pp. 246-262.

33 See Torsten Petterson, 'Det svårgripbara levet: Ett förbisett tema I dagdrivarlitteraturen', in: Sven Linnér, ed., *Från Dagdrivare till Feminister. Studier I finlandssvensk 1900-talslitteratur* (Helsinki, 1986), p. 15; Schoolfield, *A History*, p. 434.

34 For an analysis of the *dagdrivare* as a dandy, see Päivi Molarius, 'Suomenruotsalaisen dagdrivare-kirjallisuuden dandy ja modernin subjektin itsehahmotus', in: Lyytikäinen, ed., *Dekadenssi vuosisadanvaihteen taiteessa ja kirjallisuudessa*, pp. 156-182.

dagdrivare was more like a curse. The ideal life was usually to be found somewhere else than on the asphalt of the Esplanade, and attaining that ideal life was made impossible for fairly prosaic reasons, such as disease or lack of money.[35]

It is clear that in Finnish literature at the turn of the century two very different ways of adapting the *topos* of the city walker can be discerned, reflecting the social, political, linguistic and cultural background of two literary fields within the same country. In the Finland-Swedish *dagdrivare* prose of this period, the city is the self-evident background of activities distinctly connected with urban life. Social and political trouble is rarely present, with protagonists indulging in a life of aimless wandering through the cityscape, dreaming of a better life and making acute observations about the urban landscape they encounter. In this literature, reflections on the conditions of modern life become central elements. In contemporary Finnish-language prose, in contrast, the literary characters are still in the process of taking their first, uncertain steps in the city. They feel oppressed by a sense of insecurity and alienation and often lack the necessary knowledge of the unwritten social codes regulating public space. In most novels written in Finnish, urban space, however tempting and promising, is still very much an environment able to alienate and lead to the degeneration of its inhabitants; a space in which the political and social upheavals of a troubled time play a prominent, often disconcerting role.

Here, the way thematics from international literary movements are adapted by peripheral national literary traditions proves to be dependent on a number of highly complex factors[36]. Amongst these, most prominent – in the case of the flâneur – are the position of given writers within the surrounding cultural framework (peripheral Finland-Swedish writers as opposed to authors writing in Finnish, and as opposed to authors in Sweden), the social and political conditions of the time (a relative lack of political or military upheaval in Sweden, compared to extremely troubling events in Finland, with additional implications for a progressively marginalised Finland-Swedish elite) and the attraction of particular cultural movements. In the case of the *dagdrivare*, authors were spurred on by the example set by contemporary and late-nineteenth-century

....

35 See Petterson, 'Det svårgripbara levet'.
36 Cf. the remarks on multilingualism within small language communities in Meylaerts, 'The study'.

Swedish authors who were giving shape to the city walker in Stockholm, while a detached, alienated feeling, in combination with an interest in all things modern and urban, came easily to this new generation of Finland-Swedish authors, given their background as a fading, but distinctly urbanite minority. For authors writing in Finnish, to a certain degree the flâneur remained nothing more than a superficial attitude adopted by literary characters when they visited Paris, but this was lost again when these same protagonists returned to Helsinki. The Finnish capital was mostly seen as a small and peripheral capital, torn apart by party strife, in which movement was stifled by foreign oppression, and in which the urban experiences of Finnish-speaking characters were determined by a paralysing sense of outsideness, alienation and anxiety.

One Nation – Two Literatures?

From Finnish to Swedish: Some Themes in the Translation of Finnish Literature into Swedish, 1900-1950

Anders Nilsson

The history of the translation of Finnish literature into Swedish is a complex question encompassing historical, political, economic and cultural factors. It is important to know that Sweden and Finland were one country from the Middle Ages until 1809, when Finland became a part of the Russian Empire. During this period, Swedish was used in most official contexts and most of the literature produced in Finland was written in Swedish. In fact, Finnish-language literature was very unusual before the romantic nationalist revival at the beginning of the nineteenth century and the first publication of the *Kalevala* epics by Elias Lönnrot in 1835-1836.[1]

Encouraged by the works of Lönnrot and the ideas of the nationalistic Hegelian philosopher Johan Vilhelm Snellman (1806-1881), transmitted through his newspaper *Saima*, many young people began to write and discuss literature written in Finnish. However, as literature was still being written in Swedish, a new situation developed, of a 'national literature' written in two languages. Despite the stiff competition posed by Finnish during the second half of the nineteenth century, many authors and critics in Finland still read in Swedish. However, as the extent of Finnish literature grew, an interest in translations from Finnish to Swedish developed.

In discussing this issue, I refer to Gisèle Sapiro's paper, 'The global market of symbolic goods: literary books in translations', which notes four different aspects of this question of translation, under four titles or constraints: 1. the international circulation of cultural goods, 2. the construction of a global book-market, 3. the agents of intermediation:

----

1 Kari Tarkiainen, *Sveriges Österland: Från forntid till Gustav Vasa* (Helsingfors, 2008). See especially 'Tavastland became Swedish', pp. 92-101. See also 'Forskningens syn på svenskarnas ankomst', pp. 49-63 and 'Korstågen', pp. 64-105; Henrik Meinander, *Finlands historia* (Helsingfors, 2006), pp. 17-21; Kai Laitinen, *Finlands litteratur* (Helsingfors, 1988), pp. 15-21, 36-42, 68-74 and 80-85.

individuals and institutions, and 4. the dynamics of reception.[2] While aware of the importance of all these aspects, in this study I will focus on the third factor, which can of course not be separated from the increasing circulation of cultural goods and the beginnings of a more global book-market during the late-nineteenth and early twentieth century. While I will not discuss these questions here, I will use a sociological framework, and begin by embedding my investigation in a short historical account of the Finnish-Swedish situation.

Historical Background

By the end of the nineteenth century, Finland had become a part of the modern world. All the important towns were connected by rail, and the trains rolled between the cities of Helsinki and St. Petersburg as never before. Steamboat connections to cities such as Stockholm, Tallinn and Stettin were firmly established, and under the protection of the tariff wall imposed by the Russian Empire Finnish industry was expanding. From Viborg in the east to Kemi in the north, large quantities of timber and paper were being shipped all over the world. The centre of this transformation to a modern nation was the Finnish capital, Helsinki.[3]

Succeeding Turku as the 'capital' of Finland in 1812, Helsinki was still quite small compared to other European capitals. However, by the turn of the century Helsinki had over 100,000 inhabitants and the surroundings small villages were developing into suburbs.[4] In the university, the senate, the parliament and in the major companies, Swedish was still an important language. However, as most of the newcomers to the city used Finnish as their native language, this situation was changing.[5]

Supported by Snellman's idea that a country could only have one language that expressed its soul and history (which for Snellman was Finnish), a large group of influential Finns – having either Swedish or Finnish as their native language – had adopted Finnish names and become supporters of the Finnish language. This was the case for both the more

....

2   Gisèle Sapiro, 'The global market of symbolic goods: literary books in translation', http://www.peripheralautonomy.org/.

3   Meinander, *Finlands historia 3*, pp. 250-256.

4   *Finlands svenska litteraturhistoria II*, pp. 42, 47-48. See also David Kirby, *Östersjöländernas historia 1772-1993*, (Stockholm, 1996), pp. 208-209.

5   Meinander, *Finlands historia 3*, 1996, pp. 296-300.

moderate 'fennomans' and the more radical 'young fennomans'.[6] By the end of the nineteenth century, Finnish had become equal in importance to Swedish as the language of culture – and Finnish-language newspapers, periodicals and publishing houses soon outstripped those using Swedish. All this was encouraged to some extent by the Russian rulers, who were happy to weaken the connection between Finland and Sweden; however, the advance of the Finnish language was mainly a logical consequence of the increased economic and political power of Finnish-speakers.[7]

Outside the biggest and most important towns in south and west Finland, Swedish was already marginalised and in large parts of the country its role as the language of culture and administration was soon just a memory. At the same time, the Finland-Swedish population (Finns with Swedish as their native language) still held a disproportionately strong position in society as a result of the historical context in 1809. However, by the end of the nineteenth century the situation was quite different – and groups of both older and younger people began to support the idea that Finnish should become the most important – or even the only – language in the country.

During the nineteenth century, the two 'Finland-Swedish' writers [8] Johan Ludvig Runeberg (1804-1877) and Zacharias Topelius (1818-1898) were certainly regarded as writers for the whole nation. However, when Topelius and Karl August Tavaststjerna (1806-1898), two widely read and appreciated authors, died in the same year, the gap between Swedish and Finnish literature in Finland became obvious.[9] It was clear that the

....

6   A fennoman is an eager supporter of the Finnish language – especially in the nineteenth and at the beginning of the twentieth century. In the autonomous Grand Duchy of Finland during the mid-nineteenth century, J.V. Snellman developed a political programme with the intention of getting the Finnish-speaking majority involved in public life. The fennomans strove to make cultural life and the ruling classes more Finnish and less Swedish. Nationalencyklopedin, http://www.ne.se/lang/fennomaner, (2010-06-15).

7   Rainer Knapas, 'Finsk eller svensk nationallitteratur i Finland – Litteraturhistoriens frontlinjer på 1850- och 1860-talen', in: Dahl, P. and Steinfeld, T. eds., *Videnskab og National opdragelse: Studier i Nordisk Litteraturhistorieskrivning 1*, (København, 2001), p. 21; Meinander, *Finlands historia*, pp. 123-124; and *Finlands svenska litteraturhistoria II*, p. 13 and pp. 386-389

8   The concept 'Finland-Swedish' was not used at the time, therefore it is problematic to say that Runeberg and Topelius were Finland-Swedish.

9   Yrjö Varpio, 'Det nationella i den finskspråkiga litteraturhistorieskrivningen 1858-1949', in: Dahl, P. and Steinfeld, T. eds., *Videnskab og National opdragelse: Studier i Nordisk Litteraturhistorieskrivning 1*, (København, 2001), pp. 83, 92-93.

Finns were in a large majority and that the Finland-Swedish were a small minority (about 12.5 percent).[10] In an interesting article, the Finnish critic and professor of literature Kai Laitinen wrote:

The idea of a separate Swedish literature in Finland was noticeable around the turn of the century and rapidly became stronger. This was observed by the young (Finnish writer and critic) Eino Leino (1878-1926), who in an article from 1899 about Arvid Mörne's and Nino Runeberg's poem asked himself why these poems 'reflect so little that is typical for this country and this people' and wondered which feelings these poets 'feel and celebrate in song'.[11]

Leino's article also provides an answer:

By no means the feelings of our land and our people, but instead the feelings of Scandinavia, Norway and Denmark, and perhaps also Helsinki which is a part of Scandinavia. If someone were to investigate how far removed from each other Swedish and Finnish culture in our country have already become, these texts offer a good opportunity. While we find roots in Kalevala and Karelia, they turn to Iceland and the Edda. According to them, the Finnish people start with the first crusade, for us it ends there to reawaken only during this century (the twentieth). According to them, our national spirit's deepest expression is Runeberg and *Fänrik Ståls sägner* (The legends of second lieutenant Stål), in our opinion it is Alexis Kivi and *Sju Bröder* (Seven brothers).[12] [author's translation]

In his Finnish literary history, Eino Leino also regards 'Finland-Swedish' literary history as more Swedish than Finnish. Rafael Koskimies comes to a similar conclusion when he writes that Finland-Swedish literature after Topelius and Tavaststjerna isolated itself from the 'Finnish national way of looking at the world' and therefore cannot be the literature of the Finnish nation.[13]
Swedish literature in Finland soon developed themes that directly illustrated the relationships that the Finland-Swedish minority had to their own history, as well as to both Finnish and the standard Swedish culture and literature. Their poetry tried to move away from 'Saarijärvis

---

10 Meinander, *Finlands historia 4*, pp. 80-86.
11 Kai Laitinen, 'Över språkgränsen', in: *Finlands svenska litteraturhistoria II*, pp. 386-397.
12 *Finlands svenska litteraturhistoria II*, p. 389.
13 Varpio, 'Det nationella', pp. 93.

moar' and the Finnish interior, which Runeberg had used in his attempt to develop a Swedish literature.[14] Instead, the coasts and the archipelagos of Finland – with its Finland-Swedish farming districts and pine-covered cliffs – became the most important landscape for poets such as K. A. Tavaststjerna, Mikael Lybeck and Arvid Mörne.[15] Similarly, the works of prose writers such as Runar Schildt, Torsten Helsingius and Ture Janson abandoned the historical, cultural and geographical world of Topelius. They concentrated instead on the rapid changes in society and, inspired by French and Scandinavian impressionists such as Guy de Maupassant, Herman Bang and Hjalmar Söderberg, life in the towns – especially in Helsinki – became the most important topic for the new generation of Finland-Swedish prose writers at the beginning of the twentieth century. While these 'idlers' often had their roots in the countryside or in a small town, they had come to Helsinki as young students and a common theme was about leaving an increasingly Finnish countryside and moving to an increasingly Finnish Helsinki. There they would have to compete with the new and sophisticated Finnish elite.

Without an appropriate socio-scientific model to aid their analysis, these writers often came to understand and describe their situation from a biological, Darwinist or psychological perspective,[16] which provided them with many possibilities: they could use Nordic or pan-Germanic mythology

....

14 In contrast to many other 'Finland-Swedish' poets – who used the coast, the archipelago and the coastal towns as themes for their poetry – a great deal of Runeberg's poetry has motifs from the very Finnish Saarijärvi region in central Finland. He wrote about ordinary Finnish peasants in a way that made his poetry very popular among Finnish-speaking readers and critics. One of the most famous poems is the 'Idyll and epigram no. 25', which starts: 'Högt bland Saarijärvis moar bodde/ Bonden Paavo på ett frostigt hemman (...).' (High up among the heath of Saarijärvi/ Paavo the peasant had a frosty homestead (...). [author's translation]). See also Johan Wrede, *Världen enligt Runeberg*, (Helsingfors, 2005), for example, pp. 77-78 in the chapter 'Saarijärvi – naturens röst'. The Finnish author Väinö Linnas (1920-1992) also wrote a famous novel entitled *Täällä Pohjantähden alla*, which in its Swedish translation received the Runeberg-inspired title *Högt bland Saarijärvis moar*.

15 In a brief essay, entitled 'I martallsskogen', Clas Zilliacus discusses different trees and landscape types as symbols – while the inland fir forest was found to be typically Finnish, the coastal dwarf pine is – or was – typically Finland-Swedish, *Finlands svenska litteraturhistoria II*, pp. 37-38.

16 In his essay 'Dagdrivare och Runar Schildt', Massimo Ciaravolo presents this new orientation in Finland-Swedish prose, *Finlands svenska litteraturhistoria II*, pp. 47-54.

and fight against Finnish nationalism (as did Bertel Gripenberg (1878-1947)); they could try to create a small space for Swedish culture in Finland by creating parallel institutions and maintaining the coastal culture, where Swedish was still an important language (as did Arvid Mörne (1876-1946)); or they could style themselves as the last of their kind with the task of reflecting on and describing their old and rich history, and their own more or less embarrassing flaws (as did 'the idlers' and Runar Schildt (1888-1925)).[17]

Of course the atmosphere surrounding Finnish culture and literature was different. The inferiority complex towards the Swedish-speaking inhabitants was now forgotten and with Lönnrot's *Kalevala* there was a rich and deep Finnish literary tradition that could compare favourably with Nordic Viking and medieval literature. After Alexis Kivi's (1834-1872) pioneering oeuvre – with *Seitsemän veljestä* (Seven Brothers) as its crowning glory – it was obvious that modern novels could also be written in the Finnish language.[18] Finnish culture was obviously a winner.

Due to the public success of Finnish literature at the turn of the century and the fact that the Finnish cultural sphere had achieved a strong position, Finnish writers, critics and periodicals could disregard the work of their Swedish-speaking compatriots. For the Finland-Swedes the situation was quite different, and one could respond in various ways. However, if one did not choose to move to Sweden, as did Ture Janson (1886-1954), Finnish language, culture and literature were likely to become extremely influential. On the basis of personal relationships, economic necessity or a genuine interest in the Finnish language, many Finland-Swedish writers became increasingly interested in Finnish literature and culture.

Kai Laitinen suggests that the cultural relationship just before the turn of the century developed its own gravity. Some of the older leading personalities in the literary world such as Werner Söderhjelm (1859-1931), Olaf Homén (1879-1949), Gunnar Castrén (1878-1959) and Yrjö Hirn (1870-1952) particularly served as bridge-builders. Söderhjelm was an early translator of the Finnish author Juhani Aho into Swedish, and he wrote

....

17 *Finlands svenska litteraturhistoria II*, pp. 37-38, 72-76.
18 Alexis Kivi's comic drama *Nummisuutarit* (in Swedish *Sockenskomakarna* and in English *Parish Shoemaker*) from 1864 and his novel *Seitsemän veljestä* are still landmarks in the history of Finnish literature. Ilmari Havu describes *Parish Shoemaker* as Finland's most important contribution to world literature in his *Finlands litteratur 1900-1950*, p. 9. Kai Laitinen describes *Seven Brothers* as an innovative and original novel – and as the first classic piece of Finnish art prose, *Finlands litteratur*, pp. 106-108.

articles about new Finnish literature for Swedish periodicals.[19] He also wrote essays and books about Linnankoski, Kivi and Frans Eemil Sillanpää for a Scandinavian public.[20]

In his speech to the Finnish Society of Science on Werner Söderhjelm in 1934, Gunnar Castrén described him as one of the very few people in Finnish cultural life who had a strong impact on both Swedish and Finnish-language literature in Finland.[21] However, despite being regarded as an important mediator of Finnish literature and culture, the young fennoman circles would not accept Söderhjelm as one of their own.[22] Castrén, amongst others, also wrote an interesting study in Swedish on the oeuvre of Finnish author Juhani Aho (1861-1921) in 1922. This was published by Holger Schildt's publishing house in Finland and by the prestigious Albert Bonnier's publishing house in Sweden, and is an early example of Finnish-Swedish cultural and literary exchange.[23] In the case of Yrjö Hirn, despite all the distrust between the Finnish and Finland-Swedish writers, his broad web of contacts allowed him to succeed in forming a common PEN club for all writers in Finland. It is typical that both Castrén and Hirn were born into families that had an early interest in Finnish culture and literature and spent a lot of time with native Finnish-speakers.[24]

As Sapiro states, as individuals, these writers were all agents of intermediation, but even if the situation in the 'nation' of Finland was quite unique from the late nineteenth century until the mid twentieth century, the cultural exchange between Finnish and Swedish literature was 'organized by means of institutions and individual actors'.[25] The most important institutions involved in the Finnish and Swedish literary exchange during the period, and before the Nordic council's introduction of different forms of subsidising literature and translations, were the independent publishing houses. The translators were dependent on the publishing houses, while the publishing houses were dependent on the liberalised book market.

....

19 Henning Söderhjelm, *Werner Söderhjelm* (Helsingfors, 1960), p. 94.

20 Gunnar Castrén, *Humanister och humaniora* (Helsingfors, 1958), p. 24.

21 *Ibidem*, p. 26.

22 Söderhjelm, *Werner Söderhjelm*, pp. 121, 146.

23 Gunnar Castrén, *Juhani Aho 1* (Helsingfors, 1922) and *Juhani Aho 2* (Helsingfors, 1922).

24 *Finlands svenska litteraturhistoria II*, pp. 390-391. See also Gunnar Castrén, '"Yrjö Hirn", Minnestal i Finska vetenskaps-Societeten 1953', in: Castrén, *Humanister och Humaniora*, pp. 44-46.

25 Gisèle Sapiro, 'The global market of symbolic goods: literary books in translation', http://www.peripheralautonomy.org/.

However, the book market was of course influenced by the political, cultural, economic and historical situation in both Finland and Sweden, as well as the relationship between these nations.[26] Taking a step back, we can see that along with Castrén and Homén, Söderhjelm and Hirn were a part of the Snellman-inspired Finnish national romantic group of Finland-Swedish academics which formed in the last decades of the nineteenth century. They spoke, read and even wrote in Finnish, and they considered it obvious to follow Finnish literature. However, in opposition to the early Finland-Swedish fennomans, they argued for a bilingual Finnish nation and were concerned about the situation of Swedish-speaking literature in Finland. In his biography of his father, Werner Söderhjelm, Henning Söderhjelm wrote:

Even if Söderhjelm realised that his belief in national unity was utopian, he would not stop working towards this ideal. Finland having its own intellectual and cultural life was, he considered, only possible if the two language elements were united in a higher community.[27]

Finnish literature in Swedish translation 1900-1950
The numbers of books published in Finnish and the market for Finnish literature was quite small at the turn of the century compared to Sweden –

....

26 Gisèle Sapiro, 'The global market of symbolic goods: literary books in translation', http://www.peripheralautonomy.org/, p. 5.
27 Henning Söderhjelm, 1960, p. 163 [author's translation]. The Swedish original is: 'Om Söderhjelm sålunda kunde se det utopiska i sin tro på den nationella enheten ville han dock inte upphöra att arbeta med detta ideal för ögonen. Möjligheterna för Finland att andligen leva ett eget liv fanns, ansåg han, endast om de två språkelementen gick upp i en högre gemenskap.' In a long and interesting letter to George Brandes in 1909, Werner Söderhjelm wrote: 'I begin to understand that the dream that I and some others have had about assembling this people under one banner (...) will not ever come true. The gap between Finns and the Swedes is becoming bigger and bigger – they have different world-views, different traditions, different temperaments, which do not seem to match each other. And then the ground is prepared for those who understand how to use all this'. [author's translation]. 'Jag börjar förresten att tro, att den dröm som jag och några andra hysa om att man kunde samla detta folk under en fana (...) icke någonsin kommer att förverkligas. Klyftan mellan de finske och de svenske blir allt större – det äro olika världsåskådningar, olika traditioner, olika temperament, vilka icke tyckas kunna gå ihop. Och så är marken beredd för dem som förstå att begagna sig av allt detta.', p. 163.

or to Finland some decades later. Starting with Laitinen's *Finlands litteratur*, a standard work on Finnish literature in Sweden, I have examined how many titles by the authors of prose fiction mentioned there were translated into Swedish, and when and by whom. Using the Royal Library (Kungliga Biblioteket or KB) in Stockholm and the Libris catalogue, I have examined 40 authors mentioned by Laitinen and found 110 titles translated into Swedish by 33 translators during the period 1900-1950. It is possible of course that some important writers and titles have been omitted or forgotten, either by Laitinen, the library or the catalogue. However, as I wanted to be able to examine some of the books in person, this was the best method for my investigation.[28] To group the translated titles I use a simple division of years and decades, so the variations in the levels of translation from Finnish into Swedish will be explicit. However, many of the translators and translated authors are represented in more than one decade.

1900-1920

Between 1900 and 1917-1918, the years of independence and civil war, 26 titles of 'high literature' were translated from Finnish into Swedish. Most prominent in the first decade are four titles by Arvid Järnefeldt – by an unknown translator. Between 1910 and 1917 there are works by prominent authors such as Juhani Aho (translated by Ellen Snellman and Holger Nohrström), Eino Leino (translated by Bertel Gripenberg) and the nationalistic poet V.A. Koskenniemi (translated by Holger Nohrström). After a delay of some decades most of Alexis Kivi's work could be read in Swedish, from the drama *Natt och dag* (Night and day) from 1915 to *Sockenskomakarna* (Parish Shoemaker) from 1917, all translated by the painter Per Åke Lauréns. It is also interesting that Runar Schildt, one of the most important Finland-Swedish authors at the time, and Hagar Olsson, one of the most famous rising modernistic authors and critics, both translated novels by Maila Talvio in 1914 and 1915. This is the only translation from Finnish to Swedish by Runar Schildt that I have found, but Hagar Olsson subsequently translated many books from Finnish.

---

28 In this work I investigate novels and collections of short stories and poetry in more refined literary circulation. Popular fiction, nonfiction and some poetry were published, translated and mediated in other channels. On the exchange between Finnish and Swedish poetry, see Kai Laitinen's essay, 'Över språkgränsen' in *Finlands svenska litteraturhistoria II*, pp. 386-397. See also my contribution, 'Finsk-svensk lyriktrafik från tidig modernism till idag', in: Hadle Oftedal Andersen, Per Erik Ljung and Eva-Britta Ståhl, eds., *Nordisk lyrikktrafikk*, 2009, pp. 35-59.

Hagar Olsson, probably 1920s

After the bridge-builders mentioned above, a division developed between the two countries, strengthened by Finland's independence in 1917, the civil war of 1917-18 and the political, cultural and linguistic polarisation occurring during the 1920s and 1930s. It is often assumed that during this period very little work by Finland-Swedish writers was translated into Finnish, but it does not follow that the connection between the two groups of writers had broken down. Many Finland-Swedish and some Finnish writers had a good command of the other language and some critics read and commented on literature and theatre written in the other language. However, for a large group of people who were less skilled in languages this was a period of significant isolation from the other language. This was of course most noticeable in the Swedish-speaking minority, which in 1900 was 12.9 percent of the population and decreasing a little each decade; however, it was also tangible to those Finns who wished Finland to be oriented towards Sweden and the Scandinavian democracies rather than the increasingly authoritarian nations in Central and Eastern Europe.

The translation and publication of Finnish literature continued during and just after the civil war. I have found 11 translated titles of high literature completed in the very short period between 1918 and 1920. These include Alexis Kivi's very famous *Sju bröder* (Seven Brothers) by Per Åke Laurén and Juhani Aho's *Järnvägen* (The railroad), translated by Hagar Olsson. Olsson also translated one title by Onerva in 1918, two titles by Linnakoski in 1919 and one by Aho in 1920. In addition, she translated the first novel by the later Nobel Prize winner Frans Eemil Sillanpää (1888-1964) into Swedish in 1920. This period as translator from Finnish also coincides with her breakthrough as an international critic and author. Another important translator during the first decades of the twentieth century, and beyond, is the Finland-Swedish editor, critic, librarian and writer of detective stories Holger Nohrström (1855-1939). He translated a work by Aho in 1906, continued with one by Linnakoski in 1913, Aino Kallas in 1915, another from Aho in 1916, and one each by Konrad Lehtimäki and the highly thought of professor and poet Veikko Antero Koskenniemi in 1917.[29]

1921-1930

I have found 21 different works of high literature translated from Finnish into Swedish during the period 1921 to 1930. Translators such as Laurén, Gripenberg and Olsson continued with works by Kivi, Aho and Sillanpää. The most prolific is Bertel Gripenberg, with seven titles, starting with Linnakoski's famous *Sången om den eldröda blomman* (The song about the fire-reed flower) in 1921 and finishing the decade with Arvid Järnefelt's novel *Mina föräldrars roman* (My parents' novel) in 1929. The young Finland-Swedish critic, poet and painter Ragnar Ekelund (1892-1960) was also quite active as a translator during the period. He had translated a novel by Larin-Kyösti in 1916, but it was only in the 1920s that he became one of the most important translators, with titles by F.E. Sillanpää, Pentti Haanpää and

....

29 *Finlands svenska litteraturhistoria II*, pp. 104-105, 117, 164, 176.

Unto Seppänen. Seppänen's *Flyktingskolan* (The school of refugees) from 1930 also had a preface by the famous Swedish critic, poet and member of the Swedish Academy, Anders Österling. This is an example of the high ambitions of the Swedish presentation. The preface is quite short – less than two pages – but quite interesting. Österling is not very familiar with Finnish literature and suggests that the main reason for publishing this 'short novel' seems to be the Karelian milieu and the contrast between the Finnish people and the young nation of Finland, and the Russian refugees who had fled the Soviet-Russian ruin. Österling writes:

> The story is in every breath inspired by an authentic Finnish national feeling. It truthfully reflects the way the Finnish country population in the border area apprehend their neighbours; necessarily hard, cold and vigilant. Especially in this, the book is of a certain interest to a Swedish public.[30] [author's translation]

This way of characterising Finnish literature – and probably other literature from small languages areas – seems to be quite common during the period. In her paper, 'Bilden av finnen i svensk litteraturreception på 1930-talet', Pirjo Vaitinen points to key expressions such as 'Det tysta och sega folket' (The silent and the tough people), 'Naturbarn' (Child of nature), 'En finsk arbetare' (A Finnish worker) and 'Finsk kvinnomystik' (Finnish female-mystique).[31] Eva Herner's dissertation *Svenska recensenter läser finska böcker: En studie i receptionen av finsk prosa, översatt på 1960-talet* is also of interest in this regard – even if the object of investigation is outside my frame of reference. The chapter 'Attityder till "det finska"' (Attitudes to 'the Finnish') also mentions key expressions which are similar to those referred to by Vaitinen. These expressions could also be relevant to a wider

....

30 (Berättelsen är i varje andedrag inspirerad av den äktfinska nationalkänslan. Den avspeglar troget, på vad sätt den finska lantbefolkningen i gränstrakterna uppfattar sina grannar, nödvändigtvis hårt, kyligt och vaksamt. Icke minst häri har denna bok sitt givna intresse för svensk publik.) Unto Seppänen, *Flyktingskolan* 1930, preface by Anders Österling, pp. 3-4.

31 Pirjo Vaitinen, 'Bilden av finnen I svensk litteraturreception på 1930-talet', in: Raoul Granqvist, ed., *Texten och läsaren i ett historiskt perspektiv: Föredrag vid nordiskt symposium i idé- och litteraturreception 1984*, (Umeå, 1985), pp. 97-106.

discussion of the critics of and the newspaper articles about the literature.[32] There are also two translations by Lisbeth Hagfors, in 1923, of novels by the more folkloric or ethnographic authors Maila Talvio and Väinö Kataja. However, these are the only translations by Hagfors in my material and she is not mentioned in the *Finlands svenska Litteraturhistoria II*. Among other interesting titles, the Finland-Swedish playwright Hjalmar Dahl also translated a book by Sillanpää in 1923, Nino Runeberg translated a cantata by V.A. Koskenniemi and Inga Enander translated the breakthrough novel by young Mika Waltari (1908-1979), *Den stora illusionen* (Grand illusions) in 1930.

Even if it is often reported that the two literatures became isolated during the 1920s and 1930s, there were writers and critics such as Hagar Olsson (1893-1978) and Lauri Viljanen (1900-1984) who attempted to make the language barrier less definitive. Olsson's work as a critic and introducer of international literature is well known in Sweden, but her texts about and translations of Finnish literature during these decades are less known. Certainly she became a central figure through her close contact with the famous Finnish critic and writer Olavi Paavolainen (1903-1964), who would soon become a leading member of the Finnish Tulenkantajat group (Torch carrier).[33]

Olsson started her work as an intermediary some years before the first publication of the modernistic periodical *Ultra* in 1922, which published Finnish and Swedish avant-garde writers and critics together in equal numbers. It was here that Edith Södergran (1892-1923) became well known among Finnish poets, and Elmer Diktonius (1896-1961) started his activity as an intermediary between Finnish and Swedish. Unfortunately, *Ultra* proved economically – and perhaps politically – an impossible task. Instead,

....

32 Eva Herners, *Svenska recensenter läser finska böcker: En studie i receptionen av finsk prosa, översatt på 1960-talet*, dissertation (Stockholm, 1999), pp. 231-246.

33 Olsson was an important critic, translator and novelist – her novels inspired both Olavi Paavolainen and Mika Waltari, *Finlands svenska litteraturhistoria II*, p. 105. About Olsson's background in the Finnish Karelia and multicultural Viborg, see Olof Enckell, *Den unga Hagar Olsson* (Helsingfors, 1949), for example 'En svenska I förskingringen', pp. 14-20. In a letter about the situation for the Swedish minority in Viborg and Karelia – where some Swedish-speaking families had adopted the Finnish language and culture – she wrote: 'Jag tycker att jag då ej skulle hava någon rätt att leva. Såsom svensksinnad är jag visserligen blott en kvarleva, men såsom fennoman är jag en abnormitet' (I think that I then should have no right to live. As Swedish-minded I am surely a remnant, but as a Fennoman I am just an abnormality) [author's translation], p. 16.

modern literature in Finland was soon divided into two new periodicals, the Finnish *Tulenkantajat* and the Finland-Swedish *Quosego* (1928-29). The latter, which had economic support from the conservative Söderström publishing house in Helsinki, was primarily an arena for the second wave of Finland-Swedish modernist poets, with Rabbe Enckell (1903-1974), Gunnar Björling (1887-1960) and Henry Parland (1908-1930) being prominent figures. Certainly there are also some texts by Olsson and Diktonius, and in Olof Enckell's (1900-1990) history of *Quosego* he mentions that both were important in the founding of the periodical.[34] However, both Olsson and Diktonius seem to have rejected the more purely aesthetic direction which lacked interest in spiritual and political revolution. It is significant that Olsson contributed the essay, 'Finlandssvensk robinsonad'– which discusses the problematic situation of the isolated Finland-Swedish culture – and that Diktonius contributes an interpretation of a poem by the great Finnish symbolist poet Eino Leino. Diktonius also translated a selection of Eino Leino's work into Swedish in 1931. In addition to this work, the bilingual Diktonius is only represented by two translations from Finnish into Swedish: Katri Vala's *Vår sång* (Our Song) from 1943 and the highlight, a new translation of Kivi's *Sju bröder* (Seven brothers) in 1948.[35] Even if Diktonius did not translate very many titles, he was an important

....

34 In the prologue, 'Vägen till Quosego', to the new edition of *Quosego* in 1971, Olof Enckell wrote: 'Det är också hos dessa två, Hagar Olsson och Diktonius, man finner de tidigaste förebuden till en ny publikation, som efter Edith Södergrans död på midsommardagen 1923 ville föra vidare arvet efter den stora föregångerskan'. (It is also in the work by Hagar Olsson and Diktonius that you find the first suggestion of a new publication which, following the death of Edith Södergran on midsummer's day in 1923, tried to pass on the heritage of their great precursor), p. vi. On the next page Enckell continues: 'Både Hagar Olsson och Diktonius var med i det lidelsefulla och av entusiasm präglade förspel under senhösten 1927 och vintern 1928, som slutligen resulterade i att Quosegos första nummer förelåg i tryck i slutet av man 1928' (Both Hagar Olsson and Diktonius were in a passionate and enthusiastic prelude during the late autumn of 1927 and the winter of 1928), p. vii.

35 In his biography *Diktonius – ett liv* (Helsingfors, 2007) Jörn Donner writes: 'Diktonius var tvåspråkig, han medarbetade i ett stort antal tidningar, på finska och svenska'. See the chapter 'En ny finsk diktare?', where Donner discusses Diktonius as a bilingual or Finnish poet, pp. 325-332. On Diktonius's background in a bilingual, working-class milieu in Helsinki, see also pp. 38-63. Hagar Olsson also had a bilingual background and as both a critic and novelist she was interested in Finnish literature, culture and society, *Finlands svenska litteraturhistoria II*, pp. 104-106.

mediator between Swedish and Finnish literature and culture. He wrote letters to Swedish authors and critics, articles in Swedish newspapers and periodicals, and he mentioned Finnish authors such as Eino Leino, Alexis Kivi, Volter Kilpi and F.E. Sillanpää in articles and poems.[36]

1931-1940

In the period from 1931 until 1940 – a nationalistic decade dominated by the undemocratic right-wing Lappo movement and a political and military confrontation with the Soviet Union – there were 20 different titles of high literature translated from Finnish into Swedish. Numerically superior here is the 1939 Nobel Prize winner F.E. Sillanpää, who had five works translated by Ragnar Ekelund (3) and Henning Söderhjelm (2). Werner Söderhjelm's son, the author and critic Henning Söderhjelm (1888-1967), had an early orientation towards Finnish culture and literature. Later in life, in 1935, he published a book with the Swedish publishing house Natur och Kultur in Stockholm, entitled *Finsk och svenskt i Finland: En orienteering i språk- och nationalitetsfrågorna* (Finnish and Swedish in Finland: an orientation towards the language and nationality problem). He was a critic in the daily newspaper, *Göteborgs handels - och Sjöfarts-Tidning*, in Gothenburg and became an important bridge-builder between Finland and Sweden, as well as between Finnish and Swedish literature, after he moved to Gothenburg and became a Swedish citizen in 1932. However, even if the interest in Finnish literature and authors in Sweden was increasing during the 1930s it was limited in comparison to literature from many other countries, and when Söderhjelm published his book *Författarprofiler* with Bonnier's publishing house in 1938, just one of his twenty portraits

....

36 In one of his many letters to his friend, the Swedish author Eyvind Johnson, Diktonius sometimes mentions Finnish literature and his work as a translator. For example, his unfinished translation of a text by Volter Kilpi in *Och så vill jag prata med dig: Brevväxlingen mellan Eyvind Johnson och Elmer Diktonius*, 1997. Jörn Donner summed up Diktonius's role as a mediator of Finnish and Swedish in his biography: 'Vad Diktonius beträffar, gjorde han kanske inte alls sin största finska insats som översättare, utan som propagandist för finsk litteratur, i synnerhet Sillanpää, i Sverige'. (Diktonius perhaps did most not as a translator of Finnish literature, but as a propagandist for Finnish literature, especially the work of Sillanpää, in Sweden). In Donner, *Diktonius*, pp. 331. See also letters to the Finnish author Frans Eemil Sillanpää and to the editor-in-chief of the Swedish newspaper *Göteborgs-Posten*, Harry Hjörne, in Jörn Donner and Marit Lindquist, eds., *Brev. Elmer Diktonius* (Helsingfors, 1995), pp. 263, 282-283.

was about a Finnish writer, this being the popular and 'Swedish-friendly' author F.E. Sillanpää and his novel *Silja*. Sillanpää was very popular and almost his entire oeuvre was translated into Swedish after 1920, with some of his novels being published in many editions. After Sillanpää received the Noble Prize in 1939, Söderhjelm also wrote a small book on him for Bonnier's, which was published in 1940.[37]

Other writers who had two or more books translated included the Tulenkantajat group member Olavi Paavolainen, who had three essayistic works translated: one by the critic, author and later professor Olof Enckell, one by Gripenberg, and the remarkable work, *Gäst i tredje riket* (Guest of the Third Reich) from 1937, for which no translator is mentioned. Olof Enckell also translated two works by Iris Uurto and became one of the important translators and mediators between Finnish and Swedish literature during the decade. His interest in culture and literature from Karelia was especially important.[38] Helvi Hämäläinen is also represented, with two translations by Ragna Ljungdell.

1941-1950

During the next decade we can see that the translations from Finnish to Swedish were affected as the political and military situation in Finland became more vulnerable. There were 31 literary works translated into Swedish during the period – an increase of about 40 percent. One reason for this peak could be the awarding of the Noble Prize to a Finnish author in 1939. Even though only two more new titles by Sillanpää were translated after 1940, there were many new editions – especially of *Silja*, the novel translated by Ragnar Eklund in 1931. The Nobel Prize and the

---

37 Henning Söderhjelm, *Författareprofiler* (Stockholm, 1938), pp. 265-272. Kai Laitinen emphasises Sillanpää's Nordic orientation and writes: 'Praktiskt taget hela Sillanpääs produktion gavs efter 1920 ut på svenska. Till Sillanpääs popularitet bland svenska läsare bidrog hans liberala inställning i språkfrågan och hans ibland nästan demonstrativt framlyfta nordiska orientering. Allt detta bidrog till att han fick Nobelpriset i litteratur den skickelsedigra hösten 1939'. (Almost all of the titles by Sillanpää were published in Swedish after 1920. Sillanpää was popular among Swedish readers for reasons such as his liberal attitude towards the language conflict and his sometimes almost demonstratively Nordic orientation. All this contributed to the fact that he received the Noble Prize for literature in the fateful autumn of 1939), *Finlands svenska litteraturhistoria II*, p. 392.

38 Laitinen, *Finlands litteratur*, pp. 272-274; *Finlands svenska litteraturhistoria II*, pp. 127, 136-137.

political situation in Europe and the Nordic countries drew Finland closer to Sweden, and many of the larger publishing houses in Sweden were interested in translating Finnish writers.

However, the decade can be split into two shorter periods: the first five years encompassing the war to 1944, and the following five years encompassing the difficult post-war period from 1945-1950. There are some differences in the publications during the first (16 titles) and second periods 1945-1950 (19 titles). During the war there were, for example, titles translated by F.E. Sillanpää and Paavolainen, as well as three titles by the poet Elina Vaara, all translated by the Finland-Swedish working-class writer Anna Bondestam. Three titles by Toivo Pekkanen were also translated between 1942 and 1946, by Kajsa Krook, R. R. Eklund and Heidi Parland, and titles by Mika Waltari from 1947 to 1950, translated by the Finland-Swedish author and translator Ole Torvalds, the author Lorenz von Numers and Heidi Enckell.[39] In addition, Elvi Sinervo, Viljo Kajava and Arvi Järventaus are also represented, with each having two works translated during the post-war period. The socialist writer Elvi Sinervo can be found in translations by Ragna Ljungdell and Anna Bondestam, while the left-wing poet Kajava appears in a collection that involved many translators. Järventaus, who wrote historical novels and about the province of Lapland, appears in two translations by Valdemar Lindholm.

Typical of the time, and probably translated for the Scandinavian book market, was the anthology *Thirty Short Stories* from 1943, selected by Elmer Diktonius and Lauri Viljanen. After 1945, the three historical novels by Mika Waltari were more typical. Waltari, together with Olof Enckell, was also the editor of the prose anthology *Finska berättare* (Finnish storytellers) from 1946, in which the first Swedish translation of work by Volter Kilpi (by Elmer Diktonius) appeared – the short story, 'Vandraren på isen' (The wanderer on the ice). Another translator, Ragna Ljungdell, was also the editor of the poetry anthology *Modern finsk lyrik* from 1947.

Conclusion

As we have seen, the Finland-Swedish population continued to read, comment on and translate a great deal of Finnish literature during the 'cold years' from 1920 to 1950. There are of course many reasons for this: the

....

39 Heidi Enckell and Heidi Parland are the same person – and Parland is the correct name at the time.

necessity for a minority to keep in touch with the culture of the majority, a tradition of curiosity in Finnish culture,[40] and also, of course, the need for introductions and translations of Finnish literature for the market in Sweden. This mediation between Finland and Sweden also provided translators with the opportunity to earn some money and establish contact with the Swedish publishing houses. However, these possibilities remained limited, and most of the translations seem to be the result of a mixture of personal contacts, interest and the need to earn a living.[41]

Some of the well-known Finland-Swedish writers I have mentioned above, such as Hagar Olsson and Elmer Diktonius, translated novels and poetry from Finnish to Swedish. The bilingual Diktonius also translated from Swedish to Finnish. However, as we will see in the appendix below, there were also many other less famous writers and translators, and some of them were both more active and sometimes more careful in their work. In my examination of 40 different Finnish authors and more than one hundred different titles between 1900 and 1950, I found some interesting results. Among these 40 writers, 26 had one or more books translated into Swedish during the period. The others were not translated into Swedish, or were only translated after 1950. This is especially apparent for some female writers and writers with working or farming backgrounds. Of the 110 different titles I have located by writers who were regarded as producers of 'high literature' or literature regarded as historically important, it is clear that very few were translated and those who were only had some of their works translated. Among these titles I have found 33 different translators (with some unknown). A number of these translator's names occur quite often, with most of them translating a number of books, often by one or two authors.

....

40 Many of the fennomans in the nineteenth century – such as J. V. Snellman and Yrjö Koskinen – had Swedish as their mother tongue and, as well as their political and philosophical ideas, they had an interest in Finnish language and literature. Finland-Swedish writers such as Werner Söderhjelm, Yrjö Hirn and Olof Enckell, and modernists such as Hagar Olsson and Elmer Diktonius, were also interested in Finnish culture and literature. They translated, wrote articles and attempted to introduce and discuss Finnish literature in Swedish, *Finlands svenska litteraturhistoria II*, pp. 387-391.

41 It is necessary to investigate the translators' situations and the contacts between translators and publishing houses during the period. For example, was translation from Finnish to Swedish badly paid work for Diktonius, even after his breakthrough as a poet?

It is clear that Bertel Gripenberg was a very busy translator, with thirteen titles from nine different writers. It is a little surprising that this Swedish nationalistic and pan-Germanic poet actually translated so much Finnish literature. Probably this was partly due to economic reality, but an important fact seems to be that after the civil war Gripenberg made the issue of race and language secondary to that of class and political opinion. The civil war had shown him, along with many of the other bourgeois or right-wing writers and translators, that the Finnish-speaking bourgeoisie had reacted against the working class with the same seriousness and passion as their Finland-Swedish counterparts.[42] Gripenberg translated a range of different works, from Maria Jotuni's *Kärlek* (Love) in 1908 and Eino Leino's *Den unga kvinnan* (The young woman) in 1911, to Joel Lehtonen's *Ödemarkens barn* (The children of the wilderness) in 1935 and Aino Kallas's *Vargbruden* (The bride of the wolf) in 1936, and finally Juhani Aho's *Fiskelycka* (Luck at fishing) in 1948, published a year after his death. In addition, he was one of many translators of F. E. Sillanpää, translating two titles.

The appendices also reveal one exceptional 'one-writer-translator', who became the Swedish voice of that author. This is Per-Åke Laurén, who translated five titles by Alexis Kivi and who was the 'Kivi translator' until Diktonius's translation of *Sju bröder* (*Seven Brothers*) in 1948. Hjalmar Dahl and Henning Söderhjelm are to a lesser extent one-writer-translators, with their two translations each of titles by F. E. Sillanpää. To translate the well-known Sillanpää was probably a good idea economically, but also strategically as the books received a great deal of attention in Sweden and, after Sillanpää received the Noble Prize in late 1939 also in other parts of the world. However, there is nothing to indicate that translating from Finnish to Swedish – even if we include Sillanpää's novels – during the period was particularly economically attractive for the translators. Ragnar Ekelund (1892-1960) was the most prolific Sillanpää translator, with five titles, from *Änglarnas skyddslingar* (The protégés of the angels) in 1926, to the international breakthrough with *Silja: berättelsen om ett gammalt*

....

42 '1918 fann Gripenberg slutligen sin egen identitet och en grupp att identifiera sig med – inbördeskrigets vita segrare. Kriget befriade honom plötsligt från alla privata bekymmer (...). Till och med språkgränsen och de sociala skillnaderna jämnades ut på den nya samhörighetskänslans väg.' (In 1918 Gripenberg at last found his own identity and a group to identify himself with – the white victors of the civil war. The war suddenly released him from all his private problems (...). Even the language border and social differences were levelled out by the new feelings of affinity), Laitinen, *Finlands litteratur*, p. 160.

släktträds sista gröna skott (Silja: the story about an old family tree's last green sprout) in 1931 and *Färden till kvarnbäcken och andra historier* (The journey to the mill brook and other stories) in 1936. Ekelund started his career as a translator with Larin-Kyösti's *Askepilt och prinsessan* (Askepilt and the princess) in 1916.

By the beginning of the 1950s a new opening was more than apparent and new key figures began to take the places of those from the civil war or the Second World War periods. The Finnish publishing house WSOY's first yearbook from 1946, *Suomen kirjallisuuden vuosikirja* (*Yearbook for Finnish literature*), had already started an extensive presentation of Finnish literature, which included the Finland-Swedish literature of the year. In an article from 1947 the editor and writer Aaro Hellakoski started a discussion of the relationship between Finnish and Swedish literature. He also discussed the need for Finnish literature to acknowledge the different perspective provided by the nation's Swedish literature, as well as to recognise the important work done by the Finland-Swedes in introducing, translating and spreading Finnish literature into Sweden, Scandinavia and the rest of the world. This Finnish opening was also responded to by several Finland-Swedish critics and writers – and around 1950 there was renewed interest in Finnish-language literature among some younger Finland-Swedish intellectuals and writers. Examples are Jörn Donner, Bo Carpelan, Nils-Börje Storbom and – last but not least – the writer, critic and translator Thomas Warburton, who is probably the most important bridge-builder between Swedish and Finnish literature. However, that is another story.[43]

As we can see from Appendix 2 many people were translating from Finnish to Swedish during the period. Many translated just a few titles and most seem to have had other professions or sources of income. Sapiro writes: 'Performing an activity that was still weakly differentiated at the start of the twentieth century, the translator was often himself a writer, a commentator, a teacher and/or a critic'. Gripenberg and Ragnar Ekelund, as well as Anna Bondestam and R. R. Eklund, were all well-known authors of the time, while Olof Enckell, Hagar Olsson, Elmer Diktonius and Henning Söderhjelm were translators as well as writers and critics. Per Åke Laurén was a painter, Holger Nohrström was a well-known librarian and Valfrid Vasenius a professor of Nordic literature. What Sapiro calls 'a process of specialization' had not yet begun in this field of cultural exchange.[44]

....

43 *Finlands svenska litteraturhistoria II*, pp. 393-395.
44 Sapiro, 'The global market', p. 6.

Appendix 1

1900-1910

J.H. Erkko, *Fosterländsk hustafla* (1900), translation by Valfrid Vasenius.
Santeri Ivalo, *Biskop Thomas. Historisk berättelse* (1902), translation unknown.
Arvid Järnefelt, *Jordens barn* (1905), unknown translator.
Arvid Järnefelt, *Lifvets hav: Berättelser* (1905), unknown translator.
Arvid Järnefelt, *Helena* (1906), unknown translator.
Juhani Aho, *Vårdagar och frostnätter* (1906), translation by Holger Nohrström.
Arvid Järnefelt, *Jorden tillhör alla* (1908), unknown translator.
Maria Jotuni, *Kärlek* (1908), translation by Bertel Gripenberg.
Larin-Kyösti, pseudonym of Karl Gustaf Larson, *Dikter* (1908), translation by Gunnar Castrén, Dagmar Forstén, Bertel Gripenberg, Rafael Lindqvist, Wilhelm Lundström, Arvid Mörne and Jacob Tegengren.

1911-1920

Onerva, *Brytningslinier* (1910), translation by Bertel Gripenberg.
Eino Leino, *Den unga kvinnan* (1911), translation by Bertel Gripenberg.
Larin-Kyösti, pseudonym of Karl Gustaf Larson, *Ad astra: en hattmålares dröm i sex tablåer* (1911), translation by Holger Nohrström.
Juhani Aho, *Johan* (1911), translation by Ellen Snellman.
Juhani Aho, *Hafvet i lugn* (1912), translation by Ellen Snellman.
Johannes Linnankoski, *Flyktingarna. En bonderoman* (1913), translation by Holger Nohrström.
Maila Talvio, *Kärlek* (1914), translation by Runar Schildt.
Maila Talvio, *Nineves barn* (1915), translation by Hagar Olsson.
Aino Kallas, *De farande skeppens stad* (1915), translation by Holger Nohrström.
Alexis Kivi, *Natt och dag: Skådespel i en akt* (1915), translation by Per Åke Laurén.
Alexis Kivi, *Förlofningen: lustspel i en akt* (1916), translation by Per Åke Laurén.
Juhani Aho, *Fredseremiten* (1916), translation by Holger Nohrström.
Larin-Kyösti, pseudonym of Karl Gustaf Larson, *Askepilt och prinsessan* (1916), translation by Ragnar Ekelund.
Larin-Kyösti, pseudonym of Karl Gustaf Larson, *Sanning och sägen: berättelser och sagor* (1916), translation by Sven Karlén.

Konrad Lehtimäki, *Ex inferno: Roman. Bemynd* (1917), translation by Holger Nohrström.

Alexis Kivi, *Sockenskomakarna* (1917), translation by Per Åke Laurén.

V.A. Koskenniemi, *Konsul Brenners indiansommar* (1917), translation by Holger Nohrström.

Onerva, *Jungfru Marias Gåva* (1918), translation by Hagar Olsson.

Lauri Pohjanpää, *Ainos och Lisas sommarsysslor* (1918), translation by M. Nyberg.

Johannes Linnankoski, *Simson och Delila* (1919), translation by Hagar Olsson.

Johannes Linnankoski, *Jeftas dotter: poem i en akt* (1919), translation by Hagar Olsson.

Alexis Kivi, *Sju bröder* (1919), translation by Per Åke Laurén.

Juhani Aho, *Järnvägen* (1920), translation by Hagar Olsson.

Aino Kallas, *Bortom havet* (1920), translation by Ragnar Ekelund.

F.E. Sillanpää, *Det fromma eländet: ett avslutat finsk livsöde* (1920), translation by Hagar Olsson.

Maria Jotuni, *Vardagsliv* (1920), translator unknown.

Aukusti Oravala, *Ödemarkens profet; en historisk och biografisk roman från den finska pietismens gryninstid* (1920), translation by Agda Nordström.

Juho Koskimaa, *På dekadens: Historien om en svag man* (1920), translation by Erik Björkbro.

1921-1930

Maila Talvio, *Tranorna* (1921), translation by Hagar Olsson.

Johannes Linnankoski, *Kampen om Heikkilä gård och andra noveller* (1921), translation by Holger Nohrström.

Johannes Linnankoski, *Sången om den eldröda blomman* (1921), translation by Bertel Gripenberg.

Juhani Aho, *Minns du?* (1921), translation by Bertel Gripenberg.

Juhani Aho, *Småfisk och storfisk* (1922), translation by Bertel Gripenberg.

Juhani Aho, *Spånor: förra samlingen* (1923), translation by Hagar Olsson.

F.E. Sillanpää, *Två människobarn* (1923), translation by Hjalmar Dahl.

F.E. Sillanpää, *Hiltu och Ragnar: en berättelse om två människobarn* (1923), translation by Hjalmar Dahl.

Maila Talvio, *Kyrkklockan* (1923), translation by Lisbeth Hagfors.

Väinö Kataja, *Forsfararens brud* (1923), translation Lisbeth Hagfors.

Alexis Kivi, *Dikter i urval* (1923), translation by Per Åke Laurén.

Aino Kallas, *Barbara von Tisenhusen* (1924), translation by Bertel Gripenberg.

F.E. Sillanpää, *Nära jorden: anspråkslösa berättelser* (1924), translation by Bertel Gripenberg.

F.E. Sillanpää, *Änglarnas skyddslingar* (1925), translation by Ragnar Ekelund.

F.E. Sillanpää, *Livet och solen* (1926), translation by Bertel Gripenberg.

Pentti Haanpää, *Hemfolk och strykare* (1927), translation by Ragnar Ekelund.

F.E. Sillanpää, *Människobarn på livets stråt* (1928), translation by Ragnar Ekelund.

Arvid Järnefelt, *Mina föräldrars roman* (1929), translation by Bertel Gripenberg.

V.A. Koskenniemi, *Åbo lilja: Kantat vid Åbo stads 700-års jubileum* (1929), translation by Nino Runeberg.

Unto Seppänen, *Flyktingskolan* (1930), translation by Ragnar Ekelund, foreword by Anders Österling.

Mika Waltari, *Den stora illusionen* (1930), translation by Inga Enander.

Sju finska novellister (1930), translation by Sven W. Karlén.

1931-1940

Arvid Järnefelt, *Greta och hennes herre* (1931), translation by Ragnar Ekelund.

Eino Leino, *Lyriskt urval* (1931), translation by Elmer Diktonius.

F.E. Sillanpää, *Silja: Berättelsen om ett gammalt släktträds sista gröna skott* (1931), translation by Ragnar Ekelund.

F.E. Sillanpää, *Mot uppenbarelsen och andra noveller* (1932), translation by Ragnar Ekelund.

F.E. Sillanpää, *En mans väg: om förhållandena på Ahrola gård sedan Paavo blivit dess husbonde* (1933), translation by Henning Söderhjelm.

F.E. Sillanpää, *Människor i sommarnatten: episk svit* (1935), translation by Henning Söderhjelm.

Joel Lehtonen, *Ödemarkens barn* (1935), translation by Bertel Gripenberg.

F.E. Sillanpää, *Färden till Kvarnbäcken och andra historier* (1936), translation by Ragnar Ekelund.

Aino Kallas, *Vargbruden* (1936), translation by Bertel Gripenberg.

Iris Uurto, *Farväl Maria* (1936), translation by Olof Enckell.

Iris Uurto, *Den tappra kärleken* (1937), translation by Olof Enckell.

Olavi Paavolainen, *Som gäst i tredje riket* (1937), unknown translator.

Toivo Pekkanen, *I fabrikens skugga* (1938), translation by Ragnar Ekelund, foreword by Anders Österling.

Olavi Paavolainen, *Flykten till en ny värld* (1938), translation by Olof Enckell.

Olavi Paavolainen, *Korset och hakkorset: inför en ny världsbild* (1939), translation by Bertel Gripenberg.

Tatu Vaaskivi, *Tatu: Kungagunstlingen Gustaf Mauritz Armfelt* (1939), translation by Brita Hiort af Ornäs.

Helvi Hämäläinen, *Vattnet i rännstenen* (1939), translation by Ragna Ljungdell.

Arvi Järventaus, *Kyrkoeldaren* (1939), translation by Valdemar Lindholm.

Helvi Hämäläinen, *Byn brinner* (1940), translation by Ragna Ljungdell.

Unto Seppänen, *Markku och hans släkt* (1940), translation by Karl Ekman and Olof Enckell.

1941-1950

Olavi Paavolainen, *Karelen landet som var* (1941), translation by Nils-Gustav Hahl.

Uuno Kailas, *Rökskuggan: efterlämnande noveller* (1941), translation by Thomas Warburton.

F.E. Sillanpää, *Skördmånad* (1942), translation by R.R. Eklund.

Toivo Pekkanen, *Åren som gått* (1942), translation by Kajsa Krook.

Maila Mikkola, pseud. Maila Talvio, *Muntra fruarna på Sveaborg* (1942), translation by Anna Bondestam.

Katri Vala, *Vår sång* (1943), translation by Elmer Diktonius.

V.A. Koskenniemi, *Lyckans håvor: Blad ur min levnads bok* (1943), translation by Einar Spjut.

Toivo Pekkanen, *Den svåra vägen* (1943), translation by R.R. Eklund.

Iris Uurto, pseudonym of Lyyli Ester Mielonen, *Kroppens visdom* (1943), translation by Thomas Warburton.

Finland berättar: Trettio noveller (1943) – selection by Elmer Diktonius and Lauri Viljanen.

Elina Vaara, *Tornsvalan: En samling sagor* (1944), translation by Anna Bondestam.

Elina Vaara, *Slottsjungfrun och dvärgen* (1944), translation by Anna Bondestam.

Elina Vaara, *Konungen och drottningen* (1944), translation by Anna Bondestam.

Helvi Hämäläinen, *Förpliktelse* (1944), translation by Ragna Ljungdell-Erlandsson.

Elvi Sinervo, *Smeden i Palava by* (1945), translation by Ragna Ljungdell-Erlandsson.

Oiva Paloheimo, *Orolig barndom* (1945), translation by Ragnar Eklund.

K. Wilkuna, *Med tanke, svärd och plog* (1945), translation by Einar Spjut.

Pentti Haanpää, *De vandrande stövlarna* (1945), translation by Ole Torvalds.

F.E. Sillanpää, *Människolivets ljuvlighet och elände* (1946), translation by Hjalmar Dahl.

Ilmari Kianto, *Det röda strecket* (1946), translation by Olof Enckell.

Toivo Pekkanen, *Mörknande horisont* (1946), translation by Heidi Parland.

Arvi Järventaus, *Himlasnickaren* (1946), translation by Valdemar Lindholm.

Olavi Paavolainen, *Finland i moll: dagboksblad 1941-44* (1947), unknown translator.

Elvi Sinervo, *William Bortbyting: berättelsen om en gosse, som ville bli lik Danko* (1947), translation by Anna Bondestam.

Irja Salla, *Sömngångerskan* (1947), translation by Per Jansson.

Mika Waltari, *Sinuhe, egyptiern: femton böcker ur den egyptiske läkaren Sinuhes liv omkr. 1390-1335 f.kr* (1947), translation by Ole Torvalds.

Alexis Kivi, *Sju bröder* (1948), translation by Elmer Diktonius.

Juhani Aho, *Fiskelycka* (1948), translation by Bertel Gripenberg.

Arvi Järventaus, *Malmkungen: en lapplandsroman* (1948), translation by Valdemar Lindholm.

Viljo Kajava, *Till havets fåglar* (1948), translator unknown.

Mika Waltari, *Mikael Ludenfot: hans ungdom öden och äventyr ...* (1949), translation by Lorenz von Numers.

Viljo Kajava, *Någon stans* (1949), translator unknown.

Mika Waltari, *Vem mördade fru Kroll?* (1950), translation by Heidi Enckell.

Appendix 2

List of translators, number of titles and number of writers they translated from the chosen group during the period.

Translators	Number of titles	Number of writers translated
Bertel Gripenberg	13	9
Ragnar Ekelund	10	6
Holger Nohrström	7	5
Hagar Olsson	8	4
Per Åke Laurén	5	1
Anna Bondestam	5	3
Olof Enckell (one with Karl Ekman)	4	3
Ragna Ljungdell (Ljungdell-Erlandsson)	4	2
Elmer Diktonius	3	3
Hjalmar Dahl	3	1
Sven Karlén	2	2
Lisbeth Hagfors	2	2
Valdemar Lindholm	2	2
Heidi Enckell (née Parland)	2	2
Ellen Snellman	2	1
Einar Spjut	2	2
Henning Söderhjelm	2	1
Ole Torvalds	2	2
R.R. Eklund	2	2
N.G. Hahl	1	1
Inga Enander	1	1
Lorenz von Numers	1	1
Nino Runeberg	1	1
M. Nyberg	1	1
Runar Schildt	1	1
Thomas Warburton	1	1
Valfrid Vasenius	1	1
Erik Björkbro	1	1
Agda Nordström	1	1
Brita Hiort af Ornäs	1	1
Kajsa Krook	1	1
Per Jansson	1	1
Unknown	8	5

About the authors

Lieven Ameel has an MA in English and Dutch Literature and Linguistics (Ghent University) and an MA in Finnish Language and Culture (Helsinki University). He is currently working on a PhD in Finnish Literature and Comparative Literature at Helsinki University and Justus Liebig University, Giessen, Germany. The subject of his research is experiencing and imagining the city in Finnish literature in the early twentieth century. In addition to conducting research, he also works as a translator, translating novels, children's books and poetry from Finnish into Dutch.

Petra Broomans is Associate Professor of Scandinavian Linguistics and Literatures at the University of Groningen. She is the coordinator of the project 'Scandinavian Literature in Europe around 1900: the Influence of Language Politics, Gender and Aesthetics' (2004-2010) and is currently working on a new project, 'Cultural Transmission and Minor Language Areas'. One of the related projects she is working on is the 'Bibliography of Swedish and Swedish-Finnish literature in Dutch translation (1491-2007)'. She is also editor-in-chief of the series Studies on Cultural Transfer and Transmission (CTaT). Board member of the International Association for Scandinavian Studies (IASS). For further information please visit her website: www.petrabroomans.net.

Ester Jiresch has an MA in History and Scandinavian Studies and has studied in Vienna and Stockholm. She is currently conducting PhD research at the Groningen Research School for the Study of the Humanities (GRSSH) at the University of Groningen, on 'The role of networks in the work of female cultural transmitters of Scandinavian literature and culture in Europe around 1900. A comparative study of the Dutch/Flemish and the Austrian/German-speaking regions'. She has published several articles and a monograph, *Die Österreichisch-schwedische Gesellschaft. Ihre Geschichte, ideologische Hintergründe und kulturelle Konstruktion* (=Wechselbeziehungen Österreich – Norden, Vol. 6, eds. Matthias Langheiter-Tutschek and Sven Hakon Rossel) (Vienna, 2004: Edition Praesens).

Janke Klok has studied at the universities of Amsterdam, Groningen and Oslo. She is a lecturer in Scandinavian Literature and Linguistics at the University of Groningen, where she is currently completing her PhD on 'The

literary representation of the city by the Norwegian authors Amalie Skram
(1846-1905), Sigrid Undset (1882-1949), Cora Sandel (1880-1974) and Ebba
Haslund (1917-2009). She has published several articles on Scandinavian
literature in the fields of literary transfer and gender studies in *Tijdschrijft
voor Skandinavistiek* (2001), *Sekse en de city* (2002), *From Darwin to Weil.
Women as Transmitters of Ideas* (2009) and *Feminist Review. Urban Spaces*
(2010), amongst others. She has translated novels and poetry by classic
and contemporary Norwegian authors, is one of the editors of the series
'Wilde aardbeien' (2003-) and co-author of the biography *'Mijn vak werd
mijn leven'. Amy van Marken (1912-1995)'* (2010).

Anders Nilsson works as an external lecturer in Swedish at Roskilde
University Center and South Danish University in Odense and is a
postgraduate student at the Department of Comparative Literature at the
University of Lund, investigating the relationship between the Finland-
Swedish modernist Gunnar Björling and the city of Helsinki. He has
published articles about Finland-Swedish modernists such as Elmer
Diktonius and Örnulf Tigerstedt, and about the role of sport in Finnish
nation-building, based on Kjell Westö's novel *Drakarna över Helsingfors.*

Marta Ronne has a PhD in Comparative Literature from Uppsala University,
Uppsala, Sweden. Her doctoral thesis was on gender and Swedish university
novels published between 1903-1943. She has published several articles
on university novels, the sociology of culture and gender and literary
critique in Sweden and is currently working on a professional biography of
Margit Abenius (1899-1970), one of the most prominent Swedish literary
critics of the twentieth century. Ronne is also attached to the Centre for
Gender Research at Uppsala University and she works as a literary critic
for Swedish newspapers. She is a key figure in Uppsala in relation to the
project 'Peripheral autonomy? Longitudinal analyses of cultural transfer
in the literary fields of small language communities', which is run in
cooperation with the universities of Ghent and Groningen.

Roald van Elswijk specialised in Scandinavian studies and Early
Germanic at the University of Groningen and is currently working on a
PhD dissertation on the Dutch and Frisian reception of five Nordic authors
who all played a significant role in the contemporary language-politics
debate. He has published several articles on Scandinavian literature and
also works as a freelance translator from Norwegian and Icelandic. He also
really loves chocolate.

Bibliography

Abenius, M., 'Den osynlige läsaren', i: Abenius, M., *Kontakter* (Stockholm, 1944), pp. 9-25.

Abenius, M., 'Lettiskt. Några intryck', *Bonniers Litterära Magasin* 4 (1948), pp. 276-282.

Abenius, M., *Memoarer från det inre* (Stockholm, 1963).

Aho, J., *Helsinkiin* (Helsinki, 1889, 1997).

Aho, J., *Yksin* (Helsinki, 1890, 2003).

Ahokas, J., *A History of Finnish Literature* (Bloomington, 1973).

Andersen, H. C., *Mit livs eventyr* (Copenhagen, 1855).

Antti, G., 'Så skärper den ena människan den andra. Om Margit Abenius "Memoarer från det inre"', *Ord och Bild* 3 (1964), pp. 254-264.

Arnell, A., 'I takt med tiden? När Margit Abenius möter 40-talet – exemplet Lars Ahlin', *Bokcaféts Magasin* 21 (s.d.), pp. 29-33.

Arnell, A., 'Margit Abenius som Karin Boyes biograf', in: *Karin Boyes liv och diktning IV* (Huddinge, 1988), pp. 13-22.

Bachelard, G., *La Poétique de l'Espace* (Paris, 1967).

Baudelaire, C., *Selected Writings on Art and Literature* (New York, 1863, 1972).

Belpaire, M.E., ed., *Wonderland: Vertellingen*, Vol. 1-6 (Ghent, 1894-1896).

Belpaire, M.E., 'Het landleven in de letterkunde: VIII – Noorwegen', *Dietsche Warande en Belfort* (1902/3).

Belpaire, M.E., *Het landleven in de letterkunde XIXe eeuw* (Antwerp/ Ghent, 1902).

Belpaire, M.E.,'Johannes Joergensen volgens eigen getuigenis', *Dietsche Warande en Belfort* (1919/1), pp. 103-134.

Benjamin, W., *Silmä väkijoukossa; Huomioita eräistä motiiveista Baudelairen tuotannossa* (Helsinki, 1939, 1986).

Benjamin, W., *The Writer of Modern Life. Essays on Charles Baudelaire* (Cambridge, 1935, 2006).

Blicher-Clausen, J., *Inga Heine* (Utrecht, 1902).

Boer, R.C., 'Twee Noorweegsche gedichten van de eeuwigheid', *De Gids* III (1903), pp. 23-64.

Boissevain, J., *Friends of friends: Networks, manipulators and coalitions* (Oxford, 1974).

Bolckmans, A., *Scandinavische letterkunde* (Utrecht/Antwerpen, 1984).

Boshouwers, R.F.M., *Moderne Scandinavische verhalen* (Utrecht/ Antwerpen, 1967).

Broady, D., *Sociologi och epistemologi. Om Pierre Bourdieus författarskap och den historiska epistemologin* (Stockholm, 1991).

Brooker, P., *Modernity and Metropolis* (New York, 2002).

Broomans, P., '*Scandia* i Nederländerna. Om Margaretha Meijboom och hennes nordiska tidskrifter', *TijdSchrift voor Skandinavistiek* 22 (2001:a), pp. 155-166.

Broomans, P., 'Hur skapas en litteraturhistorisk bild? Den nordiska litteraturens 'fräschhet' i Nederländerna och Flandern', in: Dahl, P. and Steinfeld, T. eds., *Videnskab og national opdragelse. Studier i nordisk litteraturhistorieskrivning 2* (København, 2001:b) pp. 487-541.

Broomans, P., '"Vertalingen waar haast bij is, boeken die gerecenseerd moeten woorden." Dien Logeman-Van der Willigen (1864-1925)' in: Desmidt, I., ed., *De overzet: Een bundel over vertalen* (Ghent, 2002), p. 47-65.

Broomans, P., '"The splendid literature of the North". Women translators and intermediaries of Scandinavian women writers around 1900', in: Van Dijk, S., Broomans, P., Van der Meulen, J. and Van Oostrum, P., eds., *'I have heard about you', Foreign Women's Writing Crossing the Dutch Border: from Sappho to Selma Lagerlöf* (Hilversum, 2004) pp. 307-323.

Broomans, P., 'Ibsen als God en duivel. Scandinavische literatuur in Vlaanderen rond 1900', in: De Bont, R., Reymenants, G. and Vandevoorde, H., eds., *Niet onder één vlag. Van Nu en Straks en de paradoxen van het fin de siècle* (Gent, 2005), pp. 245-264.

Broomans, P., 'Om vårt sätt att forska i kulturförmedling. Exempel: Marie Herzfeld (1855-1940)', in: Rossel, S.H. et al., eds., *Der Norden im Ausland – das Ausland im Norden. Formung und Transformation von Konzepten und Bildern des Anderen vom Mittelalter bis heute* (Vienna, 2006), pp. 201-209.

Broomans, P., 'Literary Fields: Battles and Borders'. Opening lecture at *Cultural Transfer and Minor Language Areas*. University of Groningen 5-6 November 2008.

Broomans, P., 'Introduction: Women as Transmitters of Ideas' in: Broomans, P., ed., *From Darwin to Weil. Women as Transmitters of Ideas* (Groningen, 2009), pp. 1-20.

Broomans, P., 'Reception and Ideology. "Wild Volcanism" and Other Varieties on Strindberg', in: T. Naaijkens, ed., *Event or Incident. Special Issue, Genèses de Textes/Textgenese(n)* (Bern, 2010), pp. 107-120.

Broomans, P., 'Reception and Ideology. "Wild Volcanism" and Other Varieties on Strindberg', proposal presented at the first workshop of the project: *Peripheral autonomy? Longitudinal analyses of cultural transfer in the literary fields of small language communities* http://www.peripheralautonomy.org/files/6%20-%20Broomans_bd-1-1_0.pdf (2010-11-15).

Broomans, P., 'Scandinavische literatuur in Nederland: verslonden, verzuild en verguisd', in: Van den Braber, H.M. and Gielkens, J.A.W., eds., *In 1934. Nederlandse cultuur in internationale context* (Amsterdam/Antwerpen, 2010) pp. 407-414.

Broomans P. and Kroon, I., *Zweedse Literatuur in Nederland en Vlaanderen en supplement Fins–Zweeds in vertaling* (Groningen, forthcoming, 2011).

Brunius, T., *Ord och övertygelser* (Stockholm, 1955).

Børre Johnsen, E. and Berg Eriksen, T., eds., *Norsk litteraturhistorie – sakprosa fra 1750-1995* (Oslo, 1998).

Casanova, P., 'Consécration et accumulation de capital littéraire. La traduction comme échange inégal', *Actes de la recherche en sciences sociales* 144:2002, pp. 7-20.

Castrén, G., *Juhani Aho 1* (Helsingfors, 1922).

Castrén, G., *Juhani Aho 2* (Helsingfors, 1922).

Castrén, G., *Humanister och humaniora* (Helsingfors, 1958).

Christens, R., et al.,'Marie Elisabeth Belpaire (1853-1948). Een hoger "doel" voor de vrouwen', in: Dekeyser, D., et al., *Vrouwenfaam op straat: Vrouwen maken naam* (Leuven/Apeldoorn, 1999), pp. 61-69.

Christens, R.,'Het is moeilijk haar eigen wezen achter te halen. De vele gedaante van Marie Elisabeth Belpaire', in: Dereere, A. and van Beeck, H., eds., *Marie Elisabeth Belpaire 1853-1948: Facetten van een levenswerk* (Antwerp, 2002), pp. 9-31.

Christofferson, B., *Svenska kritiker och deras metoder* (Stockholm, 1962).

Dahllöf, Urban, *Akademiska avhandlingar vid Sveriges universitet och högskolor 1890-1939. En kompletterande sammanställning* (*Pedagogisk forskning i Uppsala*, no. 73.) (Uppsala 1987).

Dale, J.A., *Garborg-studiar* (Oslo, 1969).

Davidoff, L., 'Gender and the "Great Divide". Public and private in British Gender History', *Journal of Women's History* 15,1 (2003), pp. 11–27.

De Winde, A. and Sintobin, T., 'Theun de Vries versus Menno ter Braak: provincialisme versus internationalisme', in: Van den Braber, H.M. and Gielkens, J.A.W., eds., *In 1934. Nederlandse cultuur in internationale context* (Amsterdam, 2010,) pp. 55-64.

Diktonius, E., *Och så vill jag prata med dig: Brevväxlingen mellan Eyvind Johnson och Elmer Diktonius* (Stockholm, 1997).

Domellöf, G., *I oss är en mångfald levande – Karin Boye som kritiker och prosamodernist* (Umeå, 1986).

Donner, J., *Diktonius – Ett liv* (Helsingfors, 2007).

Donner, J. and Lindquist, M., eds., *Brev. Elmer Diktonius* (Helsingfors, 1995).

Dorleijn, G.J. and Van Rees, K., eds., *De productie van literatuur. Het literaire veld in Nederland 1800-2000* (Nijmegen, 2006).

Enckell, O., *Den unga Hagar Olsson* (Helsingfors, 1949).

Enckell, O., "Vägen till Quosego", *Quosego* (Helsingfors, 1971).

Ekman, M., ed., *Finlands svenska litteraturhistoria II* (Helsingfors, 2000).

Estelle, B.H.,'Dien Logeman van der Willigen', *Tidens kvinder: Damernas illustrerede ugeblad*, 28.2.1924, p. 1.

Even-Zohar, I., 'The position of translated literature within the literary polysystem', in: *Literature and Translation. New Perspectives in Literary Studies* (Leuven, 1978), pp. 117-127.

Fahlgren, M., 'Från periferin till centrum. Edith Södergran och kvinnorna i 1900-talets litteraturhistoriska seminarierum', in: Ronne, M., ed., *Mot normen. Kvinnors skrivande under 1900-talet* (Uppsala, 2007), pp. 113-128.

Furuland, L., *Mina dagsverken. Minnen från folkhögskolor, folkbildning, universitet och möten med arbetarförfattare* (Uppsala, 2009).

Garborg, A., *Den ny-norske Sprog- og Nationalitetsbevægelse* (Kristiania, 1877).

Garborg, A., *Vor Sprogudvikling. En Redegjørelse. Med et Tillæg* (Kristiania, 1897).

Garborg, A., 'Nieuw Noorsch', *Scandia* 6/7 (1904), pp. 86-90.

Garborg, H., 'De Færöer Eilanden', *Scandia* 4 (1904), pp. 49-54.

Govaerts, L.,'Marie Elisabeth Belpaire en haar onderwijsinitiatieven', in: Dereere, A. and van Beeck, H., eds., *Marie Elisabeth Belpaire 1853-1948: Facetten van een levenswerk* (Antwerp, 2002), pp. 31-68.

Grave, J., *Zulk vertalen is een werk van liefde. Bemiddelaars van Nederlandstalige literatuur in Duitsland 1890-1914* (Nijmegen, 2001).

Grit, D., *Dansk skønlitteratur i Nederland og Flandern 1731-1982: Bibliografi over oversættelser og studier* (Ballerup, 1986).

Grit, D., 'Bestaat de receptie van 'de' Deense literatuur in Nederlandse vertaling, 1731-1990?', in: Grit, D., *Driewerf zalig Noorden. Over literaire betrekkingen tussen de Nederlanden en Scandinavië* (Maastricht, 1994) pp. 120-129.

Groen, J., *250 jaar Noorse literatuur in Nederland en Vlaanderen 1743-1993: Bibliografie van vertalingen en recensies* (Hoorn, 1994).

Gunn, S. and Morris, R.J., eds., *Identities in Space; Contested Terrains in the Western City since 1850* (Ashgate, 2001).

Hammarlund-Larsson, C., '"I denna tid af slapp nationalkänsla". Om Artur Hazelius, vetenskapen och nationen', in: Hammarlund-Larsson, C., Nilsson, B.G. and Silvén, E., eds., *Samhällsideal och framtidsbilder. Perspektiv på Nordiska Museets dokumentation och forskning* (Stockholm, 2004), pp. 11-63.

Hammarström, C., *Karin Boye* (Stockholm, 2001).

Hamsun, K., *Markens Grøde* (Kristiania, 1917).

Hamsun, K., *De koningin van Sheba*, (The Hague, 1961) [translated by Greta Baars-Jelgersma].

Haug Frøyen, M. and Time, S., *Arne Garborgs kulturnasjonalisme. To studiar* (Oslo, 1993).

Havu, I., *Finlands litteratur 1900-1950* (Stockholm, 1958).

Heilbron, J. and Sapiro, G., 'Outline for a Sociology of Translation: Current Issues and Future Prospects', in: Wolf, M. and Fukari, A., eds., *Constructing a Sociology of Translation* (Amsterdam, 2007), pp. 93-107.

Helgesson, P., 'Karin Boye: Posthumous Escuses', *Scandinavica. An International Journal of Scandinavian Studies* 1 (2001), pp. 71-95.

Helsingius, T., *Dagdrivare* (Helsinki, 1914).

Herner, E., *Svenska recensenter läser finska böcker: En studie i receptionen av finsk prosa, översatt på 1960-talet* (Stockholm, 1999).

Het Nieuws van den dag voor Nederlandsch-Indië, 19-07-1938, Vol. 43, day edition, p. 22.

Het Vaderland 10-07-1936, 20-03-1938, 05-08-1939, 03-11-1939.

Het Vaderland 11-02-1931, evening edition.

Het Vaderland, 12-02-1936, evening edition, p. 9.

Het Vaderland, 26-02-1936, evening edition, p. 9.

Hornborg, E.,'De Finsche kwestie', *Onze Eeuw* (1911), pp. 355-372.

Houm, P., *Norges litteratur fra 1914 til 1950-årene* (1955), = 6th part of Bull, Paasche, Winsnes and Houm, eds., *Norsk litteraturhistorie* (Oslo, 1924-1955).

Hroch, M., *Social preconditions of national revival in Europe*
(New York, ²2000).

Häkkinen, A., *Rahasta – vaan ei rakkaudesta. Prostituutio Helsingissä*
1867-1939 (Helsinki, 1995).

Hølaas, O., *Livstegn og speilinger* (Oslo, 1966).

Hølaas, O., *Storm og Lys: Livstegn og speilinger 2* (Oslo, 2001).

Ingerwersen, N.,'The Modern Breakthrough', in: Rossel, S.H., ed.,
A History of Danish Literature (Nebraska, 1992), pp. 261-316.

Jiresch, E., 'The problem of demarcation in the investigation of literary
networks. Margaretha Meyboom as a cultural "border crosser"',
in: Zilliacus, C. et al., eds., *Gränser i nordisk litteratu:. Borders in*
Nordic Literature. IASS XXVI 2006 (Åbo, 2008), pp. 727-735.

Jiresch, E., *The role of networks in the work of female cultural transmitters*
of Scandinavian Literature and culture in Europe around 1900:
A comparative study of the Dutch/Flemish area and the Austrian/German
speaking regions, dissertation (Groningen, to be submitted 2010).

Jørgensen, J., *Levensleugen en levenswaarheid* (Ghent, 1900).

Jørgensen, J., *De uiterste dag* (Ghent, 1902).

Jørgensen, J., *Klokke Roeland* (Bussum, 1916).

Jørgensen, J., *Over Goethe* (Bussum, 1919).

Jørgensen, J., *Mit livs legende* (Copenhagen, 1949).

Kahila, H., *Nuoruuteni muistelmia* (Helsinki, 1919).

Keunen, B., *De verbeelding van de grootstad. Stads- en wereldbeelden in*
het proza van de moderniteit (Brussel, 2000).

Kirby, D., *Östersjöländernas historia 1772-1993* (Stockholm, 1996).

Kjellén, A., *Flanören och hans storstadsvärld: synpunkter på ett litterärt*
motiv (Stockholm, 1985).

Kleine Courant of *Het Nieuws van den Dag*, 30-11-1905, 01-12-1905,
02-12-1905, 04-12-1905.

Knapas, R., 'Finsk eller svensk nationallitteratur i Finland –
Litteraturhistoriens frontlinjer på 1850- och 1860-talen', in: Dahl,
P. and Steinfeld, T. eds., *Videnskab og National opdragelse: Studier i*
Nordisk Litteraturhistorieskrivning 1 (Köpenhamn, 2001).

Koht, K.G. and Thesen, R., eds., *Hulda Garborg. Dagbok 1903-1914*
(Oslo, 1962).

Kristoffersen, I., 'Hulda Garborg', in: *Norsk biografisk leksikon*
(Oslo, 2000), Vol. 3, p. 258.

Lagercrantz, O., 'Margit Abenius död', *Dagens Nyheter*, August 5, 1970.

Lahousse, A., *Dien Logeman-Van der Willigen (1864-1925): Een vertaalster en cultuurbemiddelaarster voor de Scandinavische literatuur met een specifiek Fins effect*, unpublished master's thesis (Ghent, 2003), p. 57.

Laitinen, K., *Finlands litteratur* (Helsingfors, 1988).

Lappalainen, P., *Koti, kansa ja maailman tahraava lika. Näkökulmia 1880- ja 1890-luvun kirjallisuuteen* (Helsinki, 2000).

Lefebvre, H., *Critique of everyday life* (London, 1947, 1991).

Lehan, R., *The city in literature: an intellectual and cultural history* (Berkeley, 1998).

Leino, E., 'Päivä Helsingissä', in: Leino, E., *Valitut Teokset* (Helsinki, 1905, 1957), pp. 343-404.

Leino, E., *Jaana Rönty*, in: Leino, E., *Routavuositrilogia* (Helsinki, 1907, 1998), pp. 183-332.

Leino, E., *Olli Suurpää*, in: Leino, E., *Routavuositrilogia* (Helsinki, 1908, 1998), pp. 333-508.

Levie, S., 'De contacten van Siegfried E. van Praag met zijn uitgevers', in: Van den Braber, H.M. and Gielkens, J.A.W., eds., *In 1934. Nederlandse cultuur in internationale context*. (Amsterdam/Antwerpen, 2010), pp. 173-182.

Linn, S., 'Meten is weten? Kanttekeningen bij de compilatie van een bibliografie als basis voor receptieonderzoek naar de Nederlandse literatuur in vertaling', in: Broomans, P., et al., eds., *Object: Nederlandse literatuur in het buitenland. Methode: onbekend* (Groningen, 2006), pp. 36-55.

Linnér, S., ed., *Från Dagdrivare till Feminister. Studier I finlandssvensk 1900-talslitteratur* (Helsinki, 1986).

Logeman-Van der Willigen, D., 'Herman Bang', *Dietsche Warande en Belfort* (1912), pp. 305-321.

Lunden, K., *Norsk grålysing. Norsk nasjonalisme 1770-1814 på allmenn bakgrunn* (Oslo, 1992).

Lundgren, S., *Dikten i etern. Radion och skönlitteraturen 1925-1955* (Uppsala, 1994).

Lundkvist, A., 'Karin Boye', a review of Abenius' *Drabbad av renhet*, *Dagens Nyheter*, December 6, 1950.

Lyytikäinen, P., ed., *Changing Scenes; Encounters between European and Finnish Fin de Siècle* (Helsinki, 2003).

Lyytikäinen, P., ed., *Dekadenssi vuosisadanvaihteen taiteessa ja kirjallisuudessa* (Helsinki, 1998).

Markusson Winkvist, H., *Som isolerade öar. De lagerkransade kvinnorna och akademin under 1900-talets första hälft* (Stockholm/Stehag, 2003).

McFadden, M.H. *Golden Cables of Sympathy. The Transatlantic Sources of Nineteenth-Century-Feminists* (Lexington, 1999).

Meinander, H., *Finlands historia 3* (Helsingfors, 2006).

Meinander, H., *Finlands historia 4* (Helsingfors, 2006).

Metzemaekers, R., 'Cora Sandel: "Krane's lunchroom" – Uitg. Wereldbibliotheek N.V. – Amsterdam-Antwerpen – 1950 – 231 blz. – Uit het Noors vertaald door Greta Baars-Jelgersma', *Arsenaal. Tijdschrift voor letterkunde 3*, Vol. 6 (1950), pp. 46-47.

Meyboom, M., 'Skandinavische literatuur in Nederland', *Boekzaal 1911*, Vol. 5, pp. 45-49.

Meylaerts, R., 'The study of cultural transfer in the literary fields of small language communities: Some preliminary thoughts', proposal presented at the first workshop of the project: *Peripheral autonomy? Longitudinal analyses of cultural transfer in the literary fields of small language communities*, in Ghent –December 1-2, 2006, http://www.peripheralautonomy.org/files/6%20-%20Broomans_bd-1-1_0.pdf (2010-11-15)

Moi, T., *Simone de Beauvoir. The making of an intellectual woman* (Oxford UK/Cambridge USA, 1994).

Molarius, P. 'Suomenruotsalaisen dagdrivare-kirjallisuuden dandy ja modernin subjektin itsehahmotus', in: Lyytikäinen, P., ed., *Dekadenssi vuosisadanvaihteen taiteessa ja kirjallisuudessa* (Helsinki, 1998), pp. 156-182.

N. N., 'Mevrouw Logeman-Van der Willigen', *Onze Eeuw* XII/1 (1926/2), pp. 2-3.

Naess, H.S., ed., *A History of Norwegian Literature* (Nebraska, 1993).

Nead, L., *Victorian Babylon. People, streets and images in nineteenth-century London* (London, 2000).

Nieuwe Rotterdamsche Courant, 19th March 1929, evening edition, p. 18.

Nieuwe Rotterdamsche Courant, 3th December 1928, evening edition, p. 2.

Nilsson, A., 'Finsk-svensk lyriktrafik från tidig modernism till idag', in: Oftedal Andersen, H., Ljung. P.E., and Ståhl, E.B., eds., *Nordisk lyrikktrafikk* (Helsingfors, 2009), pp. 35-59.

Nordenstam, A., *Begynnelser. Litteraturforskningens pionjärkvinnor 1850-1930* (Stockholm/Stehag, 2003).

Nordin, S., *Ingemar Hedenius. En filosof och hans tid* (Stockholm, 2004).

Nummi, J., *Aika Pariisissa. Juhani Ahon ranskalainen kausi* (Helsinki, 2000).

Nummi, J., 'Between time and eternity. K.A. Tavaststjerna's *Barndomsvänner*', in: Lyytikäinen, P., ed., *Changing Scenes; Encounters between European and Finnish Fin de Siècle* (Helsinki, 2003), pp. 85-120.

Obrestad, T., *Arne Garborg. Ein biografi* (Oslo, 1991).

Obrestad, T., *Hulda* (Oslo, 1992).

Oort, G.A.E., 'Arne Garborg', *De Gids* III (1896), pp. 255-283.

Palmgren, R., *Kaupunki ja tekniikka Suomen kirjallisuudessa; Kuvauslinjoja ennen ja jälkeen tulenkantajien* (Helsinki, 1989).

Pedersen, A.T., *Urbana Odysséer. Helsingfors, staden och 1910-talets finlandssvenska prosa* (Helsinki, 2007).

Persyn, J., *De wording van het tijdschrift Dietsche Warande en Belfort en zijn ontwikkeling onder de Redactie van Em. Vliebergh en Jul. Persyn* (Gent, 1963).

Persyn, J., 'Belpaire, Maria Elisa. Letterkundige en Kunstbeschermster', in: Koninklijke Vlaamse Academiën van België, eds., *Nationaal Biografisch Woordenboek* (Brussels, 1966), pp. 51-56.

Petterson, T., 'Det svårgripbara levet: Ett förbisett tema i dagdrivarlitteraturen', in: Linnér, S., ed., *Från Dagdrivare till Feminister. Studier I finlandssvensk 1900-talslitteratur* (Helsinki, 1986), pp. 9-40.

Peurell, E., *En författares väg. Jan Fridegård i det litterära fältet* (Hedemora, 1998).

Pollock, G., 'Modernity and the Spaces of Femininity', in: Pollock, G., *Vision and Difference: Femininity, Feminism and the Histories of Art* (London, 1988), pp. 50-90.

Pääjärvi, M., 'Flanööri Pohjolasta – V.A. Koskenniemen *Kevätilta Quartier Latinissä* ja kadun ulottuvuudet', *Avain* 3 (2006), pp. 40-52.

Reymenants, G., 'Marie Elisabeth Belpaire: Bezielster van het Tijdschrift DWB', in: Dereere, A. and van Beeck, H., eds., *Marie Elisabeth Belpaire 1853-1948: Facetten van een levenswerk* (Antwerp, 2002), pp. 163-195.

Reymenants, G., *Vrouweninvloed in het literaire veld: De medewerking van vrouwen aan katholieke Vlaamse tijdschriften, weekbladen en kranten 1900-1940*, unpublished dissertation (Ghent, 2005).

Ronne, M., 'Kvinnliga studenter i litteraturhistoria 1900-1940. Studier, examina och kunskapssyn', in: Landgren, B., ed., *Universitetsämne i brytningstider. Studier i svensk akademisk litteraturundervisning 1947-1995* (Uppsala, 2005), pp. 627-704.

Ronne, M., '"Så skärper den ena människan den andra". Om litteraturkritikern Margit Abenius och hennes många nätverk', in: Heggestad, E., Johannisson, K., eds., *En ny sits. Humaniora i förvandling. Vänbok till Margareta Fahlgren* (Uppsala, 2008), pp. 113-128.

Ronne, M., 'Decoding a Genius Mind. The French Philosopher Simone Weil (1909-1943) and the Swedish Critic Margit Abenius (1899-1970): a Case of Cultural Transmission' in: Broomans, P. ed., *From Darwin to Weil. Women as Transmitters of Ideas* (Groningen, 2009), pp. 139-157.

Rossi, R., *Le naturalisme finlandais. Une conception entropique du quotidien* (Helsinki, 2007).

Rydén, P., *Domedagar. Svensk litteraturkritik efter 1880* (Lund, 1987).

Rönnholm, T., *Kunskapens kvinnor. Sekelskiftets studentskor i mötet med den manliga universitetsvärlden* (Umeå, 1999).

Sandel, C., 'Rosina', *Social-Demokraten*s saterday-supplement *Lørdagskveld* (1922).

Sandel, C., *Bare Alberte* (Oslo, 1939).

Sandemose, A., *Ross Dane* (København, 1928).

Sanders, M., 'Het buitenland bekeken', in: Van den Braber, H.M. and Gielkens, J.A.W., eds., *In 1934. Nederlandse cultuur in internationale context* (Amsterdam/Antwerpen 2010), pp. 301-312.

Sapiro, G., The global market of symbolic goods: literary books in translation, Accessible at http://www.peripheralautonomy.org/node/35 (2010-10-15)

Schoolfield, G.C., *A History of Finland's Literature* (Nebraska, 1998).

Scott, J., *Social network analysis: A handbook* (London, 1991).

Sick, I.M., 'In Memoriam: Professorinde Logendal v. d. Willigen', *Berlingske Tidene* (s.d.).

Sijtsma-Oma, T., *Fra kistebunn til opphavsrett. Drakt og nasjonalidentitet. Nåtidens motiver for nasjonaldraktbruk i Norge og Fryslân – en komparativ analyse,* unpublished master's thesis (Groningen, 2010).

Simmel, G., 'The Metropolis and Mental Life', in: Sennett, R., ed., *Classic Essays on the Culture of Cities* (Englewood Cliffs, 1903, 1969), pp. 47-60.

Skouen, A., 'Lysende skrivekunst', *Dagbladet*, 29.10.2001.

Skre, A., 'Huldas liv i litteraturen', *Syn og Segn* 3 (2010), pp. 14-23.

Smets, I., 'De Katholieke Hogeschool voor Vrouwen', in: Dereere, A. and van Beeck, H., eds, *Marie Elisabeth Belpaire 1853-1948: Facetten van een levenswerk* (Antwerp, 2002), pp. 69-84.

Sniader Lanser, S. and Tornton Beck, E., '[Why] Are There No Great Women Critics? And What Difference Does It Make?', in: Sherman, J.A. and Tornton Beck, E., eds., *The Prism of Sex. Essays on the Sociology of Knowledge* (Madison, 1979), pp. 79-91.

Stolpe, S., 'Kvinnorna och litteraturen', in: Liliendahl, E., ed., *Svensk yrkeskvinna. En översikt av kvinnornas insats i svenskt näringsliv* (Göteborg, 1950), pp. 234-244.

Söderhjelm, H., *Het roode oproer in Finland 1918: Volgens officiële Documenten* (Utrecht, 1920).

Söderhjelm, H., *Författareprofiler* (Stockholm, 1938).

Söderhjelm, H., *Werner Söderhjelm* (Helsingfors, 1960).

Talvio, M., *Tähtien alla*, in: Talvio, M., *Kootut teokset III* (Helsinki, 1910), pp. 183-468.

Tarkiainen, K., *Sveriges Österland: Från forntid till Gustav Vasa* (Helsingfors, 2008).

Toikka, M., 'Kadun peli katupeilin takana; Hilja Kahilan *Nuoruuteni muistelmia*', in: Kurikka, K., ed., *Paikkoja ja tiloja suomalaisessa Kirjallisuudessa* (Turku, 1998), pp. 157-173.

Tuneld, J., *Akademiska avhandlingar vid Sveriges universitet och högskolor läsåren 1910/11-1939/40. Bibliografi* (Lund, 1945).

Undset, S., *Kristin Lavransdatter* (Oslo, 1920-1922).

Vaitinen, P., 'Bilden av finnen I svensk litteraturreception på 1930-talet', in: Granqvist, R., ed., *Texten och läsaren i ett historiskt perspektiv: Föredrag vid nordiskt symposium i idé- och litteraturreception 1984* (Umeå, 1985).

Van Buuren, A., *De taal van het hart. Retorica en receptie van de hedendaagse streekroman* (Groningen, 2005).

Van den Braber, H.M. and Gielkens, J.A.W., eds., *In 1934. Nederlandse cultuur in internationale context* (Amsterdam/Antwerp, 2010)

Van der Toorn-Piebenga, G. and Houweling, F., eds., *Bzzlletin*, 130 (Den Haag, 1985).

Van Elswijk, R., '*Noarwegen en de wrâld*. Taalstrijd in Friesland en Noorwegen', in: Boersma, P. and Jensma, G.T., eds., *Philologia Frisica. XVIIIe Frysk Filologekongres* (Ljouwert [Leeuwarden], 2010) [s.p.].

Van Kalmthout, T., '*Vertalen*, het orgaan van de Vereeniging Nederlandsche Vertalingen', in: Van den Braber, H.M. and Gielkens, J.A.W., eds., *In 1934. Nederlandse cultuur in internationale context.* (Amsterdam/Antwerpen, 2010), pp. 65-73.

Van Marken, A., 'Panorama fan it noarske proaza', in: *De Ttsjerne.*
    Noarwegennûmer 1, Vol. 11 (Leeuwarden, 1956), pp. 10-11.
Van Marken, A., 'Inn i kampen mellom ideologiene', in: Grøndahl, C.H.,
    ed., *Dyade. Sigrid Undset vurdert i utlandet* 2 (1982), pp. 7-8.
Van Rees, K. and Dorleijn, G.J., 'Het Nederlandse literaire veld 1800-2000',
    in: Dorleijn and Van Rees, eds., *De productie van literatuur* (Nijmegen,
    2006) pp. 15-37.
Varpio, Y., 'Det nationella i den finskspråkiga litteraturhistorieskrivningen
    1858-1949', in: Dahl, P. and Steinfeld, T. eds., *Videnskab og National
    opdragelse: Studier i Nordisk Litteraturhistorieskrivning* 1
    (København, 2001).
Venema, A., *Schrijvers, uitgevers & hun collaboratie* (Amsterdam,
    1988-1992).
Vidler, A., *The Architectural Uncanny; Essays in the Modern Unhomely*
    (Cambridge, Mass, 1992).
Vikør, L., 'Linjer i nyare språkhistorie', *Eigenproduksjon* 37 (1990),
    pp. 1-116.
Wassermann, S. and Faust, K., *Social network analysis: Methods and
    applications* (Cambridge, 1994).
Williams, A., *Stjärnor utan stjärnbilder. Kvinnor och kanon i
    litteraturhistoriska översiktsverk under 1900-talet* (Uppsala, 1997).
Wilson, E., 'The Invisible Flâneur', *New Left Review* I/191 (1992),
    pp. 90-110.
Wolff, J., 'The Invisible Flâneuse. Women and the Literature of
    Modernity', *Theory Culture Society* 2 (3) (1985), pp. 37-46.
Wrede, J., *Världen enligt Runeberg* (Helsingfors, 2005).
Writers' & Artists' Yearbook 2006.
Zoomers-Vermeer, J.P., *De grijze hoeve* (Amsterdam, 1947).
Österling, A., förord in: Seppänen, U., *Flyktingskolan* (Stockholm, 1930).

Websites:
http://kranten.kb.nl/, (2010-10-15).
http://peripheralautonomy.org/, (2010-10-31).
http://www.bokkilden.no/SamboWeb/produkt.do?produktId=142473), (2010-10-15).
http://www.dagbladet.no/kultur/2001/10/29/291260.html, (2010-10-15).
http://www.nrk.no/nyheter/bakgrunn/portretter/1284705.html, (2010-10-15).
http://www.snl.no/.nbl_biografi/Cora_Sandel/utdypning, (2010-6-27).

Unpublished sources
Abenius, M., letters to Klara Johanson ('KJ'), L 2 suppl,
The Royal Library, Stockholm.
Abenius, M., letters to Wilhelm Abenius, G1n:19,
Uppsala University Library.
Abenius, M., Litteraturkrönikor 1933-1940, Margit Abenius 18,
Uppsala University Library.
Abenius, M., Litteraturkrönikor 1941-1967 och andra författares
manuskript, Margit Abenius 19, Uppsala University Library.
Abenius, M., Margit Abenius 1, Diaries 1916-1932,
Uppsala University Library.
Abenius, M., two radio manuscripts, Margit Abenius 25,
Biographica, Uppsala University Library.
H., G. and Ingelman, I., *Literary Circle 1944-1984*, an unpublished
manuscript by Gertrud H. and Ingrid Ingelman.
Sandel, C., letters to Margit Abenius, G1n:18, Uppsala University Library
Stolpe, S., letters to Margit Abenius, G1n:14, Uppsala University Library.

Index